SPECIAL EDUCATION LAW WITH CASES

SPECIAL EDUCATION LAW WITH CASES

JOSEPH R. BOYLE

Virginia Commonwealth University

MARY WEISHAAR

Southern Illinois University–Edwardsville

ALLYN AND BACON

Boston ▪ London ▪ Toronto ▪ Sydney ▪ Tokyo ▪ Singapore

Senior Series Editor: *Virginia Lanigan*
Vice President and Editor-in-Chief: *Paul A. Smith*
Editorial Assistant: *Jennifer Connors*
Executive Marketing Manager: *Brad Parkins*
Production Editor: *Christopher H. Rawlings*
Editorial Production Service: *Omegatype Typography, Inc.*
Composition and Prepress Buyer: *Linda Cox*
Manufacturing Buyer: *Suzanne Lareau*
Cover Administrator: *Jenny Hart*
Electronic Composition: *Omegatype Typography, Inc.*

Library of Congress Cataloging-in-Publication Data

Boyle, Joseph R.
    Special education law with cases / Joseph R. Boyle, Mary Weishaar.
        p.   cm.
    Includes bibliographical references.
    ISBN 0-205-27468-4 (alk. paper)
    1. Special education—Law and legislation—United States.   I. Weishaar, Mary Ellen.   II.
    Title.
KF4209.3.B69   2001
344.73'0791—dc21   00-036181

BK
$60.80

Printed in the United States of America
10 9 8 7 6 5 4 3 2   05 04 03 02 01

To Carole, my loving wife and friend,
and to my special children, Joshua and Ashley

—JRB

To Phil, Paul, and Mark Weishaar
and to Pat and Joe Konya,
for their support and belief in me

—MKW

CONTENTS

Preface   xi

PART I   GENERAL OVERVIEW OF LAW IN SPECIAL EDUCATION   1

CHAPTER ONE
Overview of Statutory Law   1

INDIVIDUALS WITH DISABILITIES EDUCATION ACT   1

SECTION 504 OF THE REHABILITATION ACT OF 1973   15

AMERICANS WITH DISABILITIES ACT   20

SUMMARY   23

CHAPTER TWO
Relevant Court Cases in Special Education Law   24

ZERO REJECT   24

NONDISCRIMINATORY EVALUATION   25

IEP AND APPROPRIATE EDUCATION   26

LEAST RESTRICTIVE ENVIRONMENT   28

PROCEDURAL DUE PROCESS   30

STUDENT MISCONDUCT AND COMPENSATORY EDUCATION   30

PART II   CASE STUDIES   33

CHAPTER THREE
Zero Reject and Child Find   35

CASE 3.1 ■ Jodi/Special Education Services   35

CASE 3.2 ■ Linda/Homeschool 37

CASE 3.3 ■ Danny/Expulsion 40

CASE 3.4 ■ Peter/Health Impaired Students 42

CASE 3.5 ■ Kate/Physical Disabilities 45

CASE 3.6 ■ Andre/Age and Special Education Services 48

CHAPTER FOUR
Evaluation and Classification 52

CASE 4.1 ■ Carlos/Discriminatory Evaluations 52

CASE 4.2 ■ Tony/Inadequate Evaluations 54

CASE 4.3 ■ Scott/Procedural Errors 57

CASE 4.4 ■ Tina/Classification Issues 59

CASE 4.5 ■ Joan/Refusal to Evaluate 61

CASE 4.6 ■ Latifa/Biased Testing Procedures 64

CHAPTER FIVE
Individual Education Plan and Appropriate Education 67

CASE 5.1 ■ Walter/Transition Services 67

CASE 5.2 ■ Vernon/Improper Placement 69

CASE 5.3 ■ Yancy/General Education Participation 71

CASE 5.4 ■ Nicholas/Parent Participation 73

CASE 5.5 ■ Kelly/Related Services 75

CASE 5.6 ■ Harold/Adequate Services 77

CHAPTER SIX
Least Restrictive Environment 80

CASE 6.1 ■ John/Disruptive Behavior 80

CASE 6.2 ■ Ben/Inclusion 83

CASE 6.3 ■ James/Teacher Bias   **86**

CASE 6.4 ■ David/Threatening Behavior   **89**

CASE 6.5 ■ Jane/Refusal to Consider   **92**

CASE 6.6 ■ Jared/Legal Rights   **96**

CHAPTER SEVEN
Parent Participation   **100**

CASE 7.1 ■ Amy/Parents in Class   **100**

CASE 7.2 ■ Lansky/Parental Consent   **103**

CASE 7.3 ■ Tunita/Setting Goals   **105**

CASE 7.4 ■ Kami/Improper Evaluation   **107**

CASE 7.5 ■ Washington/Divorced Parents   **108**

CASE 7.6 ■ Armstrong/Denial of Behavior   **110**

CHAPTER EIGHT
Due Process   **113**

CASE 8.1 ■ James/Expulsion   **113**

CASE 8.2 ■ Bobby/Discipline   **116**

CASE 8.3 ■ Ann/Tuition Reimbursement   **120**

CASE 8.4 ■ Luke/Stay Put   **123**

CASE 8.5 ■ Susan/Parent Input   **125**

CASE 8.6 ■ Lori/Individualized IEP   **129**

CHAPTER NINE
Confidentiality and Privacy   **132**

CASE 9.1 ■ Darrell/Personal Notes   **132**

CASE 9.2 ■ Jeff/Improper Disclosure   **135**

CASE 9.3 ■ Kevin/Delayed Records   **138**

CASE 9.4 ■ John/Withholding Information   **141**

CASE 9.5 ■ Dean/Invasion of Privacy   **144**

CASE 9.6 ■ Carlos/Falsifying Documents   **146**

CHAPTER TEN

Student Misconduct   151

CASE 10.1 ■ Donnie/Bringing a Gun   **151**

CASE 10.2 ■ Andy/Impulsive Behavior   **154**

CASE 10.3 ■ Katie/Marijuana Cigarette   **157**

CASE 10.4 ■ Mike/Violent Threats   **160**

CASE 10.5 ■ Tim/Teacher and Parent Rebellion   **163**

CASE 10.6 ■ Mario/Expulsion Proceeding   **166**

CHAPTER ELEVEN

Compliance Techniques   170

CASE 11.1 ■ Janis/Inadequate Building   **170**

CASE 11.2 ■ Lisa/Graduation Fears   **173**

CASE 11.3 ■ Michael/Sexual Misconduct   **177**

CASE 11.4 ■ Kristen/Essential Therapy   **180**

CASE 11.5 ■ Janet/Identification of Problems   **184**

CASE 11.6 ■ Gabriel/Vocational Training   **188**

APPENDIX

Answers to Legal Issues to Consider   191

References   235

Index   237

PREFACE

This text is intended to serve as an essential supplemental text in a graduate special education law course. It is also appropriate for a graduate general education law course. The authors feel strongly that all school personnel, special and general education, would benefit from knowledge of special education legal issues. The purposes of this book include the following:

- To provide a general overview of three major laws governing special education: the Individuals with Disabilities Education Act, Part 504 of the Rehabilitation Act of 1973, and the Americans with Disabilities Act.
- To provide a general review of some influential court cases in special education interpreting statutory law.
- To provide practice in analyzing special education legal issues using real-life case studies.

The book is divided into two parts. Part I presents a general overview of statutory law and case law in special education. Chapter 1 provides a review of the general principles of the Individuals with Disabilities Education Act (IDEA), the Americans with Disabilities Act (ADA), and Section 504 of the Rehabilitation Act of 1973. Chapter 2 provides an overview of some influential case laws in special education. Both chapters provide a general review of guiding principles in special education.

Part II includes real-life case studies that address important legal issues in special education. Each chapter includes six cases, and each case is followed by two types of questions: legal questions that address specific issues of law and general questions that address the social and political influences of the law. The cases in Part II are divided into the following topics:

- zero reject and child find
- evaluation and classification
- individual education plan and appropriate education
- least restrictive environment
- parent participation
- due process
- confidentiality and privacy
- student misconduct
- compliance techniques

The Appendix contains general answers to legal questions. Because there can be several correct responses to a legal situation, the Appendix presents one possible interpretation for each situation, which can serve as guidance in seeking answers. The Appendix should be consulted after each case is read and discussed in the college/university classroom.

Although the text provides an overview of special education statutory and case law, the essence of the book is the case study approach. Each case has been developed to provide students with practice in analyzing special education legal issues in a real-life scenario. Readers, at times, might be surprised at the manner in which professionals address these issues, some of which are negative. However, all cases are based on real cases experienced by the authors or relayed to the authors by professionals, and they represent reality.

To study special education law, students must study details of the law. Often, this is where the course ends, leaving students to apply the law as situations arise in their school settings. This text bridges a gap—students can practice in the university setting applying legal principles using authentic case studies. With this practice, students will be better prepared to react and become proactive as they confront the difficult legal issues in special education.

ACKNOWLEDGMENTS

We would like to thank the following people who were involved in the production of this book: Virginia Lanigan, series editor, and Jennifer Connors, editorial assistant at Allyn and Bacon.

In addition, we would like to thank the following reviewers: Robin S. Barton, Armstrong Atlantic State University; Craig Fiedler, University of Wisconsin–Oshkosh; Sheldon Maren, Portland State University; and Mitchell Yell, University of South Carolina.

SPECIAL EDUCATION LAW WITH CASES

CHAPTER ONE

OVERVIEW OF STATUTORY LAW

INDIVIDUALS WITH DISABILITIES EDUCATION ACT

The Education for All Handicapped Children Act was passed in 1975 (Public Law 94-142). The law currently known as the Individuals with Disabilities Education Act (IDEA) was passed by Congress in 1990. The effect of this law is to ensure that children with disabilities receive a free and appropriate public education (FAPE) and are not discriminated against by any public agencies (e.g., local school districts). FAPE means special education and related services that

- have been provided at public expense (i.e., without charge to parents)
- meet the standards of the state education agency
- include an appropriate preschool, elementary, or secondary school education in the state
- are provided within the confines of the individualized education program (IEP) (IDEA Regulations, 1999, C.F.R. § 300.13)

IDEA provides federal monies to states and local school districts if they agree to comply with procedures set out in IDEA and its regulations. Before the enactment of PL 94-142 in 1975, Congress found that

1. The special educational needs of children with disabilities were not being fully met.
2. More than one-half of the children with disabilities in the United States did not receive appropriate educational services that would enable such children to have full equality of opportunity.
3. One million of the children with disabilities in the United States were excluded from the public school system and did not go through the educational process with their peers.
4. There were many children with disabilities throughout the United States participating in regular school programs whose disabilities prevented them from having a successful educational experience because their disabilities were undetected.
5. Because of the lack of adequate services within the public school system, families many times were forced to find services outside the public school system, often at great distance from their residences and at their own expense (IDEA, 20 U.S.C. § 1401[a]).

In effect, Individuals with Disabilities Education Act "opened the schoolhouse doors" to many children with disabilities who had been unserved or underserved by the public schools. To a large extent, this mission has been accomplished.

Individuals with Disabilities Education Act requires that states provide services to children with disabilities between the ages of 3 and 21 in 13 categories (Figure 1.1). Operational definitions of these disabling categories can be found in the IDEA regulations (34 C.F.R. § 300.7[a][1]–[c][13]). Each state is required to evaluate children between birth and 21, even if a state doesn't provide services for the birth-through-3 population.

PL 94-142 and then IDEA were amended by Congress in 1978, 1986, 1990, and 1997. The most significant changes were made in the last three revisions. They are summarized as follows:

1986

- Infants and Toddlers with Disabilities Act became Part H of the federal law and provided monies to states for provision of early intervention services to the birth-to-3 population.
- Handicapped Children's Protection Act of 1986 was incorporated into the law. Parents who prevailed in a due process hearing or a lawsuit could recover attorneys' fees.

1990

- General language was changed from *handicapped student* to *student with a disability.*
- Name of law changed to Individuals with Disabilities Education Act.
- Two categories of disability were added: traumatic brain injury and autism.
- Assistive technology and rehabilitation services were added and clarified as related services.
- Transition plans for all students with disabilities age 16 and older were mandated.

1997

- Annual goals and benchmarks or objectives on the IEP were required to be measurable.

FIGURE 1.1   IDEA: Thirteen Categories of Disabilities

Autism
Deaf-blindness
Deafness
Emotional disturbance
Hearing impairment
Learning disability
Mental retardation
Multiple disabilities
Orthopedic impairment
Other health impairment
Speech or language impairment
Traumatic brain injury
Visual impairment

Source: IDEA Regulations, C.F.R. § 306.7

- The IEP team was expanded to include a general education teacher.
- Students with disabilities were included in state and school-district assessments of achievement, and this decision-making process became part of the IEP.
- Mediation was required to be offered by all states on a voluntary basis.
- Specific discipline procedures were added to protect the rights of students with disabilities and to maintain safety and security in the schools.

IDEA is based on a foundation of six principles: zero reject/child find, nondiscriminatory testing, individual education plan, least restrictive environment, procedural due process, and parent participation (Figure 1.2). A summary of each principle follows.

Principle of Zero Reject/Child Find

Zero reject means that local school districts cannot exclude students with disabilities from public schools due to the nature or degree of their disabilities. All students ages 3 to 21 must be located, evaluated, and provided with appropriate education programs. States are also required to locate and evaluate children with disabilities between birth and 3 years of age. The following example illustrates this concept.

A 5-year-old child moves into a very small, rural school district. The child has significant physical, health, and mental disabilities. The child uses a wheelchair,

FIGURE 1.2   Steps to Free Appropriate Public Education (FAPE): Guiding Principles of IDEA

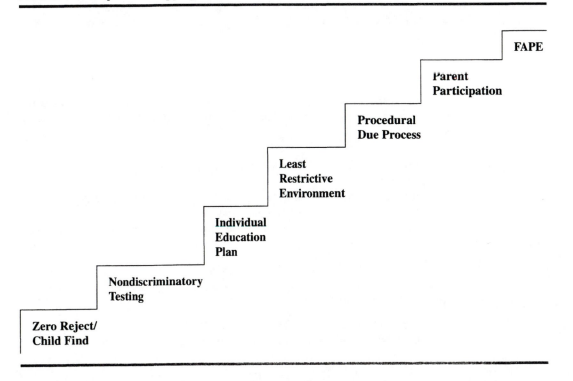

has a tracheostomy that must be suctioned daily, must be tube-fed, uses oxygen that must be monitored, must be in an air-conditioned environment, has severe mental retardation, and must be catheterized twice daily. Due to the multiple special needs of the child, his transfer IEP states that he was in a self-contained classroom with five children, a teacher, and an individual aide, with a school nurse on-site at all times. The new school district doesn't have a classroom appropriate for this child, and it would be very costly to create such a class. The zero reject principle means that this child must be provided with an appropriate education, whatever the cost to the local school district. It may mean that the new school district must pay tuition to a neighboring school district with an existing program or create a program, but the new district of residence is responsible for the child's FAPE.

An extension of the zero reject principle involves discipline. The reauthorization of IDEA in 1997 provided specific procedures for the discipline of children with disabilities. Before this revision, school districts relied largely on case law and local district policies and practice to guide their decisions. The overall theme of this section of the law is that all students, even those suspended or expelled, must be provided with FAPE (IDEA Regulations, C.F.R. § 300.121[a]). Even students not yet identified could assert the protections of IDEA in a disciplinary situation if the school district personnel had knowledge that the child might have a disability (IDEA Regulations, C.F.R. § 300.527[A]). To determine if the school district had knowledge of the potential disability, one of the following must have occurred:

- The parent of the child notified school district personnel in writing (or orally if the parent could not write) that the child was in need of special education and related services.
- The behavior or performance of the child demonstrated the need for special services.
- The parent requested an evaluation of the child.
- The child's teacher or other school personnel expressed concern about the child's behavior or performance to the special education director or other school personnel responsible for the special education referral system. (IDEA Regulations, C.F.R. § 300.527)

Specific procedures and definitions regarding discipline are summarized in Figures 1.3, 1.4, 1.5, 1.6 and 1.7.

Child find means that all states are required to implement child find procedures to locate unserved children and to inform parents of available services and programs for children with disabilities. For example, local school districts have annual early childhood screening programs, which screen the general preschool population in an attempt to locate unserved preschool children with disabilities.

Principle of Nondiscriminatory Assessment

IDEA provides strict procedures for assessing students for decisions about eligibility for special education. In the law, six general legal guidelines summarize assessment procedures.

FIGURE 1.3   Definitions: Discipline

Change of Placement: removal from school for more than 10 consecutive school days or a series of removals that constitute a pattern (must look at length of each removal, total amount of time removed, proximity of removals to each other) (C.F.R. § 300.519).

Interim alternative educational setting (IAES): must be selected to enable the child to continue to progress in the general curriculum (in another setting) and to continue to receive services that will enable the child to meet IEP goals (C.F.R. § 300.522[b][1]); must include services to address the behavior that is the subject of the discipline and must be designed to prevent the behavior from reoccurring (C.F.R. § 300.522[b][2]).

Manifestation determination: an IEP meeting whose purpose is to determine if a relationship exists between the behavior resulting in discipline and the child's disability; the IEP team must consider:

1) all relevant evaluation data
2) observation of the student
3) the student's IEP and placement (C.F.R. § 300.523[c][1][i–iii]).

The IEP team determines if the behavior is related to the disability by considering the following:

1) Was the IEP appropriate?
2) Did the disability impair the student's ability to *understand* the impact and consequences of the behavior?
3) Did the disability impair the student's ability to *control* the behavior? (C.F.R. § 300.523[c][2][i–iii])

If any of the above are not met, the behavior is a manifestation of the disability.

Functional behavioral assessment (FBA): not defined in IDEA. It could be considered as an assessment of the antecedent and consequences of the behavior that is subject to the discipline.

Behavioral intervention plan (BIP): not defined in IDEA. It could be considered as appropriate strategies and supports written as part of the IEP designed to address the problem behavior and to prevent it from reoccurring.

Adapted from *Inclusive Educational Administration: A Case Study Approach,* by M. K. Weishaar and J. C. Borsa, 2001, Boston: McGraw-Hill.

1. Discrimination in assessment is not allowed. Test instruments must not be culturally or racially biased. The following illustrates this concept:

> A school psychologist assessed an Hispanic child from Los Angeles with a reading test normed on a middle-class white population in rural Indiana. The background and experiences of the child were not likely represented in the norm group, thereby making the test culturally biased and invalid.

In addressing discrimination, IDEA states that if students do not speak English, every attempt must be made to assess them in their native languages. If students have disabilities, assessment instruments must not discriminate on the basis of the disability. An example

FIGURE 1.4   Discipline: IDEA

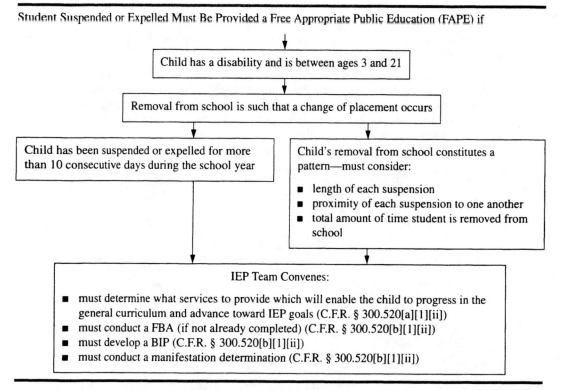

Student Suspended or Expelled Must Be Provided a Free Appropriate Public Education (FAPE) if

Child has a disability and is between ages 3 and 21

Removal from school is such that a change of placement occurs

Child has been suspended or expelled for more than 10 consecutive days during the school year

Child's removal from school constitutes a pattern—must consider:

- length of each suspension
- proximity of each suspension to one another
- total amount of time student is removed from school

IEP Team Convenes:

- must determine what services to provide which will enable the child to progress in the general curriculum and advance toward IEP goals (C.F.R. § 300.520[a][1][ii])
- must conduct a FBA (if not already completed) (C.F.R. § 300.520[b][1][ii])
- must develop a BIP (C.F.R. § 300.520[b][1][ii])
- must conduct a manifestation determination (C.F.R. § 300.520[b][1][ii])

Adapted from *Inclusive Educational Administration: A Case Study Approach,* by M. K. Weishaar and J. C. Borsa, 2001, Boston: McGraw-Hill.

might be asking children with cerebral palsy affecting their fine motor skills to write spelling words on paper as the teacher is dictating. The assessment would actually be a reflection of the children's motor skills, not spelling skills. Again, the assessment would discriminate against the children because of the nature of their disabilities.

2. The assessment must identify all of a child's educational needs, whether or not they commonly link to the child's disability category. It is not enough to simply identify a child as having a learning disability affecting reading. The assessment must address all needs of the child, including, for example, social and emotional needs.

3. Assessments must be comprehensive and use a variety of sources from a variety of professionals. The child must be assessed in all areas related to the suspected disability. Assessments must be tailored to the child's needs, not simply assessments that would yield a single intelligence quotient. Assessments must also gather functional and developmental information, include information from the parents, and include information related to helping the child to be involved in and progress in the general curriculum. In addition, assessments must be gathered by a variety of professionals representing different disciplines, including one person knowledgeable about the student's suspected disability.

FIGURE 1.5   Discipline: IDEA

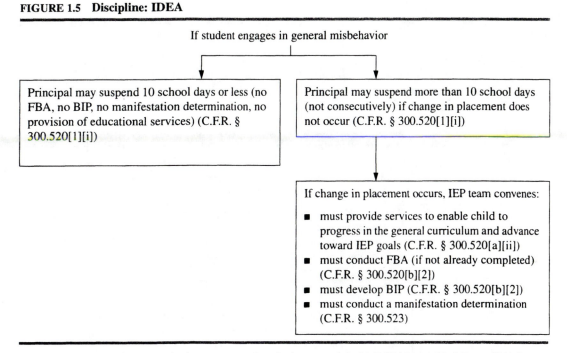

Adapted from *Inclusive Educational Administration: A Case Study Approach,* by M. K. Weishaar and J. C. Borsa, 2001, Boston: McGraw-Hill.

4. Assessments must be valid and reliable and administered by trained professionals. If any assessment is administered under nonstandard conditions, a description of the extent to which the conditions varied must be included in an evaluation report. Consider the following as an example in which a child is assessed under nonstandard conditions.

> A child with significant emotional problems is administered a standardized reading test. The child begins the test, gets frustrated when the reading becomes difficult, and refuses to complete the test. The examiner computes the scores but includes in the report that the test was not completed by the child due to refusal behavior and that any score represents a minimal estimate of the child's reading ability.

5. The rights of students with disabilities and their parents must be protected during assessment. Parents must be notified in writing when their child is referred for an evaluation, receive information on parents' rights, and give informed consent prior to the evaluation. Parents must also have an opportunity to examine records and participate in meetings when the identification, evaluation, and educational placement of their child is discussed. The child's progress toward special education goals must be provided to parents at least as often as provided in general education, and a reevaluation must be conducted at least every three years. In regard to reevaluation, if the school district determines upon review of the child's existing evaluation information that a reevaluation is not necessary, the parent may object and request that a full reevaluation be completed.

FIGURE 1.6   Discipline: IDEA

If student

1) carries a weapon to school or to a school function (C.F.R § 300.520[a][2][i]); or
2) knowingly possesses or uses illegal drugs or sells or solicits the sale of a controlled substance at school or at a school function (C.F.R. § 300.520[a][2][ii])

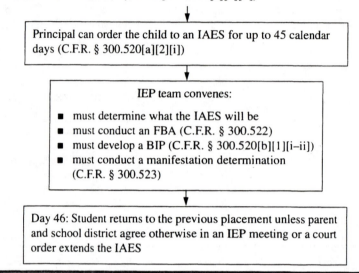

Principal can order the child to an IAES for up to 45 calendar days (C.F.R. § 300.520[a][2][i])

IEP team convenes:

■ must determine what the IAES will be
■ must conduct an FBA (C.F.R. § 300.522)
■ must develop a BIP (C.F.R. § 300.520[b][1][i–ii])
■ must conduct a manifestation determination (C.F.R. § 300.523)

Day 46: Student returns to the previous placement unless parent and school district agree otherwise in an IEP meeting or a court order extends the IAES

Adapted from *Inclusive Educational Administration: A Case Study Approach*, by M. K. Weishaar and J. C. Borsa, 2001, Boston: McGraw-Hill.

6. Children with disabilities must be included in general state and districtwide assessments, with appropriate accommodations, if needed. For children who cannot participate, as determined by the IEP team, the team must write on the IEP why the assessment is not appropriate and how the child will be assessed.

Children's rights are protected by the procedures described in IDEA. Children are evaluated and identified as having disabilities based on unbiased, fair assessments involving parents and teams of professionals.

Principle of Individual Education Plan

Each student with a disability must have a written IEP outlining services to be provided. The IEP is the heart of the law. Without an IEP, there is no way to assure that children with disabilities receive FAPE. An IEP is an appropriate education for a child, a way for parents to participate, a plan or road map for teachers, and proof of compliance for school districts. Each IEP must be developed using strict procedures and must be individualized to meet the needs of the child.

FIGURE 1.7   Discipline: IDEA

If student engages in misbehavior likely to result in injury and school wants student removed due to dangerous situation

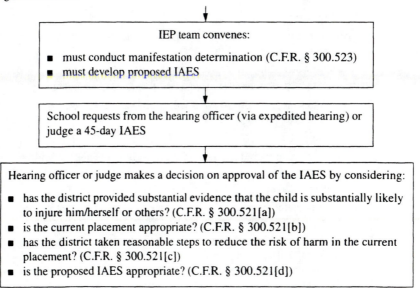

IEP team convenes:

- must conduct manifestation determination (C.F.R. § 300.523)
- must develop proposed IAES

School requests from the hearing officer (via expedited hearing) or judge a 45-day IAES

Hearing officer or judge makes a decision on approval of the IAES by considering:

- has the district provided substantial evidence that the child is substantially likely to injure him/herself or others? (C.F.R. § 300.521[a])
- is the current placement appropriate? (C.F.R. § 300.521[b])
- has the district taken reasonable steps to reduce the risk of harm in the current placement? (C.F.R. § 300.521[c])
- is the proposed IAES appropriate? (C.F.R. § 300.521[d])

Adapted from *Inclusive Educational Administration: A Case Study Approach*, by M. K. Weishaar and J. C. Borsa, 2001, Boston: McGraw-Hill.

The IEP consists of two pieces: a meeting and a document. The meeting consists of several participants, and they are clearly delineated in IDEA regulations (Figure 1.8). It is important to note that the parent is listed first in IDEA regulations, indicating that parent

FIGURE 1.8   Participants at the IEP Meeting

REQUIRED:

Child's parents

General education teacher (if child is, or may be, participating in the general education environment)

Special education teacher

LEA representative (who is qualified to provide, or supervise the provision of, special education; is knowledgeable about the general curriculum; and is knowledgeable about the availability of resources of the LEA)

Person who can interpret the instructional implications of the child's evaluation

Others at the discretion of the parents and the school district

Child, where appropriate

Source: IDEA Regulations, 34 C.F.R. § 300.344

FIGURE 1.9   IEP Components

1. Present levels of performance
2. Annual goals
3. Short-term objectives
4. Special education services to be provided (including related services, supplementary aids and services, and program modifications)
5. Extent to which child will not participate in general education
6. Anticipated date for initiation, frequency, location, and duration of services
7. How child's progress toward goals will be measured and how parents will be regularly informed of child's progress
8. Transition
   - age 14: statement of transition-service needs that focuses on child's course of study
   - age 16: statement of needed transition services, including interagency responsibilities or needed linkages
   - one year before age of maturity: statement that child was informed of rights (if adopted by state)
9. Modifications in administration of state and district assessments of student achievement (if not participating, tell why not and how child will be assessed)

Source: IDEA Regulations 34 C.F.R. § 300.347

participation is very important. In addition, a general education teacher must attend each IEP meeting if the child is or may be participating in the general education environment. Decisions cannot be made about whether a child will or may participate in general education outside of the IEP meeting, so it is assumed that general education teachers should attend all IEP meetings. The general education teacher must be present to participate in the development, review, and revision of the child's IEP, including assisting in the determination of behavioral interventions and supplementary aids and services and modifications for school personnel.

Components of the IEP are described next using examples. They also are listed in Figure 1.9.

1. *Present levels of performance* This statement is a direct reflection of the children's evaluations and the special needs that result from their disabilities. It must also include how the children's disabilities affect their involvement and progress in the general curriculum. For example, consider the following:

   A fourth-grade child with learning disabilities might have a statement that reads, "Juan has difficulty decoding words. When he reads a word incorrectly, he usually substitutes a word similar in printed form to the correct word, particularly in the first and last letters (e.g., carely/scarcely or rested for resting). He also reads slowly, generally at a rate of 20 words correct per minute. Peers generally read at a rate of 65 words correct per minute. This affects his progress in the general classroom because he is required to read stories to himself and answer comprehension questions independently. He is also required to read social studies and science information from the text and answer comprehension questions. Despite this difficulty, Juan has a positive attitude toward reading and he continues to try."

2. *Annual goals* These goals must be measurable and related to meeting the children's needs that result from their disabilities to enable them to be involved in and progress in the general curriculum. They must also meet the children's other needs that result from disability.

In the case of Juan, an appropriate goal might be, "By May 15, when shown three one-syllable words with common endings, Juan will correctly pronounce the ending sound in each word at 100 percent accuracy for sixty common endings."

3. *Benchmarks or short-term objectives* Benchmarks break down skills described in the annual goals. As an analogy, if we were taking a driving trip, the present levels of performance would describe where we were leaving, for example, Chicago. The annual goal would describe where we were going—New York City. The benchmarks describe how we would reach our destination—drive to Indianapolis, Indiana; to Columbus, Ohio; Philadelphia, Pennsylvania; and New York City.

Continuing the example with Juan, an appropriate benchmark might be, "By November 15, when shown three one-syllable words with common endings, Juan will correctly pronounce the ending sound in each word at 70 percent accuracy for thirty or sixty common endings."

4. *Special education services to be provided* This statement must include appropriate special education, related services, supplementary aids and services, and program modifications needed by the child to progress toward goals. It must also include a statement of how the child will be involved in and progress in the general curriculum and participate in nonacademic activities, and how the child will be educated with disabled and nondisabled children.

For Juan, the following services might be needed: "The special education teacher will preread all social studies and science assignments with Juan before reading the assignments in the general education classroom. He will take objective tests (written jointly by the special and general education teachers) on the material. Juan will participate in a separate reading program directed by the special education teacher."

5. *Extent to which the child will not participate in general education* An explanation must be provided of the extent to which the child will not participate in general education. The assumption is that all children will participate in general education, and if not, the IEP team must provide a reason why the child will not participate.

The following statement might be written for Juan: "Juan will participate in all aspects of the general education classroom except reading. He will receive special reading one hour per day. Juan needs one-to-one and small-group instruction to improve his ability to accurately read words. He must begin instruction at a level that is two years below the level used in the general education classroom to be successful."

6. *Anticipated date for initiation, frequency, location, and duration of services* This information must be delineated on the IEP to clearly communicate when, where, how often, and how long special services will be provided.

> With Juan, the following might be given:
>
> "Date for initiation of services: September 15
>
> Frequency: For reading, Juan will receive services daily; for social studies and science, Juan will receive services three days per week.
>
> Location: Reading instruction will take place in the special education classroom. Prereading social studies and science will take place in the general education classroom.
>
> Duration: Services will end on June 5."

7. *How the child's progress toward goals will be measured and how parents will be regularly informed of the child's progress* *Regularly informed* means at least as often as students in general education. This means that if general education students receive quarterly grade cards, parents of students in special education must be informed at least quarterly how their children are progressing toward their goals.

> For Juan, the statement might be, "Juan's progress will be evaluated by administering curriculum-based measurement probes in reading twice a week. Results will be graphed and reported to the parents on a quarterly basis."

8. *Transition* Students who are 14 years old, or younger if appropriate, must have a statement of needed transition services. For students ages 14 and 15, transition statements would focus on the child's course of study.

> For example, if a student wanted to enter the area vocational school to study welding as a ninth grader, the statement would indicate that the student needed to take a prerequisite, basic industrial arts course. At 16 and older, the statement of needed transition services would include interagency responsibilities, transition goals, and services needed to reach the transition goal. A 16-year-old girl with learning disabilities might have a transition goal to attend college after high school. Transition services might include preparation for taking the ACT and talking with the community college counselor.

9. *Modification in the administration of state and district assessments of student achievement, if appropriate* The IEP team first must determine if it is appropriate for a child with a disability to participate in state or school district assessments of student achievement. If the child will not participate, the team must provide a statement of why the child will not participate and how the child will be assessed. If the child will participate, the team must decide what, if any, modifications must be made.

> For Juan, the team might decide that he will take the state social studies test with the accommodation of having the test read aloud to him.

IDEA provides specific procedures on how to implement IEPs. IEPs must be accessible to school district personnel responsible for their implementation, and teachers and providers must be informed of their specific responsibilities in carrying out IEPs. School districts must provide what IEPs require and make good faith efforts to assist children in achieving their goals. Parents must also receive copies of IEPs.

In developing an IEP, a team must include the strengths of the child, parent input, results of the most recent evaluation, and, as appropriate, results of the child's performance on state or district assessments. In addition, special consideration must be given to the factors listed in Figure 1.10.

Principle of Least Restrictive Environment

IDEA provides four basic provisions regarding least restrictive environment (LRE). The general principle has remained unchanged since PL 94-142 was enacted in 1975, but minor changes were added in 1997. One change states that LRE includes preschool children. LRE's provisions are:

1. *General requirements* Each school district must ensure that to the maximum extent appropriate children with disabilities, including children in public and private institutions and other care facilities, are educated with children who are nondisabled; and that special classes, separate schooling, or other removal of children with disabilities from the regular educational environment occurs only if the nature or severity of the disabilities are such that education in regular classes with the use of supplementary aids and services cannot be achieved satisfactorily (IDEA Regulations, C.F.R. § 300.550).

2. *Continuum of placements* School districts must ensure that a continuum of alternative placements is available to meet the needs of children with disabilities for special education and related services...including regular classes, special classes, special schools, home instruction, instruction in hospitals and institutions, and supplementary instruction to be provided in conjunction with regular class placement (IDEA Regulations, C.F.R. § 300.551).

3. *Placements* The child's placement is determined annually, is based on the child's IEP, and is as close as possible to the child's home. Unless the IEPs of children with disabilities require some other arrangement, the children are educated in the schools that they would attend if nondisabled. Consideration should be given to any potential harmful effects on the children or on the quality of services that they need. Children

---

FIGURE 1.10   Other Factors: IEP

If behavior impedes the child's learning or that of others, team must consider strategies, including positive behavioral interventions, strategies, and supports to address that behavior

For limited-English-proficient children, team must consider language needs of the child

For blind or visually impaired children, team must consider provision of Braille instruction, if appropriate

Team must consider communication needs of child

Team must consider appropriate assistive technology

Source: IDEA Regulations, 34 C.F.R. § 300.346

FIGURE 1.11   Mediation Procedures: IDEA

Mediation is voluntary, and it cannot be used to delay or deny parents' rights to due process.

Each state must maintain a list of mediators. If a mediator is not chosen randomly, both the parents and the school must be involved in the selection process and agree upon the mediator.

The local education agency (LEA) or state education agency (SEA) may establish procedures to require parents who don't choose mediation to meet with a neutral party who would explain the benefits of and encourage mediation.

The SEA will pay the cost of mediation.

Mediation will be scheduled in a timely manner at a convenient location.

Any agreement reached in mediation must be in writing.

Procedural-safeguards notices must be given to parents engaged in mediation.

The discussions that occur during mediation must be confidential and may not be used as evidence in future due process hearings or litigation. However, the final written agreement may be used in future proceedings. Parties in the mediation may be required to sign a confidentiality pledge.

Attorneys' fees may not be awarded for mediation at the discretion of the state for a mediation conducted prior to filing a complaint.

Adapted from *Inclusive Educational Administration: A Case Study Approach,* by M. K. Weishaar and J. Borsa, 2001, Boston: McGraw-Hill.

with disabilities may not be removed from age-appropriate regular classrooms solely because of needed modifications in the general curriculum (IDEA Regulations, C.F.R. § 300.552).

4. *Nonacademic settings* With respect to nonacademic or extracurricular services, including meals and recess periods, a school district shall ensure that each child with a disability participates with nondisabled children to the maximum extent appropriate (IDEA Regulations, C.F.R. § 300.553).

Principle of Procedural Due Process

When a child experiences noticeable difficulty in school, individual determinations regarding that child's identification, evaluation, and placement are made and an IEP is developed. In this process, it is inevitable that there will be disagreement between parents and professionals at times. IDEA is based on the constitutional premise of due process; that is, if any party disagrees, that party can challenge the decision. To protect children's rights, IDEA regulates two types of conflict resolution: mediation and due process. If a conflict is not resolved by these processes, one or both parties can appeal the decision to the judicial court system.

All states must offer mediation as an option to resolve conflict. Mediation is a voluntary process in which an impartial third party assists the disputing parties in reaching a mutually satisfying agreement. Mediation does not delay due process but can occur concurrently with a request for due process. Mediation focuses on creative problem-solving and communication between all parties. It is focused on the future and does not assign blame on either party. Successful mediation results in a written agreement. Discussions during mediation are kept confidential. A summary of legal procedures during mediation is given in Figure 1.11.

Due process is a formal, adversarial procedure in which an impartial third party listens to evidence presented, including the examination and cross-examination of witnesses. Based on the evidence, the hearing officer renders a decision to resolve the conflict. The decision is binding unless it is appealed to the judicial system. In a due process hearing, there is a winner and a loser, and the focus is often on the past. Often, both parents and school districts are represented by attorneys in due process hearings. During a hearing, the provision of *stay put* applies. This means that the child who is the subject of the hearing stays in the current placement while the hearing is held. Exceptions to the provision of stay put include the following:

- The parents and school district mutually agree to a placement during the pendency of the hearing.
- The child is involved in a disciplinary situation involving weapons or illegal drugs and is placed in an interim alternative educational setting for 45 days.

Legal procedures in due process that are outlined in IDEA are summarized in Figure 1.12.

Parents may be awarded reasonable attorney's fees by a court if they prevail in a due process hearing. However, these fees may not be awarded or reduced under several circumstances detailed in IDEA regulations (see IDEA Regulations, C.F.R. § 300.513).

Principle of Parent Participation

IDEA ensures that school districts are not able to make unilateral decisions about the identification, evaluation, and placement of children with disabilities. The rights of children with disabilities and their parents are protected in many ways throughout the law. For example, parents must give informed consent before their child is evaluated for initial consideration for placement in special education and before initial placement in special education. Parents are afforded the opportunity to provide information to the evaluation team and fully participate in decisions about a child's eligibility for special education, the IEP, and placement. Before the identification, evaluation, or placement of a child is changed, parents must be given the opportunity to participate in the decision-making process. If a parent disagrees with any decision, the parent has the right to challenge the decision through mediation and due process procedures. Parents also have the right to review and obtain all records concerning their child. Rights of parents are woven throughout IDEA.

SECTION 504 OF THE REHABILITATION ACT OF 1973

Although IDEA provides critical protections for children with disabilities within the school system, Section 504 of the Rehabilitation Act of 1973 also provides important protections. Section 504 was passed by Congress in 1973, several years before the Education for All Handicapped Children Act, but regulations were not issued until 1977 (Yell, 1997).

Section 504 is a federal antidiscrimination law or a broad civil rights law. It forbids states, local governments, and any private organizations that receive federal monies from discriminating against an *otherwise qualified handicapped person* solely on the basis of a handicap. Although Section 504 provides protections for eligible individuals in agencies

FIGURE 1.12   Due Process Legal Procedures: IDEA

States are required to develop a model form to assist parents in filing a complaint.

In filing a request for a hearing to the school district, the parent must provide a written notice that includes: the name and address of the child and the name of the school the child attends; a description of the nature of the problem relating to the proposed initiation or change, including facts related to the problem; and a proposed solution to the problem.

Both parties must disclose evidence to be used at the hearing five business days before the hearing.

At least five business days before a hearing, each party shall disclose all evaluations completed by that date and recommendations based on those evaluations that are intended to be used at the hearing.

Both parties have the right to be accompanied and advised by counsel and individuals knowledgeable to children with disabilities.

Both parties have the right to present evidence and confront, cross-examine, and compel the attendance of the witnesses.

Both parties have the right to a written, verbatim record of the hearing or, at the option of the parents, an electronic verbatim.

Both parties have the right to written or, at the option of the parents, an electronic verbatim of the findings of fact and decisions.

Findings of fact decisions must be public, provided confidentiality is maintained.

The decisions and findings may be appealed to state or district courts of the United States, or first to the SEA if required in that state.

Except in cases involving alternative educational settings, unless the LEA and parents otherwise agree, the child shall remain in the then-current placement.

If applying for initial admission to school, with the consent of the parents, the child shall be placed in a public school program until proceedings end.

Parents may have the child who is subject of the hearing present.

Parents may open the hearing to the public.

Unless the hearing officer grants an extension, the final decision in a hearing must be reached within 45 days of the hearing request.

Source: IDEA Regulations, C.F.R. § 300.507–300.511

other than schools, the discussion in this chapter uses school districts to illustrate basic concepts of the law.

A person is protected by Section 504 if the person

(i) has a physical or mental impairment which substantially limits one or more of such person's major life activities, (ii) has a record of such an impairment, or (iii) is regarded as having such an impairment (Section 504, 29 U.S.C. § 706[7][B]).

The term *physical or mental impairment* means

(a) any physiological disorder or condition, cosmetic disfigurement, or anatomical loss affecting one or more of the following body systems: neurological; musculoskeletal; special sense organs; respiratory, including speech organs; cardiovascular; reproductive, digestive, genitourinary; hermic and lymphatic; skin and endocrine; or (b) any mental or psychological disorder, such as mental retardation, organic brain syndrome, emotional or mental illness and specific learning disabilities (Section 504 Regulations, 34 C.F.R. § 104.3[j][2][i]).

Major life activities include such things as walking, seeing, hearing, and learning.

Students who are eligible for services under IDEA are also eligible for protections under Section 504. However, there are a number of students who are not eligible under IDEA who are eligible for protections under Section 504. Examples of those potentially eligible under Section 504 only include:

- medical conditions, either permanent or temporary (e.g., asthma, allergies, diabetes, broken leg)
- attention deficit hyperactivity disorder (ADHD)
- behavior problems
- drug or alcohol addiction

Although IDEA has a list of 13 disabling conditions under which students can become eligible for special services, Section 504 has a very broad-based definition for eligibility: a child has or has had a physical or mental impairment that substantially limits a major life activity or is regarded as handicapped by others. Therefore, more students are eligible under Section 504 than IDEA.

There are other similarities and differences in IDEA and Section 504. Both require that FAPE be provided to students who are eligible. IDEA requires a written IEP developed using certain procedures, with specific content, and by a group of specific participants. Section 504 requires a written accommodation plan that is developed by a group of persons knowledgeable about the student. There are no specific procedures about content of the accommodation plan. Appropriate education in IDEA means a program designed to provide educational benefit, whereas in Section 504, appropriate education means to provide services comparable to those provided to nonhandicapped children. Appropriate accommodations could mean moving an English class to the first floor of a building for a student in a wheelchair, special instruction for a student with ADHD, or allowing more time for a student to complete a test.

One basic difference between IDEA and Section 504 is funding. IDEA provides funding to states for students eligible for services, but Section 504 provides no funding.

Both IDEA and Section 504 require notice to the parent about identification, evaluation, and placement. IDEA requires written notice with specific content by the school district prior to initiation or change in identification, evaluation, or placement of a child. Section 504 requires notice (but does not specify content or require written notice) when eligibility is determined or prior to a significant change in placement. Section 504 does not require written consent of the parent before the evaluation or provision of services for an eligible child, but IDEA has specific requirements regarding informed consent from the parent.

Evaluations differ between IDEA and Section 504. Section 504 evaluations are less specific. Evaluators must gather information from a variety of sources in the area of concern, and decisions are made by a group of people knowledgeable about the child, evaluation data, and service options. In contrast, IDEA requires a more-specific comprehensive evaluation by a multidisciplinary team assessing all areas of suspected disability. Reevaluations are required at least every three years under IDEA. On the other hand, Section 504 requires periodic reevaluations.

When determining placement under IDEA and Section 504, both require that school districts use information from a variety of sources, ensure that all information is considered and documented, and assure that decisions are made by a group of persons knowledgeable about the child, evaluation, and service options. Both assure that the child is placed to the maximum extent appropriate with children who are not disabled (LRE).

Section 504 requires that school districts appoint a person responsible for implementing a grievance procedure for parents and assuring compliance with the law. Parents must be notified of the grievance procedure, Section 504 procedures, and the grievance coordinator's name.

Both laws require impartial due process procedures to resolve conflict with parents who disagree with decisions made about identification, evaluation, or placement of their child. IDEA specifies procedures in due process, but Section 504 only requires that the parent have an opportunity to participate and be represented by an attorney. Other details are left for the individual school district to determine. IDEA requires that a parent pursue due process before presenting the case to the judicial system. Conversely, in Section 504, the parent may proceed directly to the judicial system.

IDEA is enforced by the U.S. Office of Special Education Programs, and the lead agency for enforcement in each state is the state education agency. Section 504 is enforced by the U.S. Office of Civil Rights, which can accept, investigate, and order compliance of a school district in which a parent has filed a complaint. The states have no regulatory authority for Section 504.

Following is an illustration of a case in which a child is eligible for services under Section 504.

> Lakisha has been diagnosed with Type I diabetes since the age of 4. She is given insulin injections three times daily. When Lakisha enrolls in kindergarten, which is a full-day program, her mother informs the teacher that she must be given an insulin injection daily before lunch. The teacher informs the building principal, and Lakisha is referred for a Section 504 evaluation. The parent receives a letter from the principal indicating that Lakisha will be evaluated for services under Section 504. Included is a document outlining parents' rights under Section 504. Lakisha's mother provides information from her doctor specifying the need for insulin injections, the time of injections, who can perform the injections, and emergency procedures. The teacher provides information about the kindergarten daily schedule, and the school nurse confers with the teacher. After information is gathered, Lakisha's mother receives notice that a meeting will be held to discuss Lakisha's health needs. At the meeting, participants include the kindergarten teacher, Lakisha's mother, the school nurse, and the building principal. The evaluation information is reviewed, and it is determined that Lakisha is eligible for protection under Section 504 as a handicapped person. An accommodation plan is written (Figure 1.13). During the school year, the school nurse administers daily injections to Lakisha before lunch. The plan is reviewed at the beginning of first grade.

FIGURE 1.13   Form for Section 504 Accommodation Plan

SECTION 504 ACCOMMODATION PLAN

Student Name: Lakisha Jones   **Grade:** K   **Address:** # 4 Harvey Drive

School: Portland   **Meeting Date:** 6/18

1. What is the concern? Lakisha must have insulin injections three times
daily. One injection must be given prior to lunch.

---

2. What is the basis for the determination of a handicap? Lakisha has Type I
diabetes, which requires insulin injections three times/day.
Lakisha's doctor provided a letter documenting her health problem.

3. How does the handicap affect a major life activity? Lakisha could not attend
school (major life activity of learning) unless the injection is
given at school.

4. What accommodations are necessary? The school nurse will give a daily
injection prior to lunch. Mrs. Jones will send necessary supplies
and medication on a weekly basis to school. In emergency, Lakisha
will be taken to the nearest hospital.

Date of Review: Prior to first grade—August

Participants: Ms. Middleton, School Nurse   Ms. Jones, Parent

Ms. Coleman, Principal

Mr. Brown, Kindergarten teacher

CC: Parent
Attached: District procedures regarding Section 504 of the Rehabilitation Act of 1973.

Section 504 is a far-reaching law, providing important protections to children with disabilities. Its importance cannot be understated because not only does it provide protection to children eligible under IDEA, but it provides protections for many children who are not eligible for services under IDEA.

AMERICANS WITH DISABILITIES ACT

The Americans with Disabilities Act (ADA) was passed by Congress in 1990 and was the most important legislation for persons with disabilities since Congress initially passed the Education for All Handicapped Children Act in 1975. The purposes of ADA include:

- to provide a clear and comprehensive national mandate for the elimination of discrimination against individuals with disabilities
- to provide clear, strong, consistent, enforceable standards addressing discrimination against individuals with disabilities
- to ensure that the federal government plays a central role in enforcing the standards established in the act on behalf of individuals with disabilities
- to invoke the sweep of congressional authority, including the powers to enforce the Fourteenth Amendment of the U.S. Constitution and to regulate commerce, in order to address the major areas of discrimination faced day-to-day by people with disabilities (ADA, 42 U.S.C. § 12101)

One important difference between ADA and Section 504 is that ADA extends coverage and protection to individuals employed by or using services provided by agencies and businesses that don't receive federal monies. Like Section 504, ADA does not provide funding to carry out the law.

Persons protected by ADA include the same persons protected under Section 504. The definition for persons with disabilities is the same—that is, a person who has, has a history of having, or is regarded as having an impairment that significantly limits one or more of life's major functions. The four major areas of coverage are reviewed next.

Employment Discrimination: Title I

Employers with 15 or more employees may not discriminate against qualified persons with disabilities. Employers must also provide reasonable accommodations for persons with disabilities unless undue hardship would result. Some of the factors considered under *undue hardship* include the nature and cost of the accommodation needed, the overall financial resources of the business, and the number of persons employed by the business (ADA 42 U.S.C. § 12111). Employment practices covered include application procedures, hiring, advancement, discharge, compensation, and job training (ADA 42 U.S.C. § 12112). Consider these as illustrations of ADA and coverage of employment practices:

> Tyrell is a person who, as a result of an accident, uses a wheelchair for mobility. Before the accident, Tyrell worked as a computer operator in a small insurance company of 25 employees. The business is located on the second floor of an old building in which there is an elevator. After months of rehabilitation, Tyrell is able to return to his position, but he is only able to work part-time until his strength and stamina improve. Tyrell is eligible for protection under ADA. The business must accommodate his disability by providing for a part-time work schedule.

David is a fifth-grade teacher in a general education classroom. He has a degenerative disease that is causing his vision to deteriorate. At this time, he is legally blind. He wants to continue teaching. David is eligible for protection under ADA, and the school district must provide reasonable accommodations. In this case, the school district employs a full-time instructional aide to assist David in the classroom.

Public Services and State and Local Governments: Title II

Title II of ADA states that qualified persons with disabilities shall not be denied participation in or be denied the benefits of the services, programs, or activities of a public entity (e.g., local and state governments) (ADA 42 U.S.C. § 12132). New construction and alterations to existing facilities must be accessible. In addition, existing facilities must meet program accessibility requirements consistent with Section 504. This is an example of Title II:

If a local school board holds monthly meetings on the second floor of a building that is not accessible to a person in a wheelchair, the school district must make arrangements for that person to attend meetings. This may involve moving the meeting to the first floor, or it may mean building a ramp to enter the building. In any case, the public entity—the school board—can't deny access to the person in a wheelchair.

In addition, Title II prohibits discrimination in public transportation services. New buses and railroad cars must be accessible, and one car per train must be accessible. Existing *key stations* in commuter rail and light rail systems must be accessible. Comparable transit must be provided to persons who can't use a fixed-route bus service to the extent that an undue financial burden is not imposed. Amtrak passenger cars must have accessible seats, and all existing Amtrak stations must be accessible. Title II specifies that public school transportation is not included (ADA 42 U.S.C. § 12141).

Privately Owned Public Accommodations and Services: Title III

The overall intent of Title III is to prohibit discrimination against a qualified person with a disability from the full and equal enjoyment of the goods, services, facilities, privileges, advantages, and accommodations of any privately owned public accommodations (ADA U.S.C. § 12182). Examples of public accommodations are listed in Figure 1.14. Public accommodations must not deny the opportunity to participate, provide for participation of unequal benefit, or provide for separate benefit (ADA U.S.C. § 12182). Participation of persons with disabilities must be provided in integrated settings appropriate to the needs of the individuals.

Title III addresses physical barriers, alterations to buildings, and new buildings. Physical barriers in existing facilities must be remodeled if readily achievable, that is, easily accomplished and able to be carried out without much difficulty or expense (ADA

FIGURE 1.14   Examples of Public Accommodations

Places of lodging—inn, motel, hotel

Food or drink establishment—restaurant, bar

Entertainment or exhibition places—movie theater, theater, concert hall, stadium

Sales or rental establishment—bakery, grocery store, clothing store, hardware store, shopping center

Service establishment—laundromat, dry cleaner, bank, barber shop, beauty shop, travel service, shoe repair service, funeral parlor, gas station, office of accountant or lawyer, pharmacy, insurance office, office of health care provider, hospital

Public transportation station—terminal, depot

Place of public display or collection—museum, library, gallery

Place of recreation—park, zoo, amusement park

Place of education—nursery; elementary, secondary, undergraduate, or postgraduate private school or public school

Social service center—day care center, senior citizen center, homeless shelter, food bank, adoption agency

Place of recreation or exercise—gymnasium, health spa, bowling alley, golf course

---

Source: ADA U.S.C. § 12181

U.S.C. § 12182). If not, services must be offered using alternative methods. Alterations to existing facilities and new construction must be accessible, which includes paths to restrooms, drinking fountains, and telephones (ADA U.S.C. § 12183).

Title III also addresses new buses and other vehicles, except automobiles. A new bus or over-the-road vehicle operated by a private entity must be accessible, or the system must provide persons with disabilities with a level of service equivalent to that provided to the general public (ADA U.S.C. § 12184).

Examples of the impact of Title III of ADA follow.

Joann is an actress who is deaf and lives in a large city. One day on her way home from work, she drives through a fast-food drive-through lane. Because of her disability, she is unable to place her order through the speaker, so she drives to the window and hands the worker a written list of what she wants to order. The worker must take the order in this manner. To do otherwise would be discriminatory and would deny Joann the ability to benefit from this service (the drive-through lane).

Wilford Junior High School is expanding the cafeteria to accommodate more students. To get into the cafeteria, one has to walk up six steps. The architect for the project informs the school-district board members that a ramp must be built to make the cafeteria accessible to people in wheelchairs. In making alterations to the building, the district must make the building accessible.

The local zoo has a train that takes visitors around the zoo grounds. One day, a fourth-grade class visits the zoo as a field trip. One fourth grader is in a wheel-chair and is unable to take the train with her classmates. The zoo ultimately has to order a special railroad car to accommodate people in wheelchairs.

Telecommunications: Title IV

In Title IV, telephone companies must provide telecommunications relay services 24 hours per day for people with hearing and speech impairments. In addition, closed captioning of public service announcements must be offered. For example, in airports, telecommunication devices (TDD) are now widely available to persons with disabilities.

ADA is a powerful and far-reaching law. As schools prepare children with disabilities with skills to live independently, to work, and to continue their education, ADA assists by removing barriers so that people with disabilities can become become full participants in the community.

SUMMARY

Three laws profoundly affect the lives of children with disabilities, IDEA, Section 504 of the Rehabilitation Act of 1973, and ADA. IDEA provides funding to school districts so they can provide FAPE to all children with disabilities.

The three laws complement one another. IDEA protects children ages 3 to 21 in one or more of 13 disabling categories. Section 504 provides protections to a broader group of children and adults with disabilities who might not be covered by IDEA. Section 504 covers agencies that accept federal funds. ADA provides protections using the same broad definition of disabilities used in Section 504, but it provides protections in most public and private businesses and agencies. With IDEA, children with disabilities can receive appropriate special education programs to enable them to become productive members of the community. When children with disabilities become young adults, ADA helps them use skills learned in school to become successfully and fully integrated into the community.

CHAPTER TWO

RELEVANT COURT CASES IN SPECIAL EDUCATION LAW

ZERO REJECT

Timothy W. v. Rochester School District

875 F.2d 954 (First Circuit 1989)

Timothy W. was born earlier than expected and weighed only 4 pounds. Timothy suffered from a number of difficulties, including respiratory problems, intracranial bleeding, hydrocephalus, and seizures. Early in his infancy, he was diagnosed as suffering from severe developmental retardation with suspected hearing and vision deficits. In February 1980, the school district's evaluation team determined that Tim did *not* qualify for special education services because of his inability to benefit from such services. In 1983, Tim was again evaluated by a team, but this time the team failed to decide whether Tim qualified for special education.

In November 1984, Tim's mother filed an action seeking injunctive relief and damages. She and her attorney requested that the school district place Tim in a special education program, paid by the district. They claimed that Tim qualified for special education under various special education laws, regardless of the severity of the disability. Despite their claims, the U.S. district court that heard the case in 1988 concluded that Tim was not capable of benefiting from special education. In addition, the court claimed that Timothy's potential for learning was "nonexistent."

In 1989, the First Circuit Court of Appeals reversed this decision. The court found that, under EHA (now IDEA), children with disabilities should receive an education that is appropriate to their unique needs. Furthermore, the court stated that states are ultimately the responsible parties in providing education to *all* children with disabilities and that proof of benefit is not required to provide services.

The Pennsylvania Association for Retarded Children v. the Commonwealth of Pennsylvania

334 F. Supp. 1257 (U.S. District Court, E.D. Pennsylvania 1972)

In 1972, the state's association for citizens with mental retardation and parents of children with mental retardation brought a class action suit against the Commonwealth because their children were excluded from public schools. The plaintiffs contended that in the process of denying a public education to children with mental retardation, they were denying them due process and equal protection.

The case was settled, and through a consent agreement the state initiated due process for students with mental retardation (or those thought to have mental retardation) before placing them in a special education program or excluding them from school. In addition, the state provided FAPE and training to children with mental retardation.

Peter Mills et al., Plaintiffs v. Board of Education of the District of Columbia

384 F. Supp.866 (U.S. District Court, District of Columbia 1972)

In August 1972, action was brought on the behalf of seven children with disabilities who had been labeled as having behavioral problems, mental retardation, emotional disturbance, or hyperactivity. They had been denied education in the District of Columbia public schools. These students had been excluded although the school system provided special education services to other students with disabilities. These particular students had been excluded through suspension, expulsion, and reassignment or transfer from regular education classes without due process. Through a judgement and decree, the court ruled in favor of the plaintiffs and found that students with disabilities, regardless of the severity of the disabilities, were entitled to a publicly supported education or alternative education. In addition, it found that prior to expulsion, public school students were entitled to hearings and periodic reviews of their status and progress.

NONDISCRIMINATORY EVALUATION

Larry P. v. Wilson Riles

793 F.2d 969 (Ninth Circuit 1981)

This complaint was filed in 1971 in the U.S. District Court for Northern California. In the complaint, the plaintiffs claimed that six African American children were placed in educable mental retardation (EMR) classes solely on the basis of Intelligence Quotient (IQ) test scores. [The case was later expanded in 1974 to include all African American school children in California who had been or were being classified as mentally retarded solely on the basis of IQ test scores.] The district court found that the use of IQ tests for placement of African American children in EMR classes violated their civil rights. The court barred schools from using standardized IQ tests for the classification or placement of African American children in EMR classes. The district court also ordered that each school district must reevaluate, without IQ tests, every African American child identified as an EMR student. The court did so in an attempt to eliminate disproportionate numbers of African Americans in EMR classes. The U.S. Court of Appeals for the Ninth Circuit later upheld this lower court's ruling. In 1994, the ban was dropped as a result of another case in the U.S. Court of Appeals for the Ninth Circuit: *Crawford v. Honig.*

Parents in Action on Special Education (PASE)
v. Joseph P. Hannon

506 F. Supp. 831 (N.D. Illinois 1980)

In this case, two African American children were placed in classes for children identified as educable mentally handicapped (EMH) after performing poorly on standard IQ tests. In 1980, plaintiffs for the children brought suit against the city board of education alleging that the IQ tests used to classify these children were culturally biased against African American children. They also claimed that the use of such tests violated the equal protection clause of the Fourteenth Amendment of the U.S. Constitution. In particular, the plaintiffs claimed that certain items on the Wechsler Intelligence Scale for Children, Revised (WISC-R) and one item on the Stanford-Binet test were culturally biased or suspected of being biased. Examples of test items included:

> What is the color of rubies?
>
> What does C.O.D. mean?
>
> Why is it better to pay bills by check than by cash?
>
> Why is it generally better to give money to an organized charity than to a street beggar?
>
> What are you supposed to do if you find someone's wallet or pocketbook in a store?
>
> What is the thing to do if a boy (girl) much smaller than yourself starts to fight with you?

The court ruled that there was no evidence that inappropriate assessment had occurred as a result of racial or cultural bias from test items. In addition, the court found that the assessment process in use in the Chicago public school system was appropriate because the number of items missed was not crucial (due to established test ceilings), some suspect test items were presented well into the test so that even nondisabled students would never have reached them, and IQ results were not the sole determinant in EMH placements.

IEP AND APPROPRIATE EDUCATION

Board of Education of the Hendrick Hudson
Central School District v. Rowley

Supreme Court of the United States, 1982

Amy Rowley was a deaf student who had minimal residual hearing yet lip-read. Before Amy started kindergarten at Furnace Woods Elementary School (Hendrick Hudson Central School District), a decision was made to place her in the general education kindergarten class for a trial period and provide her with a sign language interpreter. At the end of the trial period, it was determined that Amy should remain in the kindergarten class with the use of an FM hearing aid. Amy successfully completed kindergarten.

Before she attended first grade, an IEP was prepared for Amy. The IEP stated that Amy should be educated in a regular classroom, continue to use the FM hearing aid, receive instruction from a tutor for the deaf for one hour each day, and receive services from a speech therapist. The Rowleys agreed with the IEP but also requested that the school provide Amy with a qualified sign language interpreter in all of her academic classes. An interpreter had been used in Amy's kindergarten class for a trial period, but the interpreter reported that Amy did not need this service, and school officials agreed. When their request was denied, the Rowleys requested and received a hearing before a hearing officer. The hearing officer agreed with the school district that an interpreter was not necessary. This decision was later affirmed on appeal by the New York commissioner of education. The Rowleys then sought action in the U.S. District Court for the Southern District of New York, claiming the denial of the interpreter constituted a denial of FAPE.

The district court found that Amy was performing better than the average child in her classes and was advancing easily, but without a disability she would certainly be performing better. Because of this discrepancy between her potential and actual ability, the court agreed that she was not receiving FAPE. In other words, the court felt that Amy should be provided with an opportunity to achieve her *full potential* compared with her nondisabled peers. A divided panel of the U.S. Court of Appeals for the Second Circuit affirmed the lower court's ruling.

Next, the U.S. Supreme Court granted certiorari to review the lower courts' interpretation of IDEA. This was the first case in which the Supreme Court had been called on to interpret any provision of the Act. It was difficult for the justices to interpret the term *appropriate education*. The Court's opinion, as delivered by Justice William Rehnquist, stated that appropriate education did not mean that schools should provide services that would maximize the potential of each child with disabilities. Instead, the Court interpreted appropriate education to mean that schools should provide a basic floor of opportunity whereby students with disabilities would be provided with specially designed instruction and related services that would meet their unique needs. Through these services, students with disabilities would then be able to benefit from their education. In the process of deciding this case, the Court developed a two-part test to determine whether schools had provided a FAPE to students. First, had the school complied with the procedures set forth under IDEA? Two, were the students' IEPs (developed and written in conformance with the procedures set forth under IDEA) "reasonably calculated" to allow students to benefit from their education? In the Amy Rowley case, the Court concluded that the school had complied with requirements and procedures and that Amy was benefiting from her education, as documented by her passing grades and advancement to the next grade level. Therefore, the Court concluded that the circuit court had erred in its decision to affirm the ruling of the district court.

Cedar Rapids Community School District, Petitioner v. Garret F., a Minor, by His Mother and Next Friend, Charlene F.

Supreme Court of the United States, 1999

When Garret was 4 years old, he was involved in a severe motorcycle accident in which he suffered from a severe spinal cord injury. The accident left Garret paralyzed from the neck down, and he was restricted to a wheelchair. Despite his injuries, Garret has normal intelligence and is able to speak. Garret is, however, ventilator-dependent and requires constant assistance. For example, he has many specialized health-related needs including occasional manual pumping of an air bag attached to his tracheotomy tube, urinary bladder catheterization, and suctioning of his tracheotomy. He also needs someone near him who can perform emergency medical procedures.

Before he attended school, many of these health-related needs were met by a licensed practical nurse, who was hired by his mother with money from various sources (i.e., settlement proceeds, insurance, and other resources). Once in public school, Garret's mother asked the district to pay for his health care expenses. The district denied his mother's request. The district did not feel that it was legally obligated to provide continuous one-on-one nursing services. In a hearing before the Iowa Department of Education, an administrative law judge heard the case and sided with Garret's parents. The district appealed the decision in federal district court, but the administrative law judge's decision was upheld. Later, on appeal, the court of appeals also affirmed the lower court's ruling. It ruled that, under IDEA, schools must provide FAPE to children with disabilities and that an appropriate education includes related services. In addition, it found that Garret needed the services to attend school and that the services, although health-related, were not subject to a *medical exclusion* because a physician was not needed. Instead, the court found that a nurse or other trained personnel could provide necessary services. The school district asked to have the case reviewed by the U.S. Supreme Court. The opinion of the Court, delivered by Justice John Paul Stevens in 1999, affirmed the lower court's decision that Garret should be provided with these services and education officials should fund related services to guarantee that students like Garret can gain meaningful access to schools.

LEAST RESTRICTIVE ENVIRONMENT

Daniel R. R. v. State Board of Education

874 F.2d 1036 (Fifth Circuit 1989)

At the time of litigation, Daniel was a 6-year-old boy with Down syndrome who exhibited mental retardation and speech impairments. Daniel's developmental age and communication skills were equivalent to those of a 2-year-old child. His parents enrolled him in a half-day program devoted entirely to special education and a half-day prekindergarten (general education) class. Soon after he began prekindergarten, Daniel's teacher informed school officials that Daniel did not participate without constant, individual attention and he failed to master any of the skills that were taught. The placement committee then recommended that Daniel attend only special education classes and have lunch and recess with general education students. Daniel's parents appealed, and the hearing officer agreed with the district on the grounds that Daniel was receiving little educational benefit from his general education class and that the instructor spent the majority of her time with Daniel. In addition, the hearing officer noted that the teacher would have to modify the curriculum almost beyond recognition to meet Daniel's needs. After moving on to district court, the parents eventually filed an action in the U.S. Court of Appeals for the Fifth Circuit.

The Fifth Circuit Court used a two-part test to determine whether Daniel should be placed in the LRE. The court first had to determine whether education in the general education setting, with the use of supplementary aids and services, could be satisfactorily achieved. If it could not be achieved, the second part of the test asked whether the school had mainstreamed the student to the maximum extent possible. The court also determined that, when considering placement decisions, schools must also consider nonacademic aspects (e.g., lunch and recess) of the setting. In Daniel's case, the court decided that the teacher was spending much of her time with him at the expense of other students in the class. This third factor, according to the court, should also be taken into account when making placement decisions. The court therefore agreed that the school had met the two-part test and, in doing so, denied the parents' request that Daniel be enrolled in the general education classroom.

Sacramento City Unified School District v. Rachel H.

14 F.3d 1398 (Ninth Circuit), cert. denied, 129 L. Ed. 2d 813 (1994)

This case involves Rachel, an 11-year-old child who was diagnosed as moderately retarded. Initially, her parents requested a full-time placement in a general education classroom for their daughter. The school district refused their request and instead offered to place Rachel in a special education class for academic subjects and in a general education class for nonacademic activities such as art, music, lunch, and recess. The parents enrolled the child in a general education class at a private school while appealing the school district's decision through due process. In due process, the hearing officer agreed that the district did not make an effort to place Rachel in a mainstreamed classroom. The district then appealed to district court, and this court decided that the school district did not sufficiently prove that Rachel could not be educated in the general education classroom. In reaching their decision, the judges relied on a four-part test:

1. What are the educational benefits of general education placements (with supplemental aids and services) compared with special education class placements?
2. What are the nonacademic benefits to the children in terms of their interaction with nondisabled peers?
3. What are the effects of the children's presence on the general education teacher and nondisabled students?
4. What is the cost involved in providing supplementary aids and services in the general education setting?

In Rachel's case, the court found that the district did not sufficiently prove that the educational benefits of the special education class were equal to or better than the benefits of the general education class. The court agreed with Rachel's parents and current teacher that the nonacademic benefits (i.e., communication and social development) were sufficiently met in the general education class instead of the special education class. The court also found that Rachel's presence in the general education class was not disruptive and the teacher was not spending an inordinate amount of time with Rachel. The court did not agree with the district's claim that the general education placement was cost prohibitive. Finally, the school district appealed to the U.S. Court of Appeals for the Ninth Circuit; however, this court upheld the earlier decision of the district court.

PROCEDURAL DUE PROCESS

John Sessions v. Livingston Parish School Board

501 F. Supp. 251 (M.D. Louisiana 1980)

In 1980, parents of children with disabilities filed suit in federal district court against the Livingston Parish School Board in Louisiana for its failure to provide appropriate education for their children. Before 1979, children with disabilities received educational services from East Baton Rouge Parish (EBR). In the spring of 1979, the EBR school system notified Livingston Parish school officials that their students could no longer attend ERB schools as of the end of the school year. Early the following school year, Livingston Parish school officials placed the students in eight different classrooms throughout Livingston Parish; however, the ages and disabilities of the children were never considered. The parents of the children contended that because Livingston Parish neglected to consider the ages or disabilities of the children placed, their children were being deprived of FAPE, and they took the matter to district court. The case was dismissed by the judge because the parents had failed to exhaust the administrative remedies provided in IDEA. It was noted, however, that the parents reserved the right to renew their claims in federal district court, if necessary, but only after they had exhausted the administrative remedies that were available to them.

STUDENT MISCONDUCT AND COMPENSATORY EDUCATION

Honig, California Superintendent of Public Instruction v. Doe

484 U.S. 305, 108 S.Ct.592, 98 L. Ed. 2d 686 (1988)

In 1980, two students with emotional disturbance were suspended for inappropriate actions (in separate incidents) at their respective schools. When their five-day suspensions had concluded, school officials from the San Francisco School District sought to suspend them indefinitely and recommended them for expulsion. Doe's parents unsuccessfully protested against the indefinite expulsion and filed a suit in federal district court. (Smith later intervened.) The judge found that the proposed expulsions and indefinite suspensions for misconduct relating to their disabilities deprived the students of FAPE. In addition, the judge barred the district from suspending or expelling any students with disabilities for behavioral incidents that might be associated with their disabilities. The school district's superintendent, Honig, felt that Congress never intended (under IDEA) that potentially dangerous and violent students be returned to schools, and he appealed the decision to the U.S. Court of Appeals for the Ninth Circuit. The court, however, decided that expulsion is considered a change in placement and, therefore, regulated by the provisions under IDEA. Finally, Honig filed a request to have the U.S. Supreme Court review the case. In January 1988, the Court issued a ruling rejecting Honig's argument. In the opinion of the Court, written by Justice William Brennan, students with disabilities who are in the process of being expelled or suspended indefinitely should remain (or stay put) in their current placement until after the review. Moreover, schools could take immediate recourse against potentially dangerous and violent students via suspension for up to 10 days, change placement (following IDEA's procedures), or, if necessary, seek legal action through the courts. The IDEA Amendments of 1997 later addressed many of the unresolved issues relating to this case.

CASE STUDIES

CHAPTER THREE   ZERO REJECT AND CHILD FIND

CHAPTER FOUR   EVALUATION AND CLASSIFICATION

CHAPTER FIVE   INDIVIDUAL EDUCATION PLAN AND APPROPRIATE EDUCATION

CHAPTER SIX   LEAST RESTRICTIVE ENVIRONMENT

CHAPTER SEVEN   PARENT PARTICIPATION

CHAPTER EIGHT   DUE PROCESS

CHAPTER NINE   CONFIDENTIALITY AND PRIVACY

CHAPTER TEN   STUDENT MISCONDUCT

CHAPTER ELEVEN   COMPLIANCE TECHNIQUES

APPENDIX   ANSWERS TO LEGAL ISSUES TO CONSIDER

CHAPTER THREE

ZERO REJECT AND CHILD FIND

CASE 3.1   JODI/SPECIAL EDUCATION SERVICES

CASE 3.2   LINDA/HOMESCHOOL

CASE 3.3   DANNY/EXPULSION

CASE 3.4   PETER/HEALTH IMPAIRED STUDENTS

CASE 3.5   KATE/PHYSICAL DISABILITIES

CASE 3.6   ANDRE/AGE AND SPECIAL EDUCATION SERVICES

CASE 3.1

JODI/SPECIAL EDUCATION SERVICES

Ms. White, special education administrator, received a telephone call from Mrs. Singer on January 16. Mrs. Singer stated in a quiet and trembling voice, "My name is Debbie Singer, and my child, Jodi, is 4 years old and handicapped. She's my only child. The doctors told my husband and me that Jodi has a neurological problem and that she will die. Since she was born, Jodi's cerebellum has not fully developed, and her brain functioning is slowly deteriorating. She can't sit up by herself, and she can't hold her head up. Through my husband's insurance, Jodi has received physical therapy and part-time nursing care for the past year. My friend told me that the school district offers free physical therapy. My husband and I are concerned about health insurance. Jodi has almost reached the maximum lifetime insurance-expense cap due to her health problems. The physical therapy she receives twice a month is draining the insurance. My husband and I conduct physical therapy exercises with Jodi at home daily." Mrs. Singer began to cry as she added, "According to the doctors, Jodi will continue to deteriorate and eventually die within a few years."

Ms. White listened intently and jotted notes while Mrs. Singer spoke. She then stated, "The school district might be able to offer physical therapy, but an extensive evaluation would have to be conducted first."

Mrs. Singer, sounding disappointed, said, "Oh, Jodi isn't very strong. She might not have the stamina to go through an evaluation. Wouldn't it be possible to just provide the physical therapy services without the evaluation?"

Ms. White stated, "I'm sorry, we can't do that. However, the evaluation consists of many components, some involving Jodi directly and others not directly involving her. The psychologist and speech and language therapist will want to evaluate Jodi directly, but they will be very sensitive to your concerns about her stamina to withstand an evaluation. To gather other information, the social worker will talk to you and your husband. This information will include a developmental and health history. We'll also want to obtain copies of Jodi's medical records. If you give written permission for the evaluation, it can be completed in a short period of time, as short as three weeks."

Mrs. Singer reluctantly said, "I'll allow the evaluation. I'll stop by your office tomorrow to sign the permission forms."

During the next few weeks as the evaluation was conducted, a social worker met with both parents and gathered medical records. Jodi did have a degenerative brain disease that was quite rare. According to her mother, at the age of 2½, she was a normal child and began attending preschool. At about 3, she began to walk with an odd gait and she fell quite frequently. During this time, her speech also deteriorated and she began speaking in shorter sentences and used few words to describe objects. Her parents took her to a number of doctors and, after many tests and consultations, they were told that she had a very rare brain disease and that she would continue to degenerate as she got older. Jodi probably wouldn't live to the age of 8, and she would deteriorate to the point of needing total care. The doctors told Mrs. Singer that Jodi would become blind and deaf and lose all but spastic movement. She would be unable to sit, crawl, or talk, and eventually would have to be tube-fed. There was no treatment for the disease, and doctors said the Singers would need help caring for Jodi at home.

On receiving the news, her parents were devastated and began the task of taking care of Jodi. At first, Jodi did well for several weeks after the diagnosis. In fact, the parents said that they even had hope that the diagnosis was wrong. However, within the past few months, Jodi was hardly the child they had known. She had lost almost all of her normal functioning. Her parents took turns taking care of her day and night, with some assistance from a nurse and a physical therapist paid for by health insurance. Both parents were exhausted and distraught. It was during this time that the Singers decided to contact the school district to seek help.

As part of the evaluation, a team of evaluators went to Jodi's home to examine her directly. The team decided to evaluate Jodi at the same time on the same day. The team included a social worker, a psychologist, a speech and language therapist, and a physical therapist. When they arrived at the Singers', they found Jodi curled in a fetal position. The physical therapist tried to move her and she screamed in pain. Other forced movements resulted in the same outcome. The psychologist and speech therapist tried to see if Jodi responded to noise, light, and touch. She didn't seem to respond to any stimuli. For example, even when lightly touched on the cheek, Jodi did not respond. For the most part, she just laid curled in the fetal position. Mrs. Singer demonstrated the range-of-motion exercises that she used with Jodi. Although short in duration, Mrs. Singer preformed these exercises daily. Throughout the exercises, Jodi screamed. Often upset by watching her daughter in pain, Mrs. Singer cried and stated that she "just didn't know what else she could do."

One week after the evaluation was conducted, a multidisciplinary conference was held. At the conference, the evaluators, parents, special education teacher, and special education administrator were present. The evaluators presented their data, and all concluded that Jodi did not appear to respond to stimuli. It also appeared to hurt her when she was moved from the fetal position. The parents stated that Jodi would become more stiff if she weren't forced to move daily. The team concluded that Jodi could not benefit from any educational intervention due to her profound disability and her deteriorating condition. The special education administrator, Ms. White, concluded by saying, "Jodi is not able to benefit from any educational intervention at this time. Even physical therapy will not help her grow and develop. Therefore, it is the consensus of this team that Jodi should not be provided with special education services at this time. If her condition improves to a point where she may be able to benefit from services, the team will then reevaluate her."

The parents were astonished. How could the team conclude that they could not help her? If the parents could not give up on Jodi, how could the school district do so? Mr. and Mrs. Singer just shook their heads and left the room without saying a word.

Jodi never received special education services. Approximately one year later, on December 19, she died quietly at home.

QUESTIONS

Legal Issues to Consider

1. According to the basic principles of IDEA, did the team make a good decision not to provide special education services to Jodi? You may want to consider FAPE and equal access. Why or why not?

2. Describe any prominent court cases that address the issue of zero reject and educability.

3. Would Jodi be considered *handicapped* under Section 504 of the Rehabilitation Act of 1973? Why or why not?

4. If Jodi were considered handicapped under Section 504, what kinds of services could be provided?

Other Issues

1. Do you agree with the statement "Education must be measured by the acquirement of traditional cognitive skills"? How does this apply to Jodi's case?

2. Should children who are ill and dying be offered special education services? Why or why not?

■■■■■ **CASE 3.2** ■■■■■

LINDA/HOMESCHOOL

Linda and her mother had lived in the small town of Columbus for 10 years. When Linda was 5 years old, her mother, Mrs. Cruez, had enrolled her in kindergarten. The year did not go well. The kindergarten teacher, Mrs. West, noticed that Linda was not progressing at the same rate as the other children. Specifically, Linda had difficulty understanding the basic concepts of position, colors, and quantity. In addition, her speech was unintelligible. Concerned, Mrs. West contacted Mrs. Cruez and discussed Linda's problems. Throughout their conversation, Mrs. Cruez was angry and felt that the kindergarten teacher was not helping Linda as much as she should.

Ultimately, Mrs. Cruez took Linda to her doctor for an evaluation. Mrs. Cruez felt that Linda was not growing physically as she should, that she was immature for her age, and that her speech was very difficult to understand. After several specialists and many tests, it was determined that Linda had a rare syndrome that manifested itself overtly at about the age of 4. The characteristics of the syndrome included mental retardation, short physical stature, being overweight, social immaturity, and sterility. The condition was so rare that several doctors used Linda in a study to learn further about the syndrome. Mrs. Cruez cooperated with the doctors and even joined a support group at the hospital, but the situation at school rapidly deteriorated. At the end of kindergarten, Mrs. Cruez abruptly took Linda out of school because she felt that the school staff could not meet Linda's special needs. She decided to homeschool Linda for first grade. School personnel did not know what had happened to Linda, and no one seemed to question the fact that she was no longer in school, despite reports by several teachers that they had seen Linda at the grocery store or playing in her yard.

During the next several years, Mrs. Cruez homeschooled Linda during part of each day. No particular curriculum was used, and Mrs. Cruez felt that she had made the best decision for Linda. Mrs. Cruez consulted the State Board of Education and found that there were no rules or guidelines concerning homeschooling. Mrs. Cruez did not have to report to anyone regarding Linda's progress or attendance in school.

Linda played mostly by herself and didn't have any close friends. Occasionally, she would play with younger cousins, but, for the most part, Linda's life consisted of being with her mother. One day, Mrs. Cruez was reading the newspaper and saw an article about the local high school's work–study program for students with disabilities. Linda was now 14 years old, and her mother began to think about what would happen to Linda after she was no longer able to care for her. After reading the article, Mrs. Cruez decided to enroll Linda in the local high school.

On October 20, Mrs. Cruez and Linda walked into the high school. Linda was dressed in a summer dress, bobby socks, and old sneakers. She carried a Disney cartoon lunch box, and her hair was in a ponytail. Although Linda was very excited at the prospect of beginning school, Mrs. Cruez was quite nervous about sending her daughter to school. Mrs. Cruez enrolled Linda and met with a school counselor. It was obvious that Linda was not an ordinary transfer student. She not only looked different and acted immaturely, but her speech was somewhat unintelligible. Her mother had to interpret for her, and Linda often used gestures to communicate with her mother. The counselor talked to Mrs. Cruez about Linda's schooling. Mrs. Cruez informed the counselor that the reason she took Linda out of school was because she was afraid that the school staff wouldn't be able to meet Linda's needs. Up to this point, Mrs. Cruez did not see any useful outcome of public schooling for Linda.

"It wasn't until I saw the article about the work–study program in the newspaper that I considered sending Linda back to school," Mrs. Cruez remarked in a self-assured voice.

Mrs. Cruez wanted Linda to be part of the program and to learn to become self-sufficient because she wouldn't be around forever. The special education counselor suggested that the first step was to conduct an evaluation of Linda to determine her specific needs. Reluctantly, Mrs. Cruez agreed and signed the consent form.

Through the careful coordination of schedules among school personnel, six weeks later the evaluation was completed. A social worker met with Mrs. Cruez to obtain a medical and social developmental history and information on Linda's adaptive behavior. A psychologist met with Linda to conduct a formal assessment, using instruments including the Wechsler Intelligence Scale for Children III (WISC III) and the Wechsler Individual Achievement Test. The speech and language therapist conducted a formal assessment. In addition, vision and hearing screenings were conducted and medical records were gathered. After the evaluation components were completed, a conference was conducted to discuss the results. Members of the assessment team found that Linda had a verbal IQ of 50, a performance IQ of 49, and a full-scale IQ of 50, which was considered below average. Academically, she functioned at a prefirst-grade level in basic academic subjects. Her adaptive behavior was commensurate with her overall ability, and she had severe articulation and language delays. Based on the evaluation, the team determined that Linda was eligible for a special education program for the moderately mentally disabled. An IEP was developed that included special education classes for the full school day and participation in a work–study program. She would also receive speech and language therapy that was to be integrated into the work–study program. Mrs. Cruez signed consent for Linda's placement in the special education program at the conclusion of the meeting.

Linda successfully completed high school at age 21 and held a job at a local fast-food restaurant during her high school years. The staff worked diligently in trying to get Linda's social skills to *fit in* at the high school. In the state where Linda lived, all students regardless of their disabilities were eligible to receive high school diplomas; therefore, Linda went through graduation exercises and received a high school diploma. A state department of rehabilitation agency was available to provide assistance to Linda as a young adult. Although she would never be totally independent, she had been successfully integrated into society.

QUESTIONS

Legal Issues to Consider

1. What responsibilities did the school district have under the federal mandate for child find? Did the school district fulfill its responsibilities?

2. What responsibilities did the school district have under the federal mandate for transition? Did the school district fulfill its responsibilities?

3. How does transition in IDEA relate to the zero reject principle?

Other Issues

1. Was it appropriate for Linda's mother to homeschool Linda? Why or why not?

2. What (if anything) could the school district have done differently to get Linda in school?

3. Should students with moderate or severe disabilities receive high school diplomas? Why or why not?

━━━━━━━   **CASE 3.3**   ━━━━━━━

DANNY/EXPULSION

Danny was a 14-year-old freshman at Cole City High School. Because he behaved inappropriately, Danny was labeled behavior disordered at the age of 9, in fourth grade. His inappropriate behaviors consisted of stealing, lying, and refusing to complete work. As evidenced by his lack of friends, social relationships with his peer group were poor. In fourth grade, Danny was placed in a self-contained behavior disorders classroom, where he remained with the same teacher and students until sixth grade. In seventh and eighth grades, Danny was successfully mainstreamed into three regular classes. Despite his success in the mainstreamed classes, Danny's school attendance had become problematic, especially in eighth grade. His freshman schedule placed Danny in special education classes for English and math and general education classes for industrial arts, physical education, and science. Danny was basically a likable child who was a follower, not a leader. Easily influenced by his peers, Danny began drinking alcohol and smoking marijuana.

Danny lived with his mother, father, younger brother, and sister. The family lived in a socially depressed area of town. In this area, most children came from single-parent families, unemployment was high, most adults did not have a high school education, and drug abuse and alcohol abuse were common problems. Some families lived in substandard housing without electricity. Others lived in houses that had dirt floors. Danny's family was fortunate to live in a trailer with two bedrooms. Danny slept in the living room on the couch. His siblings shared one bedroom, and his parents shared the other bedroom. Both of Danny's parents, Tom and Sue Givens, were alcoholics, but neither actively drank. Both parents regularly attended Alcoholics Anonymous meetings. Danny's father worked in a local factory making copper tubing for plumbing. His mother did not work outside the home. Danny's mother was supportive of his education because she wanted him to graduate from high school, something neither she nor her husband had been able to accomplish. Danny's mother felt guilty about the manner in which she had raised him because she drank heavily and neglected him.

Despite his many problems, Danny began high school successfully. He liked his classes and completed all of the required work. His attendance and grades, until the "incident," were improving. It was on December 14 that the incident occurred that was to change his life in a dramatic way. On this day, in industrial arts class the students had been working with sheet metal. The students were responsible for completing a metalworking project assigned by the instructor. After initial instruction on the project, students worked independently and the instructor worked with individuals. As the other students began working on the project, Danny began creating a 10-inch-long knife. As Danny was sharpening the blade, he saw the teacher.

The teacher, Mr. Hawthorn, asked, "What are you doing, Danny?"

Danny responded, "Uh, nothing."

Mr. Hawthorn looked over Danny's shoulder and said, "It looks to me like you're making a knife."

Danny quickly said, "Well, there's a kid in school who threatened to kill me. I was making this to protect myself."

Mr. Hawthorn sighed and said, "Come on, Danny, let's go to the assistant principal's office."

Danny accompanied Mr. Hawthorn to the assistant principal's office. When questioned again, Danny admitted he was making the knife to protect himself. The principal contacted Danny's mother and suspended him 10 days for having a weapon. His mother was asked to pick him up at school. When she arrived, she was shown the weapon and given a letter of suspension. In the letter, it stated the school's policy of not permitting weapons on school grounds. As with other suspected students, Danny would receive a hearing for possible expulsion.

During the 10-day suspension from school, the special education administrator scheduled a multidisciplinary conference for Danny. On the day of the conference, Mrs. Givens, Danny, the assistant principal, a special education teacher, a school psychologist, and the special education administrator were present. Danny's father was unable to attend the meeting because of his work schedule. The team reviewed the incident, Danny's disability and its manifestation in school, his school progress, and his history of discipline problems. Danny's only discipline problems in high school involved minor incidents such as tardiness to class and unexcused absence from school. The team decided that making a knife was not a manifestation of Danny's behavior disorder and that, in this case, regular school discipline should apply. Danny's mother agreed that Danny had made a poor decision to make a knife and urged school officials not to expel him. Her pleas, however, didn't change the outcome, and the team forwarded its findings to the expulsion hearing officer, who conducted a hearing the next week.

At the expulsion hearing, the assistant superintendent, who was the hearing officer, conducted the hearing in a fair and impartial manner. Danny and his mother were able to tell what had happened, and the high school personnel reviewed the sequence of events. The special education administrator reviewed the findings of the multidisciplinary conference and stated that Danny's behavior was not related to his behavior disorder. During the hearing, the parents, school officials, and the hearing officer were afforded the opportunity to cross-examine witnesses. Mrs. Givens again made a plea for Danny not be expelled from school. She also said that she knew what he did was wrong. The hearing was recorded so that the proceedings could be transcribed for the board of education. The hearing concluded after 45 minutes, and the hearing officer stated that the hearing evidence would be presented to the board of education the next week in a closed session. It was at this time that the board would make a decision regarding Danny's expulsion from school.

At the school board meeting, all evidence was reviewed. The board members had been under pressure for some time to reduce the number of violent incidents in the school district. Therefore, they were not sympathetic toward Danny's case. Some stated that they had to do whatever was necessary to send a message to all students that weapons would not be tolerated. The board voted unanimously to expel Danny until the end of the school year. He would not be allowed to return to school until the summer session.

Angered by the board's decision, Danny's mother could only wonder what Danny would do until the summer session began. The official letter stating the decision did not offer any guidance. It simply said that Danny would be allowed to return to school in June.

QUESTIONS

Legal Issues to Consider

1. How does IDEA address the issue of expulsion?

2. Was it legal for the district to expel Danny? Why or why not?

3. Was it legal for the district to expel Danny from school during his ongoing suspension from school? What evidence supports your answer?

Other Issues

1. Did it appear from the evidence given that the behavior of making a knife was a manifestation of Danny's behavior disorder?

2. Should school districts be allowed to discontinue special education services from students for severe disciplinary incidents? Why or why not?

3. What else could the school district have done with Danny? What barriers prevented this from happening?

■■■ CASE 3.4 ■■■

PETER/HEALTH IMPAIRED STUDENTS

Amy Hernandez slowly walked into the doctor's office. She had a lump in her throat and her heart was pounding. She signed her name on the sign-in sheet. As she looked around, she noticed many children waiting with their parents to see Dr. Stevens. Some were sitting on parents' laps, and others were running around the room. The nurse called Mrs. Hernandez's name. She quickly got up and was led by the nurse to Dr. Stevens' office.

"Mrs. Hernandez, thank you for coming in so quickly. We just received the results of Peter's blood tests. I'm afraid I have some bad news."

Mrs. Hernandez felt a sick feeling in her stomach as she said, "I was afraid of that."

Dr. Stevens continued, "Peter has what is called AIDS-related complex or ARC. This means he might have what is called *acquired immune deficiency syndrome* or *AIDS*. The fevers and swollen lymph nodes he has been experiencing are symptoms of ARC."

"How could he possibly get AIDS, Dr. Stevens? I thought AIDS was contracted by drug users or homosexuals."

"No, that is not true. It is probable that Peter contracted AIDS sometime when he received blood because he is a hemophiliac. AIDS is caused by a retrovirus called *human im-*

munodeficiency virus, or *HIV.* We can treat the symptoms and there are several advances being made in treatment, but he cannot be cured of the disease. It is likely his immune system will become damaged to the point that he will be susceptible to infections and his body will be unable to fight the infections."

Mrs. Hernandez, her eyes filling with tears, quietly cried, "Oh, no." She put her head down on the edge of Dr. Stevens' desk, and he put his hand on her shoulder.

"I know this must be difficult, Mrs. Hernandez."

After a few minutes of silence, Mrs. Hernandez lifted her head and asked, "Does this mean Peter will die?"

"Mrs. Hernandez, the statistics for long-term survival are improving all the time. Much research is being conducted on HIV, and people are learning more all the time about the disease and its effects. I would like to refer Peter to a specialist who deals exclusively with HIV."

Throughout their conversation, Mrs. Hernandez frequently broke down and cried.

She finally left Dr. Stevens' office and drove home. Through a blur of tears, many thoughts went through her mind. She had known all along that something was terribly wrong. Peter was running fevers on a more frequent basis. Every time he went to the doctor, she was told that his lymph glands were swollen, and he was frequently prescribed an antibiotic. Eventually, even their family doctor became suspicious and ordered several tests. Mrs. Hernandez had always been optimistic, but this time she felt different. Now what? How would she tell Peter in a way that a first-grader could understand? What kinds of medical procedures would he have to endure? What about school? Would his school allow him to attend if they were told he had ARC? Would the school even be told? How could she possibly face the loss of her son?

Within two weeks, Mrs. Hernandez took Peter to see the specialist, and the news was very encouraging. She was told that Peter could live many years without worsening and that he would be eligible for both standard and experimental treatments. These doctors encouraged her to contact school officials so that they would be aware of any new behaviors and symptoms Peter might display. There was no reason that Peter should be excluded from school given the facts that he was relatively well and the disease could not be transmitted by casual contact.

During the next day, Mrs. Hernandez made an appointment to see the principal, Mr. Craft.

"Mr. Craft, a few weeks ago, I was told that my son, Peter, had contracted HIV from a blood transfusion. At this time, he is experiencing symptoms associated with AIDS-related complex. Basically, he is quite well at this time and taking medication".

Mr. Craft listened intently as he wrote notes and said, "What are your plans for Peter's education?"

Mrs. Hernandez, feeling confused about the question, answered, "I'm not sure what you mean."

"Children who are as ill as Peter probably don't belong in school. There will be considerable fear that Peter could spread the disease to others."

In an angry voice, Mrs. Hernandez stated, "Mr. Craft, Peter will remain in his first-grade class as long as his health is stable. At this point he is not ill, and there is no way of telling when he will develop full-blown AIDS." As she got up to leave the office, she said,

"You may have access to Peter's medical records, but Peter *will* remain in his first-grade classroom!"

Mr. Craft conferred with the district superintendent and members of the board of education. It was decided that Mr. Craft would inform Peter's teacher about Peter's condition. Peter's teacher was extremely upset. She stated, "You mean I have to teach a child with AIDS? Can you guarantee me 100 percent that this disease cannot be contracted by casual contact? I can tell you right now that I refuse to teach this child in my class, and if you don't like it, you can find another first-grade teacher!"

After further consultation with the superintendent and board of education members, it was determined that Peter should be evaluated for possible special education. Mrs. Hernandez reluctantly agreed with the evaluation. The evaluation included a review of medical records, psychological assessment, assessment of Peter's progress, and a social developmental study. Upon completion of the evaluation, a multidisciplinary conference was held to discuss the results. Mrs. Jones, Peter's teacher; a school nurse; the school psychologist; the school social worker; the special education administrator; and the principal were present. Peter's medical records confirmed what Mrs. Hernandez had previously told the principal. The records also clearly stated that it was unlikely that HIV would be transmitted by casual contact. Peter was viewed as a well-behaved student and who was highly unlikely to bite or scratch anyone. Therefore, it was unlikely that anyone would come in contact with his blood or saliva. The psychologist stated that Peter was above average in intelligence and that academically he was progressing well. Toward the end of the conference, the team stated that Peter was eligible for special education services under the label *health impaired* because he had ARC. The team then began writing an IEP to exclude Peter from the first-grade class. The team stated that other children and their parents would fear and ridicule Peter if they found out about his medical condition. They felt Peter would be protected and educated more appropriately outside of the regular classroom.

Specifically, it was proposed that Peter be placed in a portable classroom that had been used several years ago but was now unoccupied. Peter would be provided with his own teacher, who also happened to be a nurse. He would not be integrated with any other students in the school.

At the end of the meeting, Mrs. Hernandez stood up and stated, "I will not allow you to do this to my child. It is unfair and discriminatory for you to implement this plan. I am requesting a hearing, and I will be represented by an attorney." With that, Mrs. Hernandez stomped out of the room.

The case received much press in the local newspapers, and the community was divided. Some people felt that Peter should be allowed to attend his regular first-grade class, and others (a very vocal group) felt that no one should associate with this child for fear of contracting the disease. The teachers in the school district were also divided. Most did not want to teach a child with ARC in any classroom. The teachers filed a grievance with the school district stating that teaching a child with ARC would be placing teachers in a dangerous situation. In the community, citizens picketed school board meetings, and someone even sent a threatening letter to Mrs. Herrandez. Because Mrs. Herrandez feared for Peter's safety, she took him out of school and enrolled him in a homeschool program.

A due process hearing was held, and the hearing officer decided in favor of the school district. The hearing officer stated that the district had observed the child's rights by appropriately evaluating him and offering an appropriate education in the least restrictive environment. The school district was told it would be able to carry on with its proposed placement for Peter. Mrs. Herrandez immediately appealed the decision to the federal appeals court. At this level, the decision was overturned, and the district was ordered to immediately place Peter in the general education classroom. The judge reasoned that, although Peter did have a disability, it was in no way interfering with his education. Therefore, Peter was not eligible for special education services under IDEA.

By this time it was summer, and Mrs. Hernandez was weary from her fight to keep Peter in the classroom. Peter were beginning to experience night sweats, which were a symptom of his progressing disease. Peter seemed very confused about what was happening in his school. Mrs. Hernandez decided that she and Peter would move out of the state for Peter's well-being. After they moved, no one heard from them again.

QUESTIONS

Legal Issues to Consider

1. Was Peter eligible for services under IDEA? Why or why not?

2. Was Peter eligible for services under Section 504? Why or why not?

3. Should the school district have excluded Peter from the general population? Why or why not?

Other Issues

1. Many people fear contracting AIDS. How would you, as a teacher, feel about teaching a child with AIDS?

2. Why is AIDS a more fearful disease than any other communicable disease?

3. What precautions could school districts take to prevent the spread of blood-borne pathogens?

4. What questions might teachers ask about children with AIDS attending their classrooms?

CASE 3.5

KATE/PHYSICAL DISABILITIES

Mr. Watson, the principal, walked into the third-grade classroom and noted that all students were busy working on a writing task at their desks. Kate sat toward the front of the room and, from the back, looked like all of the other third-graders. As the principal moved to the front of the room to speak to Mrs. Wilke, the teacher, he noticed that Kate was writing with a pencil. Below her wrists, Kate was missing her hands. She carefully held the pencil, grasping it with both "wrists."

Mr. Watson remarked to Mrs. Wilke, "I am always amazed at how well Kate does in your classroom. She appears to write as well as anyone in the class."

Mrs. Wilke smiled and stated, "Yes. You should see her draw in art class. Her art work is just as detailed as any other child's."

As he walked out of the room, Mr. Wilke said, "Keep up the good work."

Mrs. Wilke watched Kate work. Kate was diligently working on a handwriting assignment. It was nice to have the principal notice that Kate was doing well. When Kate first moved to the school, the other teachers were reluctant to take her into their classes. Mrs. Wilke shared the initial concern, but after a few weeks, she could see that motor skills were not a major problem for Kate.

Kate's parents, Dr. and Mrs. Sims, had moved to the district at the beginning of the year. Her father, who was a physician, set up a private practice in town. Kate had two brothers, one older and one younger. Kate's mother once was a nurse but stopped working when the children were born. Kate's mother and father were pleased to finally move back to the small town where they grew up. Both parents had attended the local high school and had families within a few miles of where they purchased their new house. They finally felt settled.

Life had presented many challenges for Mrs. Sims since she left her hometown. After receiving her nursing degree, she helped her husband through medical school then through the rigors of residency. Next came the children. Bobby was born first and was an easy baby who was sweet-tempered. He was bright, walking and talking early. Two years later, Kate was born. Dr. Sims was present at Kate's delivery, and when she was born, Mrs. Sims remembered a quiet hush in the room. Then Dr. Sims, said, "It's a girl!" Mrs. Sims was thrilled. When she first held the baby, she could see that Kate was born without hands. Her little arms extended to her wrists, then stopped. Both parents were devastated. They were worried about how other people would perceive Kate and about the limitations Kate might have.

Kate was the opposite of Bobby in disposition. She was a very demanding baby, crying a considerable amount every day. When she was 3 months old, her parents consulted orthopedic specialists about her physical disability. The specialists were very encouraging and suggested that Kate be fitted with prostheses in a few years. In the meantime, they suggested that Kate be treated as normally as possible. Even though her parents were privately very upset about Kate's physical disability, they made every effort to treat her as normally as possible. Kate learned to manipulate toys, even blocks and tinker toys. As a preschooler, she learned how to hold a pencil using both arms and how to scribble. However, when Kate couldn't perform a task or didn't get what she wanted, she often threw temper tantrums, jumping up and down and crying. When Kate was 3, her younger brother, Kevin, was born. Kevin was much like his brother Bobby in temperament and intellect.

Kate attended first and second grade in a private parochial school in the city. Although she was old enough to be fitted with myoelectric prosthetic hands, Dr. and Mrs. Sims delayed having Kate fitted for them. She seemed to be doing so well without them that it seemed that the hands could wait.

When Kate's father opened his practice in his small hometown, Kate began third grade in Mrs. Wilke's room. Mrs. Sims was nervous about Kate attending a new school. She worried about children making fun of Kate because of her lack of hands and the teacher's attitude toward Kate. When Mrs. Sims enrolled Kate in school, she met Mrs. Wilke and talked with her about Kate's needs. Mrs. Sims requested that Kate be treated as normally as possible. She assured Mrs. Wilke that Kate had adequate motor skills, with the exception of fine motor skills for tasks like zipping, tying shoes, and opening a milk carton.

Kate did well in school until January of her third-grade year. It was at this midpoint in the year that Mrs. Wilke began to notice that Kate seemed to be struggling with reading. She had difficulty with new vocabulary words in her third-grade basal reader. Although she could sound out some words, as they became more difficult, Kate struggled. She also struggled with new spelling words. The curriculum was definitely more difficult for her. Mrs. Wilke kept Mrs. Sims informed about her concerns, and Mrs. Sims worked with Kate every day at home on her reading and spelling. Mrs. Sims began to see that the work was becoming too difficult for Kate.

Mrs. Wilke suggested that Kate receive extra help from the remedial reading teacher and Mrs. Sims agreed. After about six weeks, it became apparent that Kate wasn't progressing well, despite the extra help at home and at school. Mrs. Wilke suggested to Mrs. Sims that Kate be referred for a special education evaluation to determine if she had a learning disability. Mrs. Sims agreed and signed the consent form.

The evaluation was completed in about six weeks. A social worker met with Dr. and Mrs. Sims, and the school nurse screened Kate's vision and hearing. Mrs. Wilke described in writing Kate's progress in third grade, and a school psychologist met with Kate to administer a battery of tests. In addition, an a occupational therapist and a speech and language therapist assessed Kate.

After completing the evaluation, Dr. and Mrs. Sims met with the evaluation team and the building principal, the special education administrator, and the learning disabilities teacher. Each person on the team shared information from the evaluation. The social worker summarized Kate's developmental and social history and stated that the parents were going to pursue myoelectric hands for Kate. The school nurse said that Kate had passed the vision and hearing screening and that she wore glasses. Mrs. Wilke summarized Kate's progress in third grade, emphasizing that she had made adequate progress until January, when she began to experience difficulty in reading. Despite extra efforts, Kate was not progressing as Mrs. Wilke would want a third-grader to progress. For example, her second-quarter grades in reading were mostly Ds, with some Cs. The school psychologist summarized his test results. He stated that Kate had a verbal IQ of 83, a performance IQ of 90, and a full scale IQ of 88, based on the Weschler Intelligence Scale for Children III. He stated that Kate's academic performance was commensurate with her ability. Kate's standard score in reading was 86, in math it was 88, and in spelling it was 87. He noted that Kate was able to complete most writing tasks with little difficulty. The speech and language therapist concurred with the psychologist and stated that Kate's language skills were immature, but consistent with her overall ability. The occupational therapist indicated in her report that Kate had done remarkably well without hands and that she should have little difficulty adjusting to using myoelectric hands because of her age. Dr. and Mrs. Sims stated that they simply wanted Kate to receive extra assistance with her reading and spelling and extra assistance using her myoelectric hands after she was fitted for them. The meeting concluded with the following dialogue between Dr. Hart, special education administrator, and Mrs. Sims.

Dr. Hart stated, "Kate does not appear to meet the definition of learning disabilities because she does not have a severe discrepancy between her ability and achievement. She received a comprehensive evaluation, including the area of motor skills, and, although she has a physical disability, the disability does not adversely affect her education. She does not appear to need extra assistance with her motor skills. Therefore, Kate is not eligible for special education services."

As Dr. Hart talked, the evaluation team nodded in agreement.

Mrs. Sims, amazed at their decision, said, "How can you sit there and say our daughter doesn't need special help? We demand special help for Kate. She deserves this help, especially because she doesn't have hands. What's more, my husband and I have agreed that Kate should receive occupational therapy five days a week as soon as she gets her myoelectric hands. She should receive the hands over the summer and this gives you three months to plan this help for Kate."

Dr. Hart calmly stated, "I'm sorry, Dr. and Mrs. Sims. Kate is not eligible to receive special education services, and even if she was, the district couldn't afford to provide occupational therapy five days a week."

Mrs. Sims angrily retorted, "Well, we'll just see about that."

Dr. and Mrs. Sims stomped angrily out of the room. The evaluation team sat there silently.

After many meetings and much conflict, with attorneys involved, Kate was determined to be eligible for learning disabilities services. She was transferred to another school in the district and received occupational therapy three days a week to assist with her use of the new myoelectric hands. Eventually, Kate decided that she did not want to wear the myoelectric hands and refused to put them on in school and at home. Her parents gave up trying to force her to wear the prostheses.

QUESTIONS

Legal Issues to Consider

1. Based on the evidence given, was Kate eligible for services under IDEA? Why or why not?

2. What other federal law might provide legal protection to Kate? Would she have been entitled to special services?

3. Was cost the legal basis for denying occupational therapy?

Other Issues

1. How does society treat individuals who have obvious physical disabilities?

2. What can schools do to transition students who have physical disabilities into society?

3. How do you think Kate would have been educated if she were in third grade during the 1950s?

====   **CASE 3.6**   ====

ANDRE/AGE AND SPECIAL EDUCATION SERVICES

It is 10:00 A.M. in a large high school of 2,000 students located in the Midwest. Andre has been called to the counselor's office to see Mr. Dennison, his school counselor. He shows the secretary in the guidance office his hall pass, and she motions him toward Mr. Dennison's office. Andre slowly lumbers into Mr. Dennison's office. He looks at the floor as he walks.

Andre is a 6-foot-tall 18-year-old who has a learning disability. His long hair hanging in front of his eyes prevents him from making eye contact with people. He wears an old hockey T-shirt with jeans and tennis shoes. His clothes are dirty, and his hands are stained with oil from trying to fix his old car. He thinks *Man, what do they want now? I didn't do anything. I should tell them all where to go. Oh well, at least I got out of third period English, which I hate. Now I can't get in trouble for not doing my homework.*

Mr. Dennison begins the conversation by saying, "Hi, Andre. Have a seat over there. I called you in here to talk about how you are doing in school and your future here."

Andre thinks, *Here we go again. He's always on my case to come to school.* Andre makes no comment, simply staring at the floor with his hair covering his eyes.

Mr. Dennison says, "Look, I'm not going to beat around the bush. You've been here 3½ years, and you have four high school credits toward graduation. You've failed more classes than you've passed. I just received your report card from first semester, and you've failed every class except woodworking, where you got a C. You miss one day each week, usually with no excuse. What's going on here?"

Andre, staring at the floor, simply shrugs and remarks, "I don't know."

"Well, if you don't know, who does?"

Andre shrugs his shoulders.

"Look, Andre, you've had every chance at this high school. You've had special education classes since ninth grade, and you're even failing those classes. You sit in class and do nothing. Your teachers always complain that you don't complete homework assignments, don't participate in class, and fail most tests. Why do you even bother to come to school?"

"Oh, man, all you ever do is criticize me."

Mr. Dennison ignores Andre's remark and continues, "High schools are set up for students who want to graduate. It's apparent to me that you don't really want to graduate. With only four credits, you'll be almost 22 years old when you graduate, and that's assuming you start passing all of your classes right now. What do you have to say about this?"

"I hate school, but my mom makes me come."

"Andre, you're 18 years old. You can make your own decisions. I think you're wasting your time here, when you and I both know that you'll never graduate from high school. Weren't you working this semester?"

"Yeah, at the hamburger place on Main Street."

"What do they pay you?"

"Minimum wage."

"What do you do with your money?"

"Buy stuff."

"See, that's what I mean. You're not acting responsibly. You're floating through school and life without any direction. I can safely say that school doesn't seem to be the place for you. I strongly suggest that you consider quitting. Maybe you need a good dose of reality to see that life is difficult without a high school education.

"Man, I hate this place. I've had nothing but trouble here. All you do is try to get me in trouble. I hate school. Maybe I *will* quit."

"I think that would be best for you. I have a form here you can sign to show that you are quitting. Then all you have to do is hand in your books and clear out your locker. You can do that now if you want. Then tomorrow you won't have to come back.

"Yeah, okay."

Andre signs the paper and gathers his books from his locker. He turns in the books and walks out of the building. On the way out, he thinks, *I hate this place. I'm never coming back, no matter what. I don't care what my mom says. I'll get a job and find an apartment.*

Mr. Dennison walks down the hallway to the assistant principal's office, where he sees the assistant principal, Mr. White. He laughs and says, "Hey, Mac. I just got rid of that Andre Maag kid. What a loser. He decided to quit. Now he won't mess up the average-attendance and test-score averages for the school. We sure don't need kids like that in this school. Let him go out and flip hamburgers for minimum wage."

Mr. White, who knows Andre, remarks, "Yeah, I'm glad to see him leave. We sure have enough problems around here without kids like that."

Ms. Mensinger, the special education supervisor, happens to be walking down the hall and overhears the conversation between Mr. Dennison and Mr. White.

"Mr. Dennison, did I hear you say that Andre Maag quit school?"

"Yeah, I talked him into quitting. It was the only sensible thing to do. You know, he only has four credits, and he's 18 years old."

"I'm really sorry to hear that. We had planned to meet with his mother next week to talk about Andre's future. We just received a grant for an alternative education program, and Andre would have been a good candidate for the program. As a special education student, he also would have qualified for a work–study program off-campus."

"What a waste. Save your efforts for more deserving students."

"Mr. Dennison, I'm a very upset about this. Andre has an IEP with a transition plan, and you just blew it by talking him into quitting school."

"Well, who's going to know or care? His mother doesn't care what he does. I'm really tired of having to counsel special education students who are losers. They don't care, and they have rules made just for them."

"Mr. Dennison, I think we're going to have the meeting with Andre next week anyway. Maybe we can talk him into staying in school."

"Oh great, a bleeding heart. Ms. Mensinger, in case you didn't already know, you can't save everyone."

"I know that, but I'm going to try to help Andre if it's not already too late."

Ms. Mensinger walks off fuming. She thinks, *What does Mr. Dennison know about Andre's situation? Andre has a severe learning disability affecting his reading. In fact, he can hardly read at all. He needs help reading the simplest text.*

Ms. Mensinger decides that she will try to help Andre return to school, despite what Mr. Dennison has stated. She first reviews his special education file. It indicates that Andre has been in a self-contained learning disabilities class since first grade. He lives with his mother, who never has worked outside of the home. His father is in prison for armed robbery. The family is very poor and survives on food stamps and other welfare. As she reads the file, she thinks, *Andre often doesn't come to school clean. One of the teachers even offered to help him do his laundry in the home economics classroom after school. Andre often comes to school hungry. He is one of just a few students who alway use their free lunch tickets for the hot meals in the cafeteria, when most students buy fast food snacks for lunch. One reason he likes his job at the fast food restaurant is that he gets a free meal.*

After reading Andre's file, she wonders how she can get Andre back into school, or is it a lost cause, as Mr. Dennison said?

QUESTIONS

Legal Issues to Consider

1. Is is legal for the school to reject Andre at age 18? Why or why not?

2. What obligation does the school have for Andre's transition into the community?

Other Issues

1. How can society assist students like Andre to become productive members of society?

2. How do high schools deal with students like Andre?

3. How does the transition mandate help students with disabilities?

CHAPTER FOUR

EVALUATION
AND CLASSIFICATION

CASE 4.1   CARLOS/DISCRIMINATORY EVALUATIONS

CASE 4.2   TONY/INADEQUATE EVALUATIONS

CASE 4.3   SCOTT/PROCEDURAL ERRORS

CASE 4.4   TINA/CLASSIFICATION ISSUES

CASE 4.5   JOAN/REFUSAL TO EVALUATE

CASE 4.6   LATIFA/BIASED TESTING PROCEDURES

▬▬▬   CASE 4.1   ▬▬▬

CARLOS/ DISCRIMINATORY EVALUATIONS

Carlos is 7 years old and is currently enrolled in Mr. Stevens' second-grade class at Bell-view Elementary School. Although school started one month ago, Carlos is new to the class because of his late enrollment. Carlos' father, Juan Chevaz, is a migrant worker who frequently makes three to four moves a year to different parts of the country to harvest whatever crop is in season. Carlos' mother, Rivera, often finds a job working at discount department or grocery stores.

This month finds the Chevaz family in the rural town of Markus, California. Markus is a small town with a population of about 300. In Markus it is time to harvest the grapes that will later be turned into wine. Although Carlos and his family have been here before, the constant moving interrupts the education of all of the Chavez children. The two oldest brothers, Emanuel and Ricki, ages 15 and 16, dropped out of school because they make "good money" working with their father in the fields harvesting fruits and vegetables.

At school, Mr. Stevens is familiar with the routine of enrolling students in his class, only to have them leave three months later. Most of the Chevaz family members speak Spanish and broken English. Juan and Rivera have a difficult time getting Carlos to go to school on most days because he says that he does not like school. Carlos claims that the other children in the class pick on him because he wears old clothes and gets a free lunch. Considering his age, Carlos speaks English as well as any of his brothers and sisters; however, he has a poor vocabulary.

Mr. Stevens has been working with Carlos for two weeks when he begins to suspect some learning and behavioral problems. At first, Mr. Stevens believes that Carlos' problems are simply due to his lack of mastery of the English language. However, when he begins to ask Carlos questions in Spanish, Mr. Stevens begins to see that Carlos really lacks an understanding of basic skills. Mr. Stevens, whose only training in Spanish has come from a handful of courses taken in high school, often has to repeat many of his questions to Carlos because his Spanish is still rusty. To add to these suspected learning problems, Carlos often experiences bouts with otitis media, middle ear infections, which frequently go undetected and untreated.

From these informal observations, Mr. Stevens decides to speak to John Simpson, the school psychologist, to request a formal evaluation of Carlos. From their conversation, Mr. Simpson suspects that Carlos may be mildly mentally impaired, and he wants him to be evaluated after he informs his mother about his suspicions. New to the school psychological staff, Mr. Simpson calls Mrs. Chevaz and requests permission to evaluate Carlos. Mr. Simpson does not indicate that the tests used—the WISC III—will be in English. Mrs. Chevaz grants permission for the evaluation.

As Mr. Simpson assesses Carlos, he finds that he performs poorly on the test and scores well below the average range. Mrs. Chevaz, anxious for the results, is contacted by telephone by Mr. Simpson. Mrs. Chevaz is surprised to find that the results of Carlos' evaluation include only the WISC III and classroom observations.

In a written report sent by mail to Mrs. Chevaz, Mr. Simpson uses a large amount of assessment terminology and mentions that Carlos' score falls within the mentally impaired range. Uncertain of what she is reading, Mrs. Chevaz asks a neighbor to read and interpret the report. When the neighbor tries to explain, she has difficulty describing many of the terms and eventually says to Mrs. Chevaz that *mentally impaired* means "loco." Shocked to hear the news, Mrs. Chevaz cries and then begins cursing the psychologist.

As soon as the school opens the next day, Mrs. Chevaz calls Mr. Stevens and begins frantically explaining that a mistake has been made in the evaluation and that she wants something done about it. Between breaks in Mrs. Chevaz' Spanish and broken English, Mr. Stevens tries to explain that Carlos will finally get the help that he badly needs. When she requests a new evaluation, Mr. Stevens tells her that "it is out of the question." Mrs. Chevaz then tells him that she will have someone else conduct an evaluation of Carlos. Mr. Stevens agrees, but he warns her that the new evaluation may not be considered in Carlos' placement decision.

Later that day, Mrs. Chevaz calls the local college clinic and inquires about testing. Much to her surprise, the secretary informs her that the clinic will conduct the tests, but for a price of $800. When she explains her financial situation, the secretary says that they have an installment plan available. Within two weeks, the Chevaz family meets with the college clinician, Susie Walker, who explains the tests that will be used and sets up an appointment for Carlos.

For an entire day, Susie administers a series of intellectual, psychological, and academic measures to Carlos. Two weeks later, the family returns and Susie reviews the results of the assessment. She explains that Carlos' scores indicate that he is intellectually and academically slightly below average, but these scores are not indicative of mental impairment.

Relieved, Mrs. Chevaz returns home, calls the school, and tells them that she wants the college evaluation considered when making any decisions about Carlos' placement in school. In addition, she wants the school to pay for the evaluation. Mr. Stevens immediately responds that the school district will never pay for the second evaluation because evaluations that have been done in the past by the college have not been valid. According to Mr. Stevens, "Tests done by our school psychologists are better than anything around." With that statement he says good-bye and hangs up the telephone.

QUESTIONS

Legal Issues to Consider

1. What mistakes does Mr. Simpson make when evaluating Carlos?

2. What is the school's responsibility regarding the independent evaluation?

3. From the information provided, does Carlos have a disability? If yes, what is the disability? If no, what information would lead you to believe that he does not have a disability? What other information might be needed to answer this question?

Other Issues

1. The United States is often considered the melting pot of the world. Should English be the standard language by which people are taught in school?

2. How can a teacher help children of families who move frequently?

CASE 4.2

TONY/INADEQUATE EVALUATIONS

Tony currently attends Rodman Elementary School, an urban school in Chicago, Illinois. He is in Mrs. Hill's third-grade classroom. Having been diagnosed at age 5 by the family pediatrician as having attention deficit hyperactivity disorder (ADHD), Tony has been able to control most of the symptoms of ADHD with the help of the medication Ritalin. However, on those days when Tony forgets to take his medication, he becomes extremely hyperactive, unruly, and distractible.

From his earliest days, his mother, Natasha, knew that Tony was different from the rest of his peers. She recalls how Tony was always in motion and always in trouble. On one occasion, Natasha remembers how an angry neighbor knocked on her door late one night demanding to speak to Tony about his broken car mirror. It seems that Tony was seen earlier that day hanging around his neighbor's new station wagon. For Natasha, responding to complaints such as this one have become part of her daily routine.

At school, Tony encountered similar problems. He has been constantly in trouble for disrupting the class. His teacher, Mrs. Hill, writes daily notes home to his mother about his inappropriate behavior and lack of academic progress. On several occasions, Mrs. Hill has noticed that Tony has difficulty reading certain words, particularly words that are similarly spelled, for example, them and these, and which and with. At about the same time, Natasha begins to notice similar problems at home, and she decides to call Mrs. Hill. After Natasha's phone call, Mrs. Hill decides to place Tony in Mr. Jobson's special education classroom to help deal with his academic deficits, and she also requests that he be tested for learning disabilities (LD). Mr. Jobson, who is one of the school's two special education teachers, is certified to teach students with behavior disorders (BD), but his classroom is considered cross-categorical (LD/BD). Mr. Jobson agrees to transfer Tony to his classroom to work on his social and inappropriate behavior skills. After Mrs. Hill makes arrangements with Mrs. Jobson, she calls Mr. Nash, the school psychologist, to discuss the possibility of getting Tony evaluated for LD.

The next day, Tony is sent to Mr. Jobson's cross-categorical LD/BD resource classroom for a half-day, every day. Meanwhile, Mrs. Hill meets with Mr. Nash to discuss Tony. At the meeting, as Mrs. Hill describes Tony's various problems, Mr. Nash furiously scribbles down notes on his pad. With each of her comments, Mr. Nash nods his head and says, "good, keep going." Mr. Nash asks her whether Tony has had his hearing and vision tested recently. Mrs. Hill, not certain about his vision, replies, "Tony tested okay for hearing, but was absent on the day the nurse tested our class for vision."

Finally, after about 15 minutes, Mr. Nash stops Mrs. Hill in midsentence and announces that Tony definitely "sounds like an LD student." Mrs. Hill, surprised by his immediate diagnosis, asks how he knows Tony is LD.

"Well," Mr. Nash, stammering for an answer, says, "I just know he is. Besides, he will be the perfect candidate for a new test that the district has just purchased." With that, Mr. Nash informs Mrs. Hill that he will be in next Tuesday to test Tony.

The test that Mr. Nash plans to use is called the Wilson Evaluation of Learning Disabilities (WELD). The WELD is a new test, and its producers tout it as the quickest way to determine whether a child has a learning disability. Using the WELD, school psychologists can determine a learning disability in only 15 minutes, they claim. The WELD tests only the areas of spelling and math, and then it yields a quotient that helps the assessor determine whether a child qualifies for LD. The WELD, one of the hottest tests to hit schools, was normed on a population of 100 White sixth-graders from Beverly Hills, California. In addition to this test, because of Tony's language difficulties, Mr. Nash also plans to administer the Speech Only Method of Evaluation (SOME).

On Tuesday, Mr. Nash arrives as promised, toting his new test under his arm. Mrs. Hill calls Tony's name. When he does not respond, she calls his name a second time. Finally, on her third attempt to get his attention, he looks up and asks, "Are you talking to me?"

Mrs. Hill signals for Tony and introduces him to Mr. Nash. She then says, "Mr. Nash wants to work with you to see how much you've learned in school this year." Mr. Nash walks Tony to a quiet part of the room, unwraps the WELD, and begins scanning the test manual, looking for directions about starting points.

After finding the starting point for someone Tony's age, Mr. Nash begins the subtest for spelling, gives him the words, and begins to query him. After Tony misses five spelling words in a row, Mr. Nash begins working backward in an attempt to establish not only a ceiling but also a basal. Mr. Nash feels that he does not have to administer the entire subtest according to the directions in the manual because he believes Tony does not know any of the test words. Minutes later, Mr. Nash announces that they are moving on to the math sub-test. After three minutes, Mr. Nash announces that he is finished. Mr. Nash thinks how easy this test is to administer.

When Mrs. Hill doesn't hear from Mr. Nash after several weeks, she decides to call him to ask about the results of Tony's testing. When he answers the phone, Mr. Nash is surprised to hear from Mrs. Hill.

"Those test results are around here somewhere," Mr. Nash responds. When he informs her that he "can't place my finger on them," Mrs. Hill becomes concerned.

Later that day, Mr. Nash calls Mrs. Hill back to inform her that he has found the records and he will have the report to her by the end of the week. By now, three months have passed since he administered the tests to Tony.

As Mr. Nash predicted, Tony does qualify for LD services because of his poor performance on the spelling subtest and overall score on the SOME test. When Mrs. Hill finally receivs the report from Mr. Nash, she was suspicious of the results because it makes no mention of Tony's reading problems, but she is nevertheless relieved to learn that Tony qualifies for services. According to the report, Mr. Nash recommends that Tony be placed in a LD resource room.

With the report in hand, Mrs. Hill immediately calls Tony's mother, Natasha, to let her know about the test results and to discuss his IEP. In an attached note, Mr. Nash has written that he wants to combine the evaluation meeting with the IEP meeting, and wants to set up this meeting for next week because it will be more convenient for him. Natasha agrees to attend the meeting on Tuesday morning.

Before the meeting, Mrs. Hill speaks to Mr. Jobson and asks him to write the IEP for Tony. When Tuesday morning arrives, Natasha telephones the school and informs Mrs. Hill that she cannot make it because her boss wants her to work that day. Not certain what to do, Mrs. Hill tells Natasha that they will have the meeting without her, but she will receive a copy of Tony's IEP. Present at the meeting are Mrs. Hill, Mr. Nash, and Mr. Jobson. Mr. Jobson presents Tony's IEP to the other members. Mr. Nash mentions that it is well written and agrees that Tony should remain in his classroom. Mr. Jobson, a first-year teacher, has had some difficulty writing the IEP and has written only goals, no objectives. He also has not included any related services. In addition, spelling and computers are the only goal areas that are mentioned in the IEP.

QUESTIONS

Legal Issues to Consider

1. Describe the issues of parent participation that were ignored during this evaluation.

2. Describe the issues of appropriate evaluation that were ignored during this scenario.

Other Issues

1. What type of training should be given to Tony's mother to help her deal with his behavior problems?

2. How does society treat a person diagnosed with ADHD? Does society treat that person differently than it would someone without a disorder or disability?

3. How do schools respond to individuals with ADHD?

■■■■■■■■   **CASE 4.3**   ■■■■■■■■

SCOTT/PROCEDURAL ERRORS

Fred Evans arrived early at the evaluation meeting. The secretary showed him to the room and offered him a cup of coffee. As Fred sat waiting for others to join him on this warm day in mid-July, his mind began to drift. *What signs did I miss? If only I could do this over again, things would be different for Scott,* he thought. Now at the evaluation meeting, faced with the issue of trying to get the school to accept his claim that Scott, his son, should qualify under the category of severe behavior disorders, Fred could only wonder where it all began.

Scott had been an excellent student until ninth grade. He was hard-working, was trustworthy, and had his entire life ahead of him. His grades were good, and Scott was involved in intramural soccer and wrestling. Midway through ninth grade, in January, Fred began to notice marked changes in Scott's behavior. Because Fred had recently divorced Scott's natural mother, Sara, Fred naturally began to suspect that Scott's odd behavior was related to the divorce. Although both parents shared custody of their son, Scott lived with his father.

After the divorce, Scott's odd behavior began to exhibit itself in a number of ways. For example, Scott began to skip classes and would, instead, go drinking with friends. Fred also learned from the school that Scott was tardy to class on more than 60 instances and had missed 35 days of school. More troubling, however, were Fred's suspicions that Scott was using drugs.

Fred remembered one particular incident that he would never forget. For two days in March he had been unable to locate Scott. On the second day, after countless phone calls to Scott's friends, Scott appeared through the front door.

"Where have you been?" Fred demanded.

"I crashed at my friend's house. Besides, it's none of your damn business," Scott fired back.

As Fred moved closer to Scott, he began to notice that there was something odd with Scott's appearance. Aside from his eyes being bloodshot, Scott's pupils were dilated. Scott also appeared to be slurring his words as he spoke. Fred had seen these signs before and he knew they were serious. In an ugly confrontation, Scott finally admitted to using speeders (amphetamines) and trip weed (marijuana treated with LSD). To appease his parents, Scott agreed that he should quit using drugs, but he continued anyway.

Within weeks, as Scott became more rebellious, Fred began family counseling. During April, Fred called one of the school counselors, Judy Kirby, to see what could be done for Scott. Judy had known Scott for about one year, and the first words out of her mouth were about the dramatic change that she had seen in Scott during the past few months. She agreed to try to help Scott, but only if Fred would follow up on all of her recommendations. The first step that she would take was to assess Scott to see if he would qualify for special education services under IDEA. Though not officially qualified to assess students, Judy, whose degree was in physical education, wanted badly to help Scott. Judy knew that she might get into trouble, but she also knew that the school's only certified psychologist had a 2-month backlog of cases.

Fortunately for Judy, she was able to get Scott to attend school just long enough that she could test him. After administering a personality test and an achievement test, Judy was dismayed by her results. Scott's personality test results showed signs of psychosis and severe antisocial behavior. After reporting the results to her school's principal, Judy called to discuss the results with Fred and to obtain his signature for a special education evaluation.

By now it was early May. Scott appeared to be improving, and his attendance at school was much better. Still, Fred and Sara saw the need for further testing. On May 10th, both Fred and Sara stopped by the school to sign the parent-permission form for a formal evaluation. The next week, both parents met with school officials to decide whether testing should occur before summer break or during September. The school psychologist's docket was still quite full, and it seemed impossible for him to test Scott until August or September. Frustrated with the school system and reassured that Scott's behavior appeared on the upswing, they decided to wait until September to test Scott.

As the summer progressed, Scott's behavior deteriorated. In one incident, police arrested Scott at a rock concert in June for disorderly conduct and destruction of property. Scott admitted that he had been drinking beer, but he denied using drugs, despite being caught with speeders in his pocket. When his father received the call from the police, he immediately called his attorney, who was able to get all of the charges reduced. It was also during this time that Scott began to experience severe anxiety attacks and what appeared to be psychotic episodes, during which Scott would ramble on that the government was out to get him. Scott's arrest was his final straw. The next day, Scott's father called the school and requested an evaluation as soon as possible. The earliest that an evaluation could be conducted was July 3.

On that day, Fred drove Scott to the office of Mr. Barrison, the school psychologist, to be evaluated. Mr. Barrison was a certified school psychologist with 14 years of experience.

The earlier evaluation, conducted by the school counselor, was part of Scott's full evaluation. As he tested Scott during the next two days, he also had Fred complete various psychological and behavioral evaluations pertaining to Scott's behavior. Throughout the evaluation, Scott suspected that he was being evaluated for mental illness and did his best to respond in an appropriate manner.

With the evaluation complete, a meeting to discuss the results was scheduled for July 15. Fred was notified by telephone of the date and time of the meeting. Scott's mother was never notified.

In attendance at the meeting were Fred, Scott, and Mr. Barrison. The building principal was on vacation and could not attend, but he was very aware of the situation. At the meeting, the psychologist reviewed his results with Scott's father and reported, to Fred's astonishment, that he felt that Scott did not qualify under IDEA's definition of emotional disturbance. Mr. Barrison went on to mention that Scott probably needed some counseling, but his behavior was not severe enough to interfere with his education. As Fred left the meeting, he wondered what to do next.

QUESTIONS

Legal Issues to Consider

1. What was wrong with Scott's evaluation, according to IDEA?

2. From the information provided, does Scott have a disability of emotional disturbance? Why or why not?

3. Based on the meeting to discuss Scott's evaluation, what could Fred do next?

Other Issues

1. What types of behaviors are considered under the category of serious emotional disturbance?

2. If a student is a drug user and quits his drug use but continues to experience emotional instability, should he be considered in the serious emotional disturbance category?

CASE 4.4

TINA/CLASSIFICATION ISSUES

"But please, Mrs. Fromme, I promise to turn in my paper tomorrow," Tina pleaded. Tina, an attractive young lady with brown hair and dark brown eyes, had used her charm on many other occasions to turn in assignments late and request extra credit work.

Tina, a ninth-grade student in Mrs. Fromme's class, procrastinated on a consistent basis when it came to completing assignments and homework. Consequently, her grades reflected Tina's lack of enthusiasm for school. Her records showed poor academic performance and a number of in- and out-of-school suspensions. Despite her parents paying tutors over the years to help her with school, Tina had always maintained a low C–average most of her school career. Her academic problems began during Tina's first year of formal schooling.

Because her birthday fell on August 2, Tina was the youngest in her first-grade class. Throughout her first year in school, her teacher believed Tina was very immature and slow for her age. At the end of her first year, her teacher recommended to her parents that Tina repeat first grade. Tina's parents agreed, and she repeated first grade. At first, it seemed like the right decision because Tina did well during the beginning of her second year in first grade. However, as time went on, Tina's performance began to tailspin. Once again, she was just barely earning passing grades. As soon as her parents began to notice her poor performance, they hired a tutor to assist Tina with her reading and spelling skills. The tutors continued throughout much of Tina's schooling. In third grade, Tina received services from a remedial reading teacher, but one year later the program was terminated due to a lack of funds. With the help of a tutor, Tina still struggled, but she was able to maintain a slightly higher grade average. During this time, many of her teachers blamed her poor grades on laziness.

Tina was now in tenth grade, and her mother, Justine Peterman, recently attended a local workshop in which Professor Katazi discussed attention deficit disorder and students with learning problems. The information presented in the workshop prompted Justine into action. As she thought about Tina's performance, she decided that Tina was not lazy but in fact suffered from LD. As she reflected on Tina's future, Justine became quite concerned that Tina's continual reading problems might eventually cause her to drop out of school. In the past, Tina had spoken about quitting school, but her parents would always subdue such irrational talk by threatening to kick her out of the house if she quit school.

The day after the workshop, Justine saw a news special about students with learning problems who improved their reading skills with the use of colored overlays and visual tracking training. The next day, Justine called the special education director in the school district, explained Tina's learning and behavioral problems, and asked if school personnel had the training that she had seen on TV. Mrs. Bonton, the director, smiled and told Justine that those techniques didn't work for kids like Tina. Mrs. Bonton did, however, suggest that Tina be tested for LD.

A referral was completed, and three weeks later Tina was tested. Within a week, Mrs. Bonton and the school's psychologist, Missy Young, were present at a meeting to present the results to Justine. At the meeting, Missy pointed out that, despite Tina's poor performance, Tina did not qualify for LD. She tried to explain that Tina did not have a large enough discrepancy between her IQ score and her achievement test score. Despite the explanations, Justine simply shook her head in amazement, unable to believe that Tina did not qualify.

Convinced that Tina needed help, Justine pleaded with the psychologist and director to provide services to Tina. When both said that it was impossible to qualify Tina for LD, Justine said that this would not be the end of it and walked out.

As Tina's luck would have it, a few days later while she was out with some high school seniors drinking beer, she was involved in an automobile accident. Tina was knocked unconscious and rushed to the hospital. A few hours later, she regained consciousness but was disoriented and groggy. The hospital staff decided to keep her at the hospital for 24 hours of observation. After 24 hours, she was examined and released.

Two days later, Justine again called Mrs. Bonton requesting that Tina be tested because her injury might have caused additional learning problems. After speaking to the hospital staff, Mrs. Bonton decided that retesting Tina would be a waste of time. When she called Justine to inform her of the decision, Justine was furious and demanded that Tina be tested again. After Mrs. Bonton read the report from Tina's doctors, she again confirmed that no visual or serious damage had been done; therefore, she would not retest Tina.

Within two weeks, Mrs. Bonton received a call from Justine. Justine began by saying, "I told you she would qualify for special services at your school."

"Who is this?" asked Mrs. Bonton of the familiar-yet-nameless voice on the other end of the line.

"This is Justine Peterman, Tina's mother."

"Oh, Justine, how are you?" asked Mrs. Bonton.

"I just wanted to let you know that I had Tina tested by Nancy Bertel, and she says that Tina has perceptual motor and visual motor difficulties," replied Justine. Without a pause, she went on to say, "So I guess she will get those special services at your school?"

"Well," said Mrs. Bonton, "these tests didn't determine a learning disability, or did they?"

"These tests are as good as any of yours! Besides, Nancy said that Tina has lots of learning problems," Justine shot back.

"Slow down, Justine. In our district, we have dealt with Nancy Bertel before, and if I'm not mistaken, she is not trained to administer intelligence tests, is she?" queried Mrs. Bonton.

"Well, I know she has a masters degree in social work," replied Justine, "but you have to consider these test results."

"No, I don't," replied Mrs. Bonton.

QUESTIONS

Legal Issues to Consider

1. Based on the test results and the definition of a learning disability, did the school make the correct decision concerning Tina's classification during the first evaluation? How do you know?

2. After Tina's accident, was it appropriate for Justine to request additional testing? Why or why not?

3. Should the school consider the test results from Nancy Bertel? Why or why not?

Other Issues

1. Should students who are involved in serious automobile accidents be tested to receive special education services? Why or why not?

2. How does the category of learning disability (LD) differ from traumatic brain injury (TBI)?

CASE 4.5

JOAN/REFUSAL TO EVALUATE

"Pencils down. Your time is up," said Mrs. Kauffman as she began to collect the test booklets from her students. *Whew,* she thought, *two days down and one to go.* This was the second day of the Illinois Achievement Test (IAT) at Jossett Elementary School.

As she moved down the last row of students, she noticed Joan furiously erasing the answers on her bubble sheet answer form. "I said pencils down, Joan!" said Mrs. Kauffman in a stern voice.

"But, I…" Joan began to explain, but Mrs. Kauffman cut her off in midsentence.

"Joan, Joan, Joan, you have every excuse in the book for some of the things that you do."

"Mrs. Kauffman, I messed up big time," Joan stammered, as Mrs. Kauffman grabbed the answer sheet and test booklet from her hand.

Two months later the test results finally arrived. As Penny Kauffman took the package out of her mailbox, she instantly knew what they were. As a whole, her class performed well. *Now, maybe Principal Belamy will get off my back about my teaching,* she thought. As her eyes scanned down the list of individual scores, one student's score caught her eye—Joan's. *Jeez, can't she do anything right?* she thought.

As the other teachers crowded around the mailboxes, eager to see their classes' scores, Penny stuffed the test results back in the envelope and headed back to her room. Once there, she again zeroed in on Joan's scores. *Wow, she is in the twenty-eighth percentile for science, the fiftieth for math, and only the third for reading,* Penny thought. *I knew she was bad in reading, but this is ridiculous.*

The next week Penny informed her students that she had received the test scores and that they were to take them home to their parents. As the students walked out of her class that day, Penny handed each student a copy of their scores. When Joan approached, Penny remarked, "Make sure that your parents see this."

When Joan's parents, John and Anita Sedwick, saw her scores that night, they became upset with Joan. "How could you have done so poorly?" demanded John.

"That's what you get when you are too lazy to work," remarked Anita.

Joan, speechless, didn't quite know what to say. Should she explain how she lost track of her answers on the bubble sheet? Or should she simply accept the fact that she did poorly on the IATs?

After her parents calmed down, they decided that they would talk to Joan's teacher about her performance. Convinced that she might need special services, they contacted Mr. Belamy and Mrs. Kauffman to request additional help for her at school.

The next day, John and Anita traveled to Joan's school to meet with Mr. Belamy and Mrs. Kauffman. At the meeting, Mr. Belamy and Mrs. Kauffman agreed to try Joan in the Reading First program on a trial basis. The Reading First program, run by Mr. Swazy, was an after-school program that provided students with tutorial help in reading and gave Pizza Hut certificates as an incentive for reading a certain number of books. Joan's parents agreed to try Joan in the program, but they also requested testing for special services. Mrs. Kauffman was adamant that Joan was undermotivated, not disabled, and she remarked that the testing would be a waste of time for her. The principal agreed with Mrs. Kauffman that Joan should attend the Reading First Program for two weeks. They set a date for the next meeting.

At the end of the two weeks, Joan's parents felt that she had made little, if any, progress, and they set up another meeting with Joan's principal and teacher. Before this meeting, Anita made calls to the local university to see if it offered any reading programs. In talking with Dr. Dinkins, head of the Reading Department, Anita learned that there was a person in town who conducted evaluations for learning and processing problems. After calling and speaking to Mrs. Toni Butler, a private learning consultant, it was agreed that Toni would attend Joan's meeting. From her conversations with Anita, Toni felt that Joan definitely had a severe reading disability.

On the day of the meeting, Toni went to the school early to observe Joan in the classroom. Following her observations, the group convened to discuss the next step for Joan. In attendance at the meeting were Mr. Swazy, Mrs. Kauffman, Mr. Belamy, Mr. and Mrs. Sedwick, and Mrs. Butler. Mr. Swazy began the meeting by summarizing Joan's reading progress and stating that she seemed to be improving her reading, particularly when she was given reading material on her independent level. Mrs. Butler interrupted and asked how different Joan's independent level was from her grade level. Mr. Swazy checked his notes and stated that Joan did not have difficulty reading third-grade stories. Mr. and Mrs. Sedwick looked at each other, and then John blurted, "But she's in fifth grade." Mr. Swazy assured John and Anita that over time her reading would improve. Mr. Belamy and Mrs. Kauffman joined in agreeing with Mr. Swazy. John, who by now had become irritated, requested that Joan be tested to receive special services.

"You mean learning disability service," Toni chimed in.

"Yes, whatever—whatever it will take to get her to read better," responded John.

"Well, we don't agree that Joan needs any such services. She simply needs to work harder," Mr. Belamy countered.

Toni then turned to the Sedwicks and reported that she would be happy to test Joan.

However, Mr. Belamy jumped in and stated, "I would advise against using any independent testing to get services here in school. Now, if you want to use the results for your own good—then that's okay."

With that, Mr. Belamy announced, "The meeting is concluded" and left the room with Mrs. Kauffman and Mr. Swazy.

Within a week, Toni had completed testing Joan and contacted her parents with the results.

As Anita answered the phone, the voice at the other end stated, "I've got good news."

"Oh, Toni that's great. What did you find?" asked Anita. Toni reported that Joan had severe perceptual processing difficulties and poor visual motor skills. Toni further stated that Joan definitely needed specialized services to succeed in school.

QUESTIONS

Legal Questions to Consider

1. Should Joan have been required to take a state group achievement test such as the IAT? Why or why not? If Joan had been identified as a student with a disability, would your answer be different? How?

2. After the parents requested that Joan be tested for LD, was the school under any obligation to evaluate her? How should school district personnel have proceeded?

3. Was the school district under any obligation to consider the results from the independent tests obtained by the parents? Why or why not?

Other Issues

1. How does dyslexia differ from the term learning disability? When referring to services under IDEA, which is the appropriate term to use?

2. Should students with reading problems be required to take state tests of achievement? Why or why not?

3. Do you think Joan is lazy (undermotivated), or do you think that she has a disability? Why or why not?

▰▰▰▰▰▰   **CASE 4.6**   ▰▰▰▰▰▰

LATIFA/BIASED TESTING PROCEDURES

Latifa currently attends Hillman Elementary School, an urban school in a large city. She is in Mr. Green's fifth-grade classroom. Latifa and her mother, Sasha La Que, recently moved to New York after living in La Baie, a city in Quebec, Canada. Latifa is an African American 10-year-old girl who was born in Detroit, Michigan, but has been raised since the age of 2 in La Baie, a French-speaking city in the northern region of Quebec.

Latifa and her mother left Canada because they had much difficulty with Latifa's natural father, Harvey. Harvey was frequently unemployed and had a drinking problem. During his last drinking binge, he once again became violent and beat both Latifa and Sasha. Despite speaking French and English, Latifa is more fluent in French. Moving to a large city has been a cultural shock for Latifa because of language and cultural differences, but Sasha knew that moving away from her abusive husband was the only way to protect them. Sasha has found a job at the local university in the psychology department as a secretary.

As soon as they arrived in the city, Sasha enrolled Latifa in Hillman Elementary School. In Canada, Latifa had been receiving tutoring services from a remedial reading program, and Sasha wanted to make sure that these services were available in Latifa's new school. The secretary at the school was uncertain whether Latifa would receive these services, and she sent a note to the principal, Joanne Griffin, and the school psychologist, Larry Burns, alerting them about Sasha's request.

When the school's staff finally received Latifa's records from Canada, they were not familiar with the reading tests that had been used to assess Latifa. They immediately informed Sasha that they were going to conduct an informal preassessment to determine if Latifa needed further testing. After using a diagnostic screening reading test, Mr. Burns found that further testing might be warranted due to Latifa's borderline scores in reading.

After a conversation with Sasha, Mr. Burns informed her that he would be testing Latifa during the next few weeks for either LD or mental retardation. Sasha reluctantly agreed to the testing and said that she would sign the consent form, but she never did. Sasha had second thoughts about testing Latifa using such standardized "American" measures. Her fear was that Latifa would be classified retarded or disabled, when all that she really needed was some tutoring or help with her reading.

Using an individual intelligence test, an individual achievement test, and an adaptive behavior assessment, Mr. Burns tested Latifa in English during two weeks. In scoring the measures, Mr. Burns found that Latifa performed poorly on all measures. Instead of finding that Latifa qualified for remedial reading services, as her mother had hoped, Mr. Burns found that Latifa qualified for the EMH program.

When Mr. Burns called Sasha to inform her of the results, he told her that her daughter qualified for mental retardation services. Sasha was shocked to hear that her daughter was mentally retarded. After a few minutes, she began asking Mr. Burns a barrage of questions concerning the norming of the test and the types of questions on the test.

The next day Sasha asked Dr. Johnson, her boss and a faculty member in the psychology department, about the test. She showed Sasha where they stored copies of all of their psychology and education tests, located the intelligence test, and began describing it to her. As she reviewed the test, Sasha found that it was normed using mostly Caucasian children from large suburban areas. Moreover, as she began to review some of the test questions, she found that many of the questions were based on the children's culture, not necessarily their intelligence. A few questions stuck in her mind that Sasha felt were biased for children from non-U.S. cultures. For example, she found the following test questions troubling:

Which president is on a five-dollar bill?

Why is it better to pay for inexpensive items by cash or check rather than a charge card?

What is an escalator?

A pilot does what?

What does a bellhop do?

Who is the president of the United States?

Hollywood is located in what state?

What does a microwave do?

That night, Sasha asked her daughter the same questions and found that Latifa could not answer any of them. The next day she called Mr. Burns and informed him that she felt that the questions were biased against students from different cultures. He told her that because the questions were normed on children from different regions of the United States, the questions were valid for any child who wants to grow up in an American culture.

"These are commonsense questions; besides, this test has a reliability of .95," he further explained.

Sasha replied that not only were the questions culturally and racially biased, but Latifa did not trust men. "She never works well around men," Sasha explained. "She just doesn't trust them."

In defense of his test results, Mr. Burns said he believed that the results were more than valid and that Latifa really needed help with most academic subjects.

"Sasha, what are you complaining about? You requested the testing!" Mr. Burns pointed out.

"Yeah, but my child is smarter than your tests show," Sasha responded.

"Well, there is nothing that can be done now—the testing is over," replied Mr. Burns.

The following day, Sasha asked a professor in the psychology department to test Latifa using measures that were not culturally or racially biased. She could only find one faculty member who was willing to test Latifa. Dr. Shannon Thompson was familiar with IQ testing and was able to find a culturally sensitive IQ test. Although this test was normed on larger, more culturally diverse groups of students, it reported a low (.75) reliability and validity (.72).

Within a week, Dr. Thompson tested Latifa using this IQ test, the WEAT, and ABCDE. After scoring the test, she found that Latifa had scored slightly lower than average, but her IQ scores did not fall within the mentally retarded range. In addition, she found that Latifa's scores on the other two measures were low, but Latifa should be classified as borderline LD.

QUESTIONS

Legal Issues to Consider

1. Describe how the school district handled the issue of parental consent for evaluation and its impact on the evaluation process.

2. Should the school have tested Latifa in her native French? Why or why not?

3. How have the courts interpreted issues of cultural or racial bias of standardized tests?

Other Issues

1. Latifa is now attending schools in the United States; therefore, should she be tested using measures that were developed in the United States?

2. What activities could schools do to address issues of cultural diversity in the classroom?

CHAPTER FIVE

INDIVIDUAL EDUCATION PLAN
AND APPROPRIATE EDUCATION

CASE 5.1   WALTER/TRANSITION SERVICES

CASE 5.2   VERNON/IMPROPER PLACEMENT

CASE 5.3   YANCY/GENERAL EDUCATION PARTICIPATION

CASE 5.4   NICHOLAS/PARENT PARTICIPATION

CASE 5.5   KELLY/RELATED SERVICES

CASE 5.6   HAROLD/ADEQUATE SERVICES

CASE 5.1

WALTER/TRANSITION SERVICES

Walter Thompson despised working on the menial tasks that Frank Moser assigned to him on a daily basis. "I hate these jobs," said Walter as he closed the lid on the box of another assembly task.

"Walter, do I hear you complaining again?" Mr. Moser shouted from the back of the room.

Walter, who was now frustrated by the task, responded in a grumpy "yes."

"I'm sick of doin' this stuff while all you do is sit at your desk and drink your coffee," Walter continued in an angry and indignant voice.

By the time Walter finished his statement, the other students in the class had stopped working and were commenting about how Walter was in "big trouble" now. Walter, quite pleased that he made the statement, smiled and stuck out his tongue at his classmates. (Walter was correct in noting that Mr. Moser usually took a prolonged coffee break, complete with doughnuts, in the morning while all around him the students busily worked.) By now, Mr. Moser was on his feet and heading, rather quickly, toward Walter. As he saw him approach, Walter made his next move: He tossed a box from his assembly task on the ground. In a loud crash, small pieces from his assembly task were now strewn on the floor. It was clear that another "Walter incident" was well under way, and Mrs. Massey took off in Walter's direction. She knew that when Walter got upset, he usually tried to destroy whatever property was within his grasp. Meanwhile, Mr. Moser had managed to grab Walter's hands and was trying to prevent him from knocking over more boxes of completed tasks when Mrs. Massey arrived to help physically escort Walter out of the classroom.

Walter had been working on one of the prevocational tasks that were designed by Mr. Moser. The tasks were meant to mimic vocational and work-related tasks that students would be performing in later school years. Specifically, the task that Walter was working on was very similar to the assembly tasks that he would complete in three years, when he was 15 and old enough to work in the district's vocational program. The program was composed of students with and without disabilities who completed tasks such as assembling electronic components, packaging products, and organizing materials for local companies. In turn, the local companies paid the program, and students were rewarded with small paychecks.

When Walter's parents first heard about the vocational program, they quickly made an appointment and toured the facility. What made this program so appealing to Walter's parents was the fact that Walter would be rewarded (earn) a paycheck for "real work." They had long felt that school had lost its appeal to Walter and that the only solution was to begin training him for real-world experiences. *Finally, a program that would allow Walter to learn to his maximum potential,* they thought. In a nutshell, they felt that he was destined for the district's vocational program.

Mike and Julie Thompson had watched Walter's behavior slowly deteriorate since his initial placement in Mr. Moser's class, and they placed the blame for his inappropriate behavior and his lack of progress squarely on the shoulders of Mr. Moser. Moreover, they saw the prevocational tasks for a trainable mentally retarded (TMR) child as meaningless and viewed the setting as too restrictive for such a "bright and well-behaved" child. As evidenced by Walter's nondisabled (neighborhood) friends and his participation in community activities with other nondisabled children, they felt that he was capable of participating and benefiting from an environment in which there were many students without disabilities.

On the other hand, Mr. Moser continually expressed his concern to the Thompsons about Walter's frequent outbursts and his aggressiveness toward other children. In fact, he felt that Walter would make better progress if he could first bring his inappropriate behaviors "in check." In Mr. Moser's mind, Walter's education was appropriate in his current setting.

Finally in desperation, the Thompsons decided to arrange a meeting with the director of special education, Kenny Watson, to get Walter into the district's vocational program, because they felt that this program better addressed Walter's IEP goals and objectives. Mr. Watson had been director for the past several years and sided with his teachers on most issues. Present at the meeting were Mr. Watson, Mr. Moser, and Mr. and Mrs. Thompson. Along with typical record-keeping data, Mr. Moser brought Walter's student records, which were piled on the table approximately 6 inches high. The Thompsons decided to open the meeting by directly asking Mr. Watson to place Walter in the vocational program and requesting changes in his IEP to include transition goals and objectives.

Mr. Moser addressed the issue by pointing to Walter's records and saying, "Walter's records include prevocational goals and objectives that are in line for someone his age. Besides, he is achieving his goals and objectives in my classroom. What makes you think that he'll do better in the vocational program?"

Mr. Thompson responded by saying that he felt Walter would do better in a program in which he would be working on tasks more appropriate for someone his age, and the vocational program would help him reach his maximum potential. Mr. Moser simply sat quietly and shook his head in dismay. As Mr. Watson shuffled through Walter's records, he pulled out and read Walter's IEP goals and objectives, which the Thompsons had previously approved.

"Look, these goals and objectives would not change much if Walter were in the vocational program," commented Mr. Watson.

Halfway through the recitation of Walter's IEP, Mr. Thompson grabbed his wife's hand and remarked, "Its obvious you have no intention of moving our son. As far as we are concerned, this meeting was a waste of our time." The Thompsons then got up and walked out.

QUESTIONS

Legal Issues to Consider

1. Was Mr. Watson justified in keeping Walter in his current classroom?

2. Were the Thompsons justified in requesting that Walter be placed in the vocational setting?

3. If Walter is achieving the goals and objectives set forth in his IEP, should he be moved?

Other Issues

1. At what age should vocational training begin for students like Walter?

2. What could Mr. Moser do to help Walter better adjust to working on vocational tasks?

CASE 5.2

VERNON/IMPROPER PLACEMENT

Vernon sat looking around and began to wonder what was wrong with the other students in his class. *They all act so bad,* he thought. Vernon was correct. Billy was always depressed and often acted out if he did not get enough attention from the teacher. Susie was constantly hitting whoever was near her. Robin would frequently curse the teacher or other students. Frankie would usually come to school high on drugs or intoxicated by booze. The other students also displayed similar behavioral problems. To Vernon, this was a new environment, one of constant chaos.

Vernon had been placed in the learning disabilities/emotional disturbance (LD/ED) classroom because he qualified as LD on a recent evaluation from a multidisciplinary team (MDT). Because he was evaluated at midyear, many of the special education classes were at full capacity; however, Mark Parson's class was still below capacity. Mr. Parson was certified in ED and was working on his LD certification. At the MDT meeting, it was Mr. Parson who encouraged Vernon's parents, Sam and Willie Rewey, to send Vernon to his class. *Thank God,* thought Mr. Parson, *I might finally get a student who doesn't have behavioral problems.* Mr. Parson saw Vernon as someone who could serve (behaviorally) as a role model for his other students.

When Vernon arrived in the class, he knew that he didn't quite fit in. First, Vernon was diagnosed as having mild LD, and the other students were moderately ED. It was suspected that Vernon could also be diagnosed as having an attention problem or ADD, but this type of evaluation was beyond the scope of the educational personnel at Vernon's school. Second, he did not exhibit any disruptive behaviors or aggressive behaviors, unlike his classmates. Third, Vernon's slightly higher intelligence score made him one of the smartest students in the class. Despite these obvious differences between Vernon and the other students, he was to become one of the first students with LD to be placed in the class. Unfortunately for Vernon, his mild learning problems and high IQ meant he could easily complete the daily learning packets. All of the students in the class were expected to complete the learning packets, replete with worksheets.

At first, Sam and Willie Rewey liked the idea that Vernon would be getting more attention because of a lower student-to-teacher ratio, but after a few weeks they began to question their original decision. Even with assurances from Mr. Parson that Vernon could easily meet his IEP goals and objectives in his class, Vernon's parents were suspicious. In the weeks after Vernon's placement, his parents began to notice a change in their son's behavior. For example, Vernon had problems at home with his younger brother and neighbors. At school, similar problems were occurring, such as altercations or arguments with other students in his class. Slowly, his school work began to suffer. After one quarter in Mr. Parson's class, Vernon was earning Ds and Fs. It was at this point that the Reweys decided it was time to visit Mr. Parson's classroom.

Mr. Parson generously asked the Reweys to drop by whenever they had free time to see the classroom. On the day that they decided to visit, the classroom was chaotic. When they first walked into the classroom, two students were fighting, and Mr. Parson was busy breaking up the fight. After the students had settled, Mr. Rewey noticed that Vernon finished his work very quickly and became bored sitting at his desk waiting for his next assignment. At one point, as Mr. Parson was busy talking to his parents, Vernon fell asleep at his desk. To the Reweys, it appeared that Vernon was not challenged and, worse yet, was in a class that lacked structure. Mr. Parson assured his parents that Vernon was improving in his class and that he was working on Vernon's IEP goals and objectives. When the Reweys pulled out Vernon's IEP and asked, objective by objective, when and how Vernon was learning these, Mr. Parson became defensive and said, "Well, we can't work on all of the objectives at once."

"By the end of the week, we usually cover many of the objectives," Mr. Parson added. Upset over what they had seen and heard, the Rowleys immediately went to speak to the special education director, Mrs. Cathy Holliday, about moving Vernon back to a school in which he could receive more academics.

During their brief meeting, Mrs. Holliday made it clear to Vernon's parents that Mr. Parson's LD/ED classroom was the appropriate placement. Mrs. Holliday pointed out to the Reweys that Vernon's behavior had become worse since he had moved, an indication that he should remain in the LD/ED classroom, and that Mr. Parson was teaching Vernon based on the goals and objectives in his IEP.

"I'm sorry, Mr. and Mrs. Rewey, but I think Mr. Parson's classroom is the best placement for Vernon, and I feel that his educational environment is very appropriate," Mrs.

Holliday spoke defiantly. These were the last words that the Reweys heard before leaving Mrs. Holliday's office. On the drive home, the Reweys discussed their meeting and were convinced that Vernon should be moved to a more academically challenging environment and that they would do whatever they could to get Vernon moved.

QUESTIONS

Legal Issues to Consider

1. Is Vernon achieving the goals and objectives set forth in his IEP?

2. Did the MDT make the proper decision in the placement of Vernon?

3. Is the full continuum of placement available at this district?

Other Issues

1. What training should ED teachers have to deal with and use cutting-edge behavioral techniques for children with emotional disturbance?

2. Using the findings from the Daniel R. R. case, is Vernon's placement appropriate in terms of LRE?

3. What role should academic demands play when dealing with children with ED? How can using effective teaching techniques prevent behavioral problems in the classroom?

CASE 5.3

YANCY/GENERAL EDUCATION PARTICIPATION

As Yancy sat at her desk, she kept repeating to herself, "I can't do this. I can't do this."

"Come on now. You can do this worksheet. Just multiply the top with the bottom number," her personal aide, Henry Hudson, encouraged.

"I hate this stuff," said Yancy as she pressed harder with her pencil on the paper. Finally, she applied so much pressure that her pencil point went through the paper.

"Now, look what you've done. You've ruined the paper," said an exasperated Mr. Hudson.

With that, Yancy crumbled up the worksheet and threw it across the room into the trashcan. When Mrs. Jenkins, the classroom teacher, saw the commotion coming from Yancy's desk, she went back to address the problem. By now the other students in the class had stopped working and all eyes were focused on Yancy.

"Yancy, this is the last time that you are going to disrupt my class," said Mrs. Jenkins as she handed Yancy a suspension slip. With the slip in her hand, Yancy ran out of the room toward the office. As Mr. Hudson followed, Yancy ran into the office and plopped herself down on a seat.

Principal Mendel shook his head when he saw Yancy. "Yancy, this is the third time this week. When are you going to learn? You know what this means? Don't you?" Yancy did not speak a word; instead, she sat quietly with her head down. "I'll have to call your mom to set up a meeting to have you transferred to Kimmel Junior High," said Mr. Mendel in a firm, yet pleasant tone.

Mr. Mendel and Mrs. Jenkins both felt that they had made a concerted effort to keep Yancy in the fifth-grade class and not place her in the BD classroom at Kimmel. If not for the plea of Yancy's mother, Hanna Esquin, and her threat of due process, Mr. Mendel would have placed her in the BD classroom already. When Mr. Mendel had seen the results of Yancy's psychological assessment weeks ago, he immediately had thought that Kimmel would be the best placement for Yancy, but her mother had claimed that her daughter exhibited only mild behavioral problems and had insisted on keeping her in the classroom. Hanna had visited the BD classroom at Kimmel and had not liked what she had seen. On the day of her visit, the classroom teacher, Mr. Keiv, had been ill, and a substitute teacher was teaching. Actually, the substitute could not teach because he was too busy trying to break up fights or quieting down the students. If not for the agreement between Hanna and Mr. Mendel of a six-week trial period, Yancy would have been transferred to Kimmel weeks ago.

At the time, Mrs. Jenkins couldn't believe that Yancy was staying in her classroom. She, too, was exasperated with Yancy's behavioral problems and disruptive behavior. At the MDT meeting, Mrs. Jenkins had been shocked to hear Mr. Mendel give in to the demands of Hanna. Despite the evidence supporting a label of emotional disturbance, Yancy would remain in her class. The only positive outcome of the meeting had been that Yancy would have an aide for most of the day. Henry Hudson had been working in the LD classroom on a part-time basis. Now, he would be reassigned to work with Yancy full-time. *Well, at least now I can let Hudson teach Yancy and focus my attention on the rest of the students in my class,* Mrs. Jenkins had thought as she left that meeting 10 weeks ago.

During the trial period, Mrs. Jenkins and Mr. Hudson kept detailed documentation of Yancy's behavior. At least daily, there was an incident involving Yancy and another student. The only time of the day when there were no problems was when Hanna was in the classroom. Since her daughter's evaluation, Hanna had made daily visits to the classroom to see firsthand if Yancy was causing any problems. Of course, when Hanna was in the classroom, Yancy was on her best behavior.

Since the MDT meeting, Mr. Mendel had insisted that Mrs. Jenkins incorporate a behavioral program into her teaching for Yancy. "Great, the kid gets rewards for being bad," was Mrs. Jenkins' first reaction. Mrs. Jenkins started a behavioral point system in which Yancy would earn five points per day for behaving. Unfortunately, Mrs. Jenkins was not consistent with her use of reinforcement, when she gave it, and she did not really believe that this behavioral system would work.

Ten weeks later, assembled in the conference room were Mr. Mendel, Mrs. Jenkins, Hanna Esquin, Mr. Keiv, and Yancy. "We are here today to discuss Yancy's current placement," said Mr. Mendel as he started the meeting. "We tried Yancy in Mrs. Jenkins' fifth-grade class for a longer period of time than we originally agreed upon," he said, "and we feel that this placement isn't meeting Yancy's needs."

Next, Mr. Keiv spoke, adding, "I've observed Yancy, and I think my classroom would be ideal for her. We have a better teacher-to-student ratio and provide a support system that we almost guarantee will improve her behavior."

Hanna suspected that school officials wanted to change Yancy's placement, so she had come to the meeting with a list of suggestions as alternatives to moving her. She started by pointing out that Yancy had friends at this school (friends who were also her neighbors) and that she felt that Yancy was slowly making progress on IEP goals. She also expressed her concern about how far Yancy would have to travel to attend Kimmel (30 minutes). She also suggested that perhaps Mr. Hudson, who had no training in dealing with students with emotional disturbance, could obtain training in behavior management. Despite her innovative ideas, Mr. Mendel, Mr. Keiv, Mrs. Jenkins, and Mr. Hudson all agreed that Yancy needed a more supportive environment, such as Kimmel's BD class.

QUESTIONS

Legal Issues to Consider

1. Did Mr. Mendel make the proper decision by allowing Yancy to remain in the classroom for a 10-week trial period?

2. Does Hanna have any grounds for requesting that the aide, Mr. Hudson, receive more training?

3. Should Hanna request a placement closer to Yancy's home? Is the school obligated to create such a placement?

Other Issues

1. What special training should the general education teacher have for dealing with students with behavioral problems?

CASE 5.4

NICHOLAS/PARENT PARTICIPATION

David Radison was the new coordinator for the Learning Disabilities Program at Blue Quail Middle School. As part of his job, he supervised MDT and IEP meetings in his school. His input was valuable to parents and others because he could describe, in detail, all of the LD classes in the school and the teachers who taught them. It was after his fifth MDT meeting that he became suspicious about the manner in which children with LD were being classified. *Before the next meeting,* David thought, *I'm going to try to find out why all of these kids are being labeled LD.*

At the next meeting, Nicholas Drumage was the latest to be evaluated and recommended by the school's psychologist, Wendy Wesson, for the LD program. At David's request, Wendy met him in the conference room early to discuss the Drumage evaluation. Present in the room were Wendy and Kelly Flaherty, the LD teacher. As David entered the door, he said hello to Kelly and commented to Wendy, "Not another one for the LD program. That makes five this month."

Wendy replied with a sarcastic, "I don't disable them: I just evaluate 'em."

David and Kelly simply looked at each other. Kelly also knew that there was an increased rate of placements in LD classes.

"The reason why I asked you to show up early is that I want to ask you a few questions about this Drumage case," David explained. "I'm just surprised at the rate of students being recommended for LD, and I really don't understand why you are using this Nonverbal Intellectual Test of Personal Individual Creativity (NITPIC) to assess students with suspected learning disabilities."

"Well," Wendy began, "I think it's a great test to assess students with cognitive impairments. Besides, I use the Wide Range Achievement Measure (WRAM) to show a discrepancy between IQ and achievement." No one had ever challenged her before, so it came as a surprise to see the "new guy" ask about her evaluations. "You know, David, I've been doing this job for 25 years. I know what I'm doing," Wendy continued.

"Yeah, I know about your reputation in the district as a school psychologist," David replied. As Wendy glared at him, he spoke again, "Okay, I just think that next time you need more documentation about intellectual or cognitive skills. I really don't feel that a 15-minute IQ test is the best measure to classify a student as LD."

"Well, for your information, this IQ test has acceptable levels of reliability," Wendy replied in defense of her recommendation.

Jumping in, David added, "But, it was not normed on students with LD."

"That's irrelevant," Wendy shot back.

David sensed that he had pushed Wendy as far as he could, so he decided to change the topic. "Well, let's talk about Nicholas Drumage. From your evaluation it looks as if David needs a more-intensive setting such as Kelly Flaherty's self-contained classroom."

"Yeah," confirmed Wendy.

"Okay," said David, "if the parents agree, we should try to place him in her classroom." Throughout the entire conversation, Kelly sat quietly in her chair. Being new to the district, Kelly was hesitant to speak.

After waiting for 15 minutes and making a lot of small talk, David realized that the Drumages were not going to come to the meeting. "Well, I need to get Mrs. Nelson (the school secretary) to give them a call," David announced. A few minutes later, the phone rang in the conference room and David commented, "It looks like a no show."

After hanging up the phone, David then gave a number of directives to Kelly and Wendy. "Kelly, why don't you write up some goals on Nicholas, and Wendy, why don't you fill out the placement forms." As he made another telephone call, Kelly wrote five goals and signed the IEP while Wendy and David filled out the forms on Nicholas' classification and placement. Despite the lack of information on the IEP and placement and classification forms, everyone signed all of the forms. When Kelly asked about Nicholas' parents, David said that he would send them a copy of the forms.

"But, shouldn't we try to get his parents in here to explain our decision and his IEP?" Kelly asked.

David just smiled and told her, "We'll never hear from them. On Monday, Nicholas will start in your class."

As Kelly walked out of the room, she felt uncomfortable that David didn't make more of an effort to contact the parents, especially for such an important decision. She also felt badly that the IEP was so poorly written, lacking dates and specifics (objectives), but David told her not to worry about that—she could fill in the details later.

QUESTIONS

Legal Issues to Consider

1. What members should be present at an MDT meeting?

2. What members should be present at the IEP meeting?

3. What procedures or processes did the team fail to follow concerning the evaluation, parent participation, and IEP development? What role does parental consent play in the school's responsibility in the IEP process?

Other Issues

1. What are some possible school and home objectives that might be included in a typical IEP?

2. For a student suspected of having learning disabilities, what type of tests and measures should be included in the evaluation?

■■■■■ **CASE 5.5** ■■■■■

KELLY/RELATED SERVICES

Kelly diligently worked placing pegs through small holes in the lid of a coffee can. With her tiny hands shaking, she picked up the small pegs and then fit them in the holes. While she did this, Kelly made grunting sounds with each attempt. Having practiced this task for the past several months, Kelly had become quite good at completing it within the 15-minute period. As she worked at her task, Norman Pretzman, her teacher, gave her positive encouragement, saying "great job" and "keep going." Norman made his rounds about every 10 minutes, walking around the class to make sure that all of his students were working.

Kelly was one of eight students in Mr. Pretzman's classroom for students with autism. She could only communicate through a series of grunts and noises. She seemed to understand basic commands and could follow simple directions. Other than her grunts, she was considered uncommunicative. Despite her lack of communication skills and low cognitive ability, Kelly was pleasant to have in class because she smiled often and was very cooperative. On this particular day, Kelly's task, a vocational task, was meant to strengthen her fine motor skills and improve her stamina at repetitive tasks. Mr. Pretzman had designed a series of tasks to prepare his students for later vocational and work settings. Jobs in the city were scarce, except those at the local electronics factory, which hired persons with disabilities, in part because of a financial incentive provided by the city.

Mr. Pretzman's class was located in an inner-city school in the middle of an area commonly referred to as the "combat zone." The combat zone earned its name because of the various gun fights that took place among local gangs. Jenkins Middle School was locked at all times and from the outside looked like a condemned building. Like most of the schools in the district, Jenkins was poorly maintained. Inside, the lights were dim and the windows had bars to keep its inhabitants safe from outsiders. Most of the buildings in the combat zone were either vacant or poorly maintained.

Although most of the residents of the area were poorly educated, a few parents were motivated enough to form parent groups in an attempt to change education at Jenkins. Through one local church, a special education parent group was formed. Its main focus was to ensure that the "best" special education services were provided to their children. One night several months ago, a speaker named Dr. Elliot Hobson had presented information to the group about alternative communication for students with severe disabilities. One technique that he mentioned was called an assistive communication machine (ACM). The machine was a handheld device that helped students who had never talked communicate through a human "assister." Using these devices, assisters helped students—usually by moving their arms or tugging on their sleeves—spell out basic requests and responses to requests. In the audience on this night was Kelly's mom, Havana Fasler, who saw the ACM as a means to break through to Kelly to help her communicate to her and others. The only problems were the cost of the device (about $2,000 per machine) and the cost of the assister. Immediately after Dr. Hobson's talk, Havana ran up to the stage to speak to him. After about 15 minutes, Havana was armed with enough information to pursue the idea for Kelly.

The very next day Havana called Mr. Pretzman and asked him about the machine. As she dialed the school telephone number, she could hardly contain her excitement. "I'd like to speak to Mr. Pretzman please," Havana requested when the secretary answered the phone.

"Hello, this is Mr. Pretzman. Can I help you?" asked Norman.

"Mr. Pretzman, this is Havana Fasler. Have you ever heard of the 'assistive communication machine' or ACM?" Havana asked.

"Why yes, it's a machine that is supposed to help kids communicate," Mr. Pretzman replied.

"That's right," Havana responded, "and I really want to try this with…"

"Whoa, slow down Havana," Mr. Pretzman interrupted, "this machine is not guaranteed to work. What I mean is that there is no conclusive evidence that this machine works for all kids, or, for that matter, any kids. It's a new gimmick, and, quite frankly, I think it would be foolish to buy it until we find out if it *really* works. Besides, Kelly is achieving the goals and objectives listed on her IEP."

On the other end of the line was silence as a stunned Havana stammered to find something to say.

"Havana, are you still there?" Mr. Pretzman asked.

"Yes, I am," Havana replied, adding, "according to Dr. Elliot Hobson from Klaston University, this machine works with the kids who he's tried it with, many of whom are just like Kelly."

"Look Havana, if you want to spend—waste—your money on this contraption, feel free, but don't expect too much," Mr. Pretzman pessimistically responded.

"Why should I pay? The district needs to pay for this. After all isn't it a free education? Paid for by taxpayers like me?" Havana asked. Mr. Pretzman had heard enough and politely excused himself from the conversation to take another call. The next day Havana called the director of special education and again requested that the district pay for this machine and train an assister because Kelly currently was not receiving an appropriate education.

QUESTIONS

Legal Issues to Consider

1. From the information provided, was Kelly receiving an appropriate education?

2. What is meant by *appropriate education*? How have recent court cases or IDEA defined it? Was a good faith effort made to provide appropriate education?

3. By law, what would prevent the district from purchasing a machine and training an assister for Kelly?

Other Issues

1. If the use of such a machine is written into the IEP, would the district be obligated to purchase it and train an assister?

2. How could the tasks, used in this class, be changed to reflect more real-world tasks?

CASE 5.6

HAROLD/ADEQUATE SERVICES

Harold Green twisted his tongue and squinched his face as he worked on the math worksheet. With Marcus Grace, his peer tutor, looking on, Harold looked up after finishing his second problem and asked Marcus, "Is this right?" Marcus looked at the problem, checked it, and responded, "Yep." When Harold finished the tenth problem, Marcus checked it and marked a star next to it. Harold then raised his hand and Mrs. Daphane Lee walked up to his desk to check his progress.

"Good, those tutors must really be doing a good job," remarked Mrs. Lee, referring to Harold's participation in the after-school tutoring program. Indeed, Harold has managed to maintain steady growth in most of his academic subjects, mostly Bs and Cs, because of the two hours of daily tutoring from the program. Mrs. Lee and Harold's parents, Oscar and Leslie Green, realized that Harold probably would not be succeeding in his general education classroom without the program.

Harold had always been classified as having learning problems. First identified in preschool as having a cognitive delay, he was now labeled educable mentally retarded

(EMR). Results from his most recent psychological testing indicated that Harold's IQ scores were borderline between mild (EMR) and moderate (trainable mentally retarded—TMR) retardation. If not for the tutoring program, Harold would probably be in the district's self-contained EMR classroom.

The district had recently found out that its tutoring program, now in its fourth year, was running out of funding. It had run out of money last year and had since managed to crawl along with leftover funds. Despite the program's success in helping a number of identified (special education) and nonidentified students, administrators had already decided to discontinue it because it was too costly and utilized too many personnel.

When the program's parents were informed about the decision to close the program, there was a resilient outcry, but after a few weeks things died down. Some of the parents hired private tutors for their children, but other parents, many of whom could not afford to hire tutors, simply tried tutoring their children on their own. Because many of the children received tutoring on such a frequent basis, without the program, their academic progress slowly declined. Harold, who benefited from the program, saw his test scores (grades) decrease as he fell further and further behind. Although Harold had managed to maintain passing grades in his fourth-grade classroom, his slow rate of learning had caused Mrs. Lee to slow her pace in order to accommodate him.

Seeing that his grades were falling, Mrs. Lee decided to consult with Mrs. Nancy Folksberg, the special education teacher. Mrs. Folksberg was certified in three areas, mental retardation, learning disabilities, and emotional disturbance, and had several years of experience consulting with general education teachers. After speaking with her, Mrs. Folksberg agreed to increase the amount of time she spent with Harold in the general education classroom. Despite Mrs. Folksberg's increased appearances in the general education classroom, Harold's grades continued their slow slide. After three weeks, Mrs. Folksberg suggested to Mrs. Lee that Harold be placed under her guidance for at least three-quarters of the school day. In doing so, he would be pulled from his general education class and be placed in a self-contained class.

When Mrs. Lee called the Greens about the change in placement, the Greens quickly responded by telling her that the district needed to supplement Harold's general education learning with either an aide or tutor to help him remain in the classroom. "There is no reason why Harold should be pulled," Oscar remarked. "The district is responsible for him remaining in your class, and for all the promises that were made and all of the friends that he made. I will not let him be pulled."

Mrs. Lee realized that Mr. Green was upset so she told him that she would speak to the principal, Mr. Neagly, about helping Harold. Within a few days, Mr. Neagly called Oscar and informed him that Harold needed to be in Mrs. Folksberg's class.

QUESTIONS

Legal Issues to Consider

1. From the information provided, was Harold receiving an appropriate education without the tutoring program?

2. Is the school obligated to provide a tutor or aide for Harold? What role should cost play in deciding an appropriate education?

3. What can Harold's parents do to get better services for him in the general education classroom?

Other Issues

1. Should general education teachers modify their instruction to accommodate students with different cognitive levels, such as an EMR or TMR student? Should they be asked to modify their curriculum for such students?

CHAPTER SIX

LEAST RESTRICTIVE ENVIRONMENT

CASE 6.1   JOHN/DISRUPTIVE BEHAVIOR

CASE 6.2   BEN/ INCLUSION

CASE 6.3   JAMES/TEACHER BIAS

CASE 6.4   DAVID/THREATENING BEHAVIOR

CASE 6.5   JANE/REFUSAL TO CONSIDER

CASE 6.6   JARED/LEGAL RIGHTS

CASE 6.1

JOHN/DISRUPTIVE BEHAVIOR

Ms. Chen had been retained as an attorney by Mr. and Mrs. Smith, parents of John. Ms. Chen remembered the first time she met Mr. and Mrs. Smith. They were upset and angry with the school district. Mrs. Smith stated in her initial telephone call, "I can't believe that the school people want John out of the school! We just came from an IEP meeting, and they had the audacity to tell us that John needs to be in a private day school for behavior disordered students. I just told them, 'Over my dead body! You'll be hearing from my attorney.' We left immediately and called you. Will you take the case?"

Ms. Chen was an experienced attorney and had handled many cases for parents challenging school districts' decisions. She was known as a tough and aggressive attorney. She didn't always win all issues in her cases, but she almost always prevailed on some issues. Ms. Chen took the case, in part because she had a personal interest in cases that involved students with disabilities. She had a niece in California who was placed in a private school for mentally retarded children. She vividly recalled her conversations with her frantic sister, the child's mother. It was difficult enough for a parent to have a child challenged by a disability, let alone without the school district rejecting the child. Ms. Chen's sister never quite got over the fact that the district would not allow her daughter to attend public school and instead placed her in a private school. One of the reasons that Ms. Chen decided to study law was that she felt that she could be of assistance to other parents like her sister.

After informing the school district that she would be representing Mr. and Mrs. Smith and John, Ms. Chen reviewed the records in preparation for a due process hearing. John was a 13-year-old boy who had attended Martin Luther King Middle School since sixth grade. He was now in eighth grade. The records indicated that since the sixth grade, John had exhibited minor behavioral problems, including noncompliance (e.g., verbal refusal to take his hat off in the building), poor peer relationships (e.g., fighting with other students), and poor motivation (e.g., not completing assigned tasks in the classroom). Through the seventh grade, these behaviors did not significantly affect John's school performance; however, eighth grade was a different story.

During that school year, John's behavior deteriorated. During the first semester, John had 45 discipline referrals to the principal's office. A number of the referrals were the result of John's disruptive classroom behavior (e.g., use of foul language directed toward the teachers), intimidation of other students and teachers, and physical assault on other students. In addition, John had a number of unexcused absences from school and was frequently late. John exhibited these behaviors across all school settings including classrooms, hallways, and the bus. John was failing all classes, had been suspended 10 days, and had been arrested by the police once for a fight. John was in special education for all academic classes.

In review of John's file, Ms. Chen noted that his teachers were carefully selected to include those who had smaller class sizes and who had structured classroom management. John had multiple schedule changes, and his parents were frequently contacted. Special accommodations had been made to allow John to remove himself from class if he felt upset. In addition, the IEP indicated that John was receiving a special behavioral management program, one-to-one tutoring during study hall, small group instruction, and group counseling by the social worker.

At the beginning of the school year, John physically assaulted another student and was arrested. Charges were filed against John by the other student's parents. John had to make a court appearance and was placed on a short-term probation. After the incident, a reevaluation was conducted on John. At the multidisciplinary conference, it was determined that John was still eligible for services as a student with behavior disorders. It was also determined that John could not benefit from the special education program being provided, due to his rapidly deteriorating behavior. At the meeting, Mr. and Mrs. Smith were in agreement with John's disability diagnosis of behavior disorder. According to the minutes of the meeting, John was in need of a very small group setting to avoid the possibility of violence. He also needed intense support services to assist him in controlling his anger, improving his self-concept, improving peer relationships, and developing coping strategies. The school staff proposed a program in a private day treatment facility for students with behavior disorders in a neighboring town. However, his parents disagreed.

Mr. and Mrs. Smith told Ms. Chen that school personnel were biased against John and that they were picking on him, just waiting for him to misbehave. Mrs. Smith stated that she rejected any significant changes in the placement for John. She said that the proposed placement change would mean that John would be in a class with students who exhibited severe behavior disorders, and she felt that these students would have a negative influence on John. She said that John was a follower and would quickly learn these more severe behaviors. She also feared that John would not be challenged academically. John was a very bright child (IQ 130), and Mrs. Smith felt that special schools for students moved at a slower pace. Mrs. Smith also stated that there were 11 meetings held about John during the past year. She said she did not receive notice for all of the meetings, and she attended only eight or nine of them.

The due process hearing, requested in October, was finally held in January. The hearing lasted eight hours. Ms. Chen questioned many witnesses, including the principal, special education teachers, school psychologist, and special education administrator.

The special education administrator summarized the school's position by stating that "John was properly evaluated by the school district. There is no dispute between the school and parents that John has a behavior disorder. The district has also acted properly in providing an appropriate program for John. School staff made numerous attempts to address John's behavioral difficulties in the school program. John's proposed IEP is appropriate to meet his educational needs. John needs a more restrictive environment."

The only procedural error against the school district that Ms. Chen was able to find was that Mr. and Mrs. Smith were not properly notified about two meetings that were held. As they indicated earlier, the Smiths attended the other nine meetings.

Ms. Chen also asked Mr. and Mrs. Smith to tell the hearing officer their side of the story. Mrs. Jones stated, "My husband and I feel that John needs to stay at Martin Luther King Middle School. He needs and has a right to associate with 'normal' students. If he is placed in a behavior disorder school, we feel that he will learn more inappropriate behaviors. Besides, John does not want to change schools. He has promised us that he will work harder in school, and we are willing to seek counseling outside of school."

Two weeks later, Ms. Chen received a written order from the hearing officer. The order stated the following:

1. Within two weeks of this order, the district shall convene an IEP meeting for the purpose of modifying John's IEP to include the placement at the private day treatment school for students with behavior disorders. Staff from the private school shall assist in developing the objectives and services needed. The IEP shall be reviewed every semester to evaluate John's progress. The long-term goal should be the reintegration of John back to the public school.

2. This hearing officer finds that, on two occasions, the parents were not properly notified of meetings concerning John. However, this failure did not result in John's parents being misinformed about the placement options being considered for John or disruption in the educational services being provided to John. This violation represents a technical violation only, which occurred in the context of numerous IEP meetings and contacts between the school and parents.

QUESTIONS

Legal Issues to Consider

1. What is the legal basis for the proposed placement of John in a private day treatment facility for students with behavior disorders?

2. Did the parents have a legal basis to demand that John stay in Martin Luther King Middle School (e.g., John would pick up severe behaviors from other BD students)?

3. If the district had not attempted to assist John by selecting particular teachers, changing his schedule, providing a behavior management program, and so forth, would that have changed the outcome of this case? Why or why not?

Other Issues

1. Do you think that John had a right to stay in the public school? Why or why not?

2. In your experience, how do schools deal with students who exhibit significant behavior problems?

3. How does society treat adults who exhibit severe behavior problems? Can and should schools take the same approach?

CASE 6.2

BEN/INCLUSION

Ben's family had lived in Oakville all of Ben's life. His father graduated from Oakville High School, and his grandparents lived two blocks from his home. Ben's father was the manager of a local factory that made air conditioners, and his mother owned a small dress shop on Main Street. Ben had a sister who was one year younger. Most people in the small town of Oakville knew and respected Ben and his family. The family was average in every way except one: Ben had a disability and was labeled autistic.

Ben's family noticed that when Ben was a baby he had little eye contact with anyone. When he was about a 1½, he began rocking, and his language and speech weren't developing as rapidly as they should. Ben's sister quickly surpassed Ben in every developmental milestone. The parents took Ben to a teaching pediatric hospital for an evaluation. The doctors confirmed what the parents had feared. Ben displayed what was termed autistic-like tendencies that were considered moderate in nature. The doctors encouraged Ben's parents to place him in an early childhood program for students with special needs.

At 2½, Ben's parents requested an evaluation through the local school district. The school district sent the referral to the local special education cooperative, whose personnel conducted the evaluation. The school district evaluation consisted of a battery of psychological tests, speech and language testing, observation of Ben at home, a detailed developmental history from his parents, and a review of medical records. After the evaluation was completed, an evaluation conference was held. The participants included Ben's parents, a psychologist, a social worker, a speech and language therapist, an early childhood teacher, and a special education administrator. Again, the evaluation confirmed what the doctors had told Ben's parents. Ben had autistic-like behaviors that affected his speech and language skills, social skills, and cognitive skills. Ben's parents readily agreed to place Ben in a half-day early childhood class at the local elementary school.

During the early childhood program, Ben made slow but steady progress. At the end of three years, Ben could say his name, tell in one or two words what he wanted, scribble with a crayon on paper, and sit for a period of 5 minutes listening while the teacher read a story. The only area in which Ben did not make good progress was in his socialization skills. His lack of eye contact was still a concern, and Ben had difficulty relating to other children. In fact, he didn't seem particularly interested in other children. Ben's parents were very pleased with his progress during his three years in the early childhood program. Although they were concerned about his socialization skills, they felt that Ben's sister could help with the skills at home because they were similar in age. Ben's sister included Ben in most activities at home. Ben was beginning to engage in parallel play.

Before the fall term in school, at Ben's IEP meeting, the parents stated that they wanted Ben to enter regular kindergarten as an inclusion student in the same kindergarten class as his sister. Present at the meeting were both parents, a general education teacher, a special education teacher, the principal, the special education supervisor, and a speech and language therapist.

After listening to the parents' comments, the principal sat back in his chair and said, "We don't have inclusion here. Ben will need to go to the special education class in the building."

The parents were very insistent upon placing Ben in kindergarten. They said that Ben had been treated in a normal manner at home and was accepted in the community. They felt that he would have good language role models and opportunities to improve socialization skills in kindergarten, something that would be limited in a special education classroom.

After considerable discussion, the special education administrator said, "Wait a minute. Just because we haven't included a student with special needs in kindergarten before doesn't mean we aren't willing to consider the possibility. Let's stop this meeting and reconvene in a planning meeting to discuss the possibility in more detail."

Over the next month, three planning meetings were held, each lasting approximately two hours. At each planning meeting, the principal, special education teacher, kindergarten teacher, special education administrator, and the parents were present. The focus at each meeting centered around the kindergarten teacher's expectations, Ben's skills in each area, and the appropriate modifications for each skill area. The meetings were positive in nature, and the parents were active participants. The parents agreed that the most important priorities for Ben were academic, speech, and language growth. A secondary priority was socialization skill development. It was also agreed that the curriculum could be modified for Ben, but it would not be modified beyond recognition to become a "class within a class." In other words, the teacher could not teach a completely different curriculum for Ben while at the same time teaching all other children from the standard curriculum. Ultimately, it was determined that Ben's needs could be met within the regular kindergarten with some adaptations from the teacher. Related services were to include speech and language services and the services of a full-time assistant for Ben. Information from the planning meetings was translated into Ben's IEP.

Ben's parents were very pleased with his progress in kindergarten, and it was not a problem to have Ben's sister in the same class. In fact, Ben's parents felt like they were more aware of what was happening with Ben's sister in the class because she was able to tell them how Ben was adjusting. Ben's parents met frequently with the kindergarten teacher and his aide to discuss progress.

In planning for the next year, first grade, the parents again requested inclusion for Ben in the regular classroom. Several planning meetings were held with the first-grade teacher, special education teacher, speech and language therapist, principal, and special education administrator. Again the focus was on teacher expectations in first grade, Ben's skills, and the appropriate accommodations. The discussion this year seemed to center more around Ben's skill level in reading. Ben was beginning to experience difficulty with prereading skills. He was unable to recognize the alphabet and unable to write his name without assistance. He speech was at times unintelligible, although his sister often interpreted for him in school. The special education teacher and first-grade teacher recommended that Ben receive "pull out" assistance in reading one hour per day. They felt that if Ben stayed in first grade for reading, the curriculum would have to be completely changed to become a class within a class. Ben's parents were not happy about taking him out of the first-grade classroom, but they could see that he would be unsuccessful without special assistance. They reluctantly agreed to the one hour of special instruction for first grade in reading. Both parents and teachers stated that the primary goal for Ben was academic growth. The information from the planning meetings was finalized in Ben's IEP. Again, Ben had a successful year in first grade.

The same planning process was used for second grade. However, some changes were made in Ben's program. It was agreed that Ben would be taken out of the regular classroom for reading, language arts, spelling, and speech therapy. In January, the second-grade teacher began to notice behavioral changes in Ben. She noticed that when he couldn't complete the work, Ben bit his nails until bleeding and became visibly upset. He appeared to rely completely on his aide and his sister for assistance. For example, Ben wouldn't answer oral questions unless the aide gave her verbal encouragement and approval. In the lunchroom, Ben would not leave the cafeteria unless his sister told him to leave. Ben's reliance on his sister was beginning to be a detriment to his sister and to Ben. In addition, the teacher noticed that the curriculum was far too difficult for Ben in mathematics. Even with many accommodations, Ben was becoming more and more frustrated.

An IEP meeting was arranged at the school personnel's request. The parents brought their attorney with them. The discussion centered on classroom expectations (with modifications), Ben's skills, and any other accommodations that could be made without altering the curriculum beyond recognition. The end result was a recommendation by the school personnel that Ben receive special education assistance for math, reading, language arts, spelling, and speech therapy. Ben would be out of the classroom for approximately 60 percent of the day. Ben's parents were very unhappy and insisted on Ben being fully included. Their attorney supported the position of full inclusion.

Ultimately, the parents requested a due process hearing, and the matter was heard by an impartial due process hearing officer. The due process hearing officer ruled in favor of the district, stating that the district had provided appropriate supplemental aids and services and that the proposed change in placement was appropriate. The district was ordered to provide the proposed placement.

QUESTIONS

Legal Issues to Consider

1. According to IDEA, was the principal correct when he made the statement, "We don't have inclusion here. Ben will have to go to the special education class in the building"? Why or why not?

2. Describe some of the case law that has helped set standards for determining FAPE and LRE. Did the school district in this case meet the standards?

3. How does Section 504 address the issue of LRE? Did the district in this case meet the intent of Section 504?

4. Is the term *inclusion* a legal term? How does IDEA address inclusion?

Other Issues

1. How do advocacy groups define full inclusion? How is this different from LRE and FAPE as used in IDEA?

2. What are some examples in the community and society in general that people with disabilities are becoming fully included? What are some barriers that need to be removed in order for people with disabilities to be fully included?

3. Do you think that schools will ever fully include students with disabilities? Why or why not?

CASE 6.3

JAMES/TEACHER BIAS

Ann pulled the mail from her mailbox on her way to the teacher's lounge for lunch. She glanced at a familiar form—an invitation to a multidisciplinary conference.

Oh, great, she thought, *another student. I already have 14 students who have learning problems, and we have just settled into a routine, and our daily schedule is set. Another student would upset my groups. Oh, well, I'll just wait and see. I think I've heard about this child from Mrs. Pace, the first-grade teacher. I think he's having trouble in reading.*

Ann didn't give any more thought to the upcoming staffing. She went about her daily schedule as a special education teacher for first- and second-graders.

Each morning, Ann taught reading, language arts, and spelling. In the afternoon, she taught math, science, and social studies. Some children received speech and language services, and the speech therapist tried to see the children from Ann's class twice a week in a group, to minimize taking children from the classroom. One child received occupational therapy on a weekly basis. Ann knew these were important services for her students, yet she did not like any children taken out of her room when she taught reading. So far, the related services personnel had tried to accommodate her request. Most of Ann's students were self-contained, meaning that they spent most of their days in her special class. Ann's philosophy was to attempt mainstreaming only if the child had all of the prerequisite skills necessary to achieve in the regular class. Therefore, few students left her classroom for mainstreaming because few had strong academic skills. She felt pleased with her class this year, and, as a third-year teacher, she finally felt confident in her teaching.

The next Monday, Ann arrived at school early for the staffing. Mr. Cattaneo, the principal, told Ann that someone would take her class if the staffing wasn't completed by the time students went to class. Staffings started at 8:15 A.M., and students went to class at 8:45 A.M.

Ann walked into the crowded principal's office for the staffing at 8:10 A.M. Seated around the room in a circle were the school psychologist, the school social worker, the first-grade teacher, and the special education supervisor. Mr. Cattaneo stood at the doorway and said he would be in the meeting when he was available. Then he left. Ann took the last chair.

The psychologist made final arrangements for the meeting by stating, "I guess we should get another chair for Mrs. Compton, if she comes. Does anyone know if she's coming?" Before anyone could answer, Mrs. Compton, the parent of James, was ushered into the crowded room by the school secretary. The psychologist quickly got a folding chair from the office for Mrs. Compton and she sat down. Mrs. Compton looked around the room and didn't say anything.

The special education supervisor began the meeting by saying, "Mrs. Compton, thank you for coming today. We are here to discuss the evaluation recently completed on James. You know he has been having difficulty in first grade, and we completed the evaluation to help us gain a clear picture of how he learns and to determine if we can help him in any way. As we go through the evaluation, please feel free to ask questions. Now, we'll start by introducing ourselves. My name is Ms. Tame, and I'm the special education supervisor."

All school staff went around the room and introduced themselves.

"My name is Mr. Gordon, and I'm the school psychologist who tested James."

"I'm Ms. Sanders. You and I met at your home last month, Mrs. Compton."

"And, of course, you and I know one another, Mrs. Compton. I'm Mrs. Pace, James' teacher."

"My name is Ann Wilson. I'm the special education teacher." The special education supervisor then asked Mrs. Pace to review James' progress in first grade.

"James has been with me for the entire school year. He is a hard worker and is very well behaved. The children like James. I first noticed that James was having trouble with reading at the end of September. He still was not able to consistently name all letters of the alphabet. Some days he knew them, and other days he didn't. He was completely unable to sound out three-letter words. It just didn't make sense to him. I have worked very hard with James. He is in a reading group by himself, and a volunteer tutors him daily. Now, in January, I am very concerned about his reading skills. He can barely read three-letter words and doesn't seem to understand sound–symbol relationships. He tries to memorize the words, but if they are in a different order, often he can only sound out the first letter, and he then guesses what the word is. James has made progress since the beginning of the year, but he is far behind all other first graders. In other subjects, he tries hard and is able to do okay as long as reading isn't involved. He seems to be keeping up in math, for example."

The social worker, Mrs. Sanders, was then asked to summarize her findings.

"I met with Mrs. Compton last month in her home. We talked about how James is doing at home and his developmental history. As far as developmental history, there is nothing remarkable, except that James had tubes inserted in his ears when he was 2 years old, and they fell out when he was 4 years old. The school nurse screened his hearing and vision, and he passed both screenings. Mrs. Compton is a single parent, and James is the only child in the home. Mrs. Compton often has to work evenings as a cashier, and her mother watches James. James has little contact with his father. Mrs. Compton sees James as well behaved and compliant. He does some chores around the house and has some friends. Do you have anything to add, Mrs. Compton?"

Mrs. Compton shook her head, and then the psychologist was asked to review his assessment of James.

"I saw James last week in the morning. He came with me to the testing room willingly. During testing, he was quiet and didn't offer information unless he was asked a direct question. He spoke quietly and was cooperative. James said he was having difficulty in reading and that he liked school. When asked what his favorite subject was, he said lunch. I administered a battery of tests to James. The first was the Weschler Intelligence Scale for Children III (WISC III). James was asked to answer some questions and solve some problems. Overall, James' ability fell into the average range. This means that he has the ability to do as well as any first grader. His verbal skills were in the low-average range, and his performance skills were average. He had some weaknesses. He had some difficulty with verbal-comprehension skills. When asked to define a word, for example, he often said, 'I don't know' or gave two- or three-word answers. He had some difficulty answering questions such as 'What are some reasons why we need firemen?' I also administered a general achievement test. James did average work in math and performed far below average in reading and spelling skills. James needs assistance with these skills. He didn't seem to know how to blend three-letter words such as cap and tan. He also had difficulty with sight words such as the and and. I am recommending special education help for James in the area of reading."

The special education supervisor then asked Mrs. Compton if she had any questions, and she answered, "No, I know he needs help."

To summarize, the special education supervisor stated, "Okay, it has been suggested that James become eligible for learning disabilities assistance in the area of reading skills. Is everyone in agreement with this suggestion?" All school personnel nodded in agreement. The special education supervisor continued by stating, "We now need to talk about the kinds of services James needs."

Mrs. Pace, James' teacher, quickly stated, "I think James needs help only in reading. He may need help in spelling later in the year, but, so far, first-graders do little spelling. He is doing well in math. We have reading right after lunch, and if he could have help during that time, he wouldn't miss any other classes."

Ann Wilson disagreed by saying, "My experience has been that children like James who have difficulty in reading tend to have difficulty in all academic areas in which there is any reading. I teach reading in the morning, and James would fit right into an existing group. I also think he would benefit from my program in math, social studies, and science. James could take physical education, music, and art with the other first-graders, as well as lunch and recess. My program is structured to reinforce reading during the entire day. With his limited skills, he would benefit from the full day in the special education class."

Trying to be agreeable, Mrs. Pace continued, "I certainly could keep James in first grade for every subject except reading, but if you think he could benefit from placement in special education all day, perhaps this would be best."

After some discussion and Mrs. Compton's agreement, James was placed in the special education classroom for most of the day.

Questions on the proposed IEP requested answers to the following questions: (1) What is the nature or severity of the student's disability that precludes placement in a regular class? (2) Explain why supplementary aids and services cannot be used to educate the student in a general education class. Ann Wilson smiled to herself as she wrote the standard answers on the IEP. She wrote, "James has severe learning disabilities that affect his ability to learn how to read. He cannot benefit from placement in the regular classroom due to his disability."

On the following Monday, James was placed in Ann Wilson's special education class. James fit in with the other children, and Ann placed him in existing groups for reading and math. James worked well with the other children and seemed happy.

QUESTIONS

Legal Issues to Consider

1. Did the team meet the requirements for LRE as stated in IDEA? Why or why not?

2. Did the team meet the requirements for continuum of services as stated in IDEA? Why or why not?

3. Was James' IEP individualized to meet his special needs? What evidence supports your statement?

Other Issues

1. Is it best to place a child like James in a full-day special education program so that he can benefit as much as possible from special assistance? Why or why not?

2. Conversely, do children with needs similar to James' benefit more from integration in general education? Why or why not?

3. How does the configuration of the special education class and attitude of Ann Wilson contribute to the segregation of students with disabilities from the general education population?

━━━━━━ **CASE 6.4** ━━━━━━

DAVID/THREATENING BEHAVIOR

Ms. Richardson, the special education coordinator and a teacher at East High School, sat at her desk after school completing some student-schedule changes. Mr. and Mrs. Patterson walked into the classroom.

Mr. Patterson began by stating, "We understand that we need to talk to you about our son having trouble in school."

Ms. Richardson asked, "Who is your son?"

"David Patterson. He is a sophomore here, and he's failing his classes. We can't handle him at home anymore. We think he belongs in a residential placement. We're afraid of him."

Ms. Richardson didn't recognize the name and stated, "Wait a minute. Let's look up your son's record. I don't know him."

Ms. Richardson pulled David's permanent record from the guidance office and brought it back to her room where the parents waited.

Ms. Richardson continued as she read the record, "David has been in this district since second grade. His grades were all As and Bs through seventh grade. Then he made Cs and Ds in eighth grade. His grade card for ninth grade shows that he failed English, math, science, and physical education. He passed woodworking with a D." Looking at the parents, she added, "You said you're afraid of him. What do you mean by this?"

Mr. Patterson answered, "He's threatened us. He says he's going to kill us. He leaves the house in the middle of the night and comes home two days later. He becomes very angry when we try to set a curfew. He hangs around with a group of kids who I know are using drugs. In fact, I have noticed lately that he comes home smelling of alcohol. He does what he wants when he wants. We understand that the school district is responsible for his education until he's 21 if he has a disability, and we think he has a behavior problem. He definitely belongs in a residential placement."

Ms. Richardson said, "Mr. Patterson, even if your son became eligible for special education, we wouldn't automatically place him in a residential placement. We would try to educate him here in this high school first."

Mr. Patterson sighed, "Well, any help is better than no help. Anyway, you'll see how bad he is."

Ms. Richardson said, "In order for us to determine if David has a disability, we first have to evaluate him. The evaluation will include a review of his progress in school, a social developmental study, a health history, an assessment of his current learning environment, and a psychological evaluation. Do you want to sign permission for the evaluation now?"

Mr. Patterson quickly said, "We sure do."

Ms. Richardson completed some forms, then said, "Okay, please sign here. The evaluation could take 60 school days to complete, but it probably will be completed in less time."

The evaluation was completed in four weeks, and an evaluation conference was held to review the results. The social developmental study revealed interesting information about David and his family. David was adopted at the age of 1. Apparently, he was taken away from his biological parents because of physical abuse. His biological father was in prison. David knew he was adopted but never sought information about his biological parents. The Pattersons were a very religious family. Mr. Patterson was the assistant minister of a local evangelical church. Mrs. Patterson did not work outside the home. The Pattersons stated that they tried hard to raise David. However, he wasn't always a happy child. He had strict rules at home and defied authority even as a young child. He did well in school until junior high school, where he got involved with a group of "rough" students. Mr. Patterson allowed David to go out with these boys on weekends to the bowling alley and skating rink, but David would smell of tobacco and sometimes alcohol when he came home. A major conflict began at home over David's friends. David was prohibited from seeing his friends, and he began to sneak out of the house in the middle of the night to see them. The conflict at home escalated to shouting, pushing, and cursing. David refused to talk to his father, and his grades in school began to drop. David began to wear long hair and dirty clothes that were ill-fitting. He rarely took a bath or ate at home. Even though David attended school on a regular basis, he began to fail classes in high school.

In a review of David's school progress, it was apparent that David wasn't successful in high school. He failed three of four classes in ninth grade, but he was never referred to the office for any misbehavior. David's tenth-grade teachers stated that he never caused any trouble in class, but he often did not turn in assigned work, and he failed most tests. The teachers viewed David as a student who lacked motivation but who had some academic skills.

The psychologist reviewed his assessment of David. On the WISC III, David scored within the average range of intelligence in verbal, performance, and overall intelligence. His achievement fell within the low-average range in reading, mathematics, and written language. There were no significant strengths or weaknesses noted in David's profile. Based on his interview with David, the psychologist felt that David was somewhat depressed.

David passed recent vision and hearing screenings at school. It was stated that David's overall health was adequate, but he didn't eat very much.

Mr. Patterson was very insistent on help for David as he stated, "We have done everything possible to help David. We have even suggested counseling, and David refused to attend. We feel that something serious will happen unless David receives help. He really needs to be in a residential placement."

The evaluation team discussed in detail David's assessment. He certainly wasn't the typical child referred and eligible for special education. Most students with disabilities were identified at a much-younger age. It was unusual that David had been referred for special education in high school. David also wasn't an acting-out child who brought attention to himself at school. However, David certainly did have some emotional problems complicated by possible drug and alcohol use. These problems were affecting his progress in school. After much discussion, the team agreed that David was eligible for special education services under the label behavior disorders. An IEP was written to include support for David during his study hall and one special education class in English.

The parents were unhappy about the program. Mr. Patterson said, "You'll see. This kind of program will not work with David. He needs a residential placement." Despite their concerns, the Patterson's agreed to the initial placement.

One month later, the parents requested an IEP meeting. Over the phone, Mr. Patterson said, "David is still failing his classes. He is not doing any better at home. In fact, he seems more angry." An IEP meeting was convened and the team agreed to place David in a self-contained class for students with behavior disorders.

Six weeks later, the parents requested another IEP meeting. Mr. Patterson said, "David is failing miserably. Last night, he came home drunk at 2:00 A.M. He almost hurt his mother when he threw a chair at her." David's teachers confirmed that David was not passing any classes. He was not a discipline problem, but he appeared to be passive–aggressive. He completed very little work in class, passed very few tests, and never did homework. The IEP team concluded that the regular high school was not able to meet David's needs. They recommended a private day treatment program for students with behavior disorders for David.

The parents were not satisfied. Mr. Patterson said, "We told you David would not do well at the high school. He really needs to be in a residential placement, but we will agree to a trial placement in this day treatment program. At least he will have counseling."

David attended the day treatment school for one semester. He rarely talked to anyone, even the teachers and counselors. The staff tried to get him involved in activities that might interest him, such as art or current events. David often just sat in the classroom with his hair hanging in front of his eyes and slept. He also began to skip school. At the end of the school year, David was 16, the legal age for dropping out of school.

At the beginning of the next school year, David did not return to school. In October of that year, Ms. Richardson, special education coordinator and teacher at the high school, was reading the local newspaper one day. The headlines stated that a 16-year old boy had been arrested for burning down his parents' house. Fortunately, no one was hurt. The boy who allegedly set the fire was David Patterson.

QUESTIONS

Legal Issues to Consider

1. Was it legal for the special education teacher to tell the parents that David would not be considered for a residential placement before the evaluation and evaluation conference? Why or why not?

2. According to IDEA, what issues of eligibility did the evaluation team consider in deciding if David were eligible for special education?

3. Should the evaluation team have placed David in a residential program initially? Why or why not?

Other Issues

1. An increasing number of adolescents have serious problems in the family, community, and school. Is it appropriate to label all of them behavior disordered? Why or why not?

2. What alternatives to residential placement are available?

━━━━━━━━━ **CASE 6.5** ━━━━━━━━━

JANE/REFUSAL TO CONSIDER

Mr. and Mrs. Konya were very happy with their new neighborhood. They were equally happy with the local, neighborhood public school. They were especially looking forward to meeting Mr. Timko, the school principal, to discuss their daughter's enrollment in first grade. As they entered Mr. Timko's office, Mr. and Mrs. Konya shook hands with Mr. Timko. Mrs. Konya spoke first.

"Thank you for much for seeing us, Mr. Timko. We are most anxious to enroll our daughter, Jane, in first grade. We wanted to learn a little about the first-grade class and help plan for Jane."

Mr. Konya continued, "Yes, we appreciate your time. Jane is really excited about her new school. We moved here a month early so that she can visit the school and become familiar with our new neighborhood before school begins this fall."

Mr. Timko looked pleased as he said, "We are always happy to have new families move into our area. As you know, we have an excellent school, with high expectations for students and a high degree of parental involvement. As a matter of fact, our students' state test scores are the second highest in the entire state. We also have very few discipline problems. We are a very traditional school, and we're very proud of our teachers and students."

Mrs. Konya agreed, "Yes, we know that this is an excellent school. In fact, the reason we moved to this neighborhood is so that Jane could attend this school. We have high hopes for her continued progress."

Mr. Timko said, "Let me tell you a little about the first grade, and then we can tour the school. Jane would probably be assigned to Mrs. Bush's classroom. Mrs. Bush is a veteran first-grade teacher. She won an award last year for her excellence in teaching. Students in her class learn to read well and develop higher-level thinking skills. She does some writing with the children, which is very interesting given that many of the children aren't reading and writing when they come to school. Why, at the end of the year, the children have "published" several stories! The classroom will probably have about 20 students. Students receive the normal special classes—library, physical education, art, vocal music, and computer classes. I think you'll be very pleased with the class."

Mr. Konya said, "This sounds great. Now, we have brought some records for Jane from her previous kindergarten and her evaluation. You'll probably want to look them over and arrange an IEP meeting to plan her program."

Mr. Timko looked surprised as he said, "IEP?"

Mrs. Banks answered, "Yes, Jane has special needs. She has Down syndrome."

Mr. Timko had a puzzled look on his face and said, "Down what?"

Mrs. Konya continued as she showed Mr. Timko Jane's report card, "Down syndrome. As a result of the Down syndrome, Jane has severe cognitive delays and moderate speech and language delays. She attended a regular kindergarten last year. She did so well! We were very pleased with her progress, both academically and socially. The school district provided a one-on-one aide and speech therapy three times a week. You can see on her progress report here that Jane did well. We chose this school district because we know Jane will do well here. You've already been so encouraging and welcoming to us. We're looking forward to working with you and Mrs. Bush and the other teachers. In terms of scheduling an IEP meeting, my husband and I are available any time during the next three weeks. We are both taking this time off from work to help Jane adjust to the move and will meet at your convenience to plan her program. Now, can we take a tour of the building?"

Mr. Timko fumbled with his words as he said, "Uh, sure. Before we go, I need to tell you that Jane will not be placed in regular first grade. It sounds like she needs to be placed in our special education class for mentally impaired children. It's a great classroom with an excellent teacher. Of course, there are only 12 children with the teacher and a full-time teacher's aide. These children are considered a part of our school, and we are happy to have the classroom here."

Mr. Konya stated in a concerned voice, "Mr. Timko, please don't misunderstand me, but we don't want Jane placed in a special education class. We have spent years trying to help Jane feel as normal as possible. We certainly understand her cognitive limitations, but we feel that she will gain in terms of language and social skills if she is with other normal children for the entire school day. Jane is not disruptive in the classroom. She may need help from an aide, as she did in kindergarten, and she'll certainly need speech and language therapy."

Mr. Timko adamantly stated, "I'm sorry Mr. and Mrs. Konya, we just don't do that here."

Mr. Konya looked concerned as he said, "What do you mean?"

"We just don't do that inclusion stuff here. We have a traditional program and feel that we adequately meet all students' needs. If a student needs special education, we have a special education class."

Mrs. Konya pleaded, "Mr. Timko, please look over Jane's records and arrange an IEP meeting. We'll discuss this at the meeting."

Mr. and Mrs. Konya walked out abruptly. Mr. Timko sat and looked stunned. He had never been faced with a situation like this. However, this was his building, and he would not compromise the needs of the other 19 first-graders simply to place a child with significant special education needs in the class. If a child needed special education, there was a special education class.

Mr. Timko contacted the special education administrator, Mr. Weiss, to arrange an IEP meeting. The meeting was conducted the following week in Mr. Timko's office. Along with the parents were Mrs. Bush, the first-grade teacher; Mr. Timko; Mr. Weiss, the special education administrator; Mrs. Wells, the special education teacher; and Mrs. Mercer, speech and language therapist. When the meeting convened, all school staff had reviewed Jane's records. Jane had an IQ of 45 on the WISC III. She functioned at a prekindergarten level in reading, writing, and math skills. She could scribble, listen to a five-minute story from the teacher, and count to three. She was cooperative and had one or two friends in her previous school. Jane's speech was at times unintelligible, and her language was significantly delayed. She functioned at a 3-year-old level in language.

At the meeting, the content of Jane's records was reviewed, and there was considerable discussion regarding Jane's placement.

Mr. Konya stated, "As my wife and I told Mr. Timko, we want Jane fully included in first grade. She attended regular kindergarten last year and made good progress. We are aware that Jane does not have first-grade skills, but we think that academic achievement is not the only reason to mainstream Jane. She will benefit greatly in terms of language modeling and social skills modeling from the other first-graders. If she were in a special education class, she wouldn't have these normal role models."

Mrs. Wells talked about her class, stating, "Mr. and Mrs. Konya, Jane will do well in my special education class. We are with other children during recess, physical education, music, and lunch. So you see, Jane will have good role models, but she will also get the individualized instruction that she needs. Other children like Jane are very successful in my classroom."

Mrs. Mercer supported the position of Mrs. Wells, saying, "I am in Mrs. Wells' classroom every day to assist with language instruction. In addition, I will see Jane twice a week for small-group speech and language therapy. Mrs. Well's class has a great group of children, and Jane will adjust well there and make good progress."

Mrs. Bush, in a strong voice, said, "I have never had a child like Jane in first grade. I am not trained to help a child in special education. I am worried that I will have to spend an extraordinary amount of time with her, and the other children will suffer."

Mrs. Konya stated in a very direct manner, "I want you to know that we will not accept anything less than full inclusion of Jane in regular first grade. I'm sure the special education class is a good class, but we feel it is our right to request that Jane be placed in first grade. We also want to request a full-time aide to assist Jane in first grade as a supplemental service."

Mr. Timko was angry as he said, "As I told you last week, we don't include children like Jane in regular classes. We just don't do that here. We have special education classes for children like Jane."

Mrs. Konya pleaded, "What is preventing you from placing Jane in first grade?"

Mr. Weiss answered, "As special education administrator, I can tell you that I fully support Mr. Timko. What would prohibit Jane from being placed in first grade is we do not believe it is appropriate. It seems the staff feels that Jane will make more academic progress in the special education class. The only supplemental service Jane needs is speech and language therapy. Now, let's complete our IEP to formalize the special education placement. Mr. and Mrs. Konya, I will give you some information on your rights as parents before you leave today."

Three months later, a due process hearing officer ordered the school district to place Jane in the first-grade classroom with supplemental services of speech and language therapy and a full-time individual aide.

QUESTIONS

Legal Issues to Consider

1. According to IDEA, describe how the school district failed to follow the LRE doctrine.

2. According to case law on LRE, what factors should the district have considered in making the placement decision?

Other Issues

1. Should academic achievement be the primary purpose of mainstreaming? Why or why not?

2. Should language modeling and social skills modeling be considered when mainstreaming a child into a regular class? Why or why not?

3. Should language and social skills modeling be a priority over academic achievement in mainstreaming?

4. Do you agree with the due process hearing officer's decision? Why or why not?

JARED/LEGAL RIGHTS

Ms. Schlesinger, a veteran teacher of students with BD, was not easily upset. However, her hands shook as she dialed the telephone to speak to Ms. Boyne, the special education supervisor.

"Hello, this is Mary Schlesinger from Dayton School. May I speak to Ms. Boyne? Thank you. Ms. Boyne? I am calling you because I am totally frustrated and I don't know what else to do. You know that my aide and I have 12 BD students in our class this year. We are doing well with all students except one, Jared Jackson, a second-grader who transferred here this year. He is impossible. We've had him in school now for six months, and he is continuing to regress. We need to place him in another setting, possibly a day treatment facility for BD students."

Ms. Schlesinger paused and then continued, "You ask what he does? This morning, he crawled under the teacher's desk and made animal sounds, which he does frequently. He refused to move. I tried ignoring him, then I used physical force to remove him because the entire class was watching and was off-task. Last Friday, Jared became angry at another child, and he kicked the child in the knee and hit the child in the face. As the aide was trying to pull Jared off of this child, Jared bit the aide and spit in her face. Two weeks ago, Jared ripped a necklace off of the aide's neck. Another time, when he was angry, he ripped my blouse. Jared also has poor academic skills, and he is very inattentive. He can stay on-task about one minute before he gets up and wanders around the room. Jared's mother has difficulty with him at home, and she is not home every evening because she works nights as a custodian at the high school. His grandmother takes care of him after school, and she tends to blame the school for Jared's problems. I need help!"

Ms. Boyne calmly stated, "It sounds like this is a difficult situation. Have you approached Mrs. Jackson about your concerns?"

Ms. Schlesinger said, "Yes, frequently. I'm at a point now that if he is violent toward anyone, I call the home. Unfortunately, his grandmother is the primary contact person because of Mrs. Jackson's work schedule. Jared's grandmother doesn't view Jared's problems as severe, and she feels that the school should be able to work with Jared. When I have called Mrs. Jackson at work, she is sympathetic but can't do much."

Ms. Boyne suggested, "Let's arrange an IEP meeting to discuss the options. I will schedule the meeting and make contact with Mrs. Jackson."

One week later, the IEP meeting was held. Sitting in the conference room were all of the school staff with whom Jared had worked. They included Ms. Boyne, special education administrator; Ms. Schlesinger, BD teacher; and Ms. Ling, principal. The meeting was scheduled to begin at 3:30 P.M. At 3:45 P.M.; the staff questioned whether Mrs. Jackson was attending. At 4:00 P.M., Mrs. Jackson arrived, along with her mother, Mrs. Summers, and another person unknown to the school staff.

Mrs. Jackson stated, "I'm sorry we're late. I had trouble getting off of work."

Everyone introduced themselves. The unknown person introduced herself as Ms. Leiter, the director of the Society for Inclusion and Jared's advocate.

Ms. Boyne began the conference by stating, "We are here today to discuss Jared's progress in the BD class and to decide if changes need to be made in his IEP. As you know, Mrs. Jackson, Jared has been having a great deal of difficulty at school."

Ms. Schlesinger, BD teacher, explained in detail Jared's progress in school, in much the same manner she used in talking to Ms. Boyne in her initial telephone conversation. As she spoke, Mrs. Jackson, Mrs. Summers, and the advocate, Ms. Leiter, quietly listened.

Ms. Leiter said in a confident voice, "My client, Mrs. Jackson, and I have thoroughly discussed Jared's placement in this BD class. You're right, he's not getting any better here. The reason his behavior is not improving is that he is in the wrong placement. He needs to be fully included in a regular classroom at his home school. It is ridiculous to think that placing Jared in a classroom of BD students who misbehave will help him improve. What he needs and what is his right is a full-time placement in a regular classroom. He needs to be around other normal children to see positive role models. Also, I understand that there are no African American children in the BD class. Is that correct?"

Mrs. Schlesinger answered, "Yes, that's correct. But there is one African American boy in the third grade here, and he and Jared have talked on occasion. I have observed them playing on the playground."

Ms. Leiter continued in an assured voice, "That's good, but part of the problem here is that Jared has few male role models. His home school is only 2 miles away, and I understand that 50 percent of the children there are African American. He would have many positive male role models there. He has a right to be placed in a regular classroom in his home school. With some support, perhaps an individual aide, Jared's IEP goals could be met in the regular classroom in his home school. The federal law states that all children should be educated with normal children in their home schools. I think Jared's behavior is not appropriate because of the environment in which he is placed."

Ms. Schlesinger argued, "I would be really concerned about Jared if he were placed in a regular classroom. He needs small-group instruction and constantly needs cues to remain on-task and to finish assignments. Of course, his behavior would be very disruptive to other children in a regular classroom. Crawling under desks and making animal sounds would draw attention to Jared, and other children probably would not want to be near him. His violence is also a concern. Jared easily becomes angry, often without warning. I am concerned that he could harm another child. As I said earlier, he has kicked, hit, bit, and spit on other children and staff. This would be very disruptive in the regular classroom. The teacher would have to spend considerable time with Jared, and she couldn't teach. Even if Jared had an individual aide, it would be very disruptive to the class to have the aide physically restraining Jared if he attacked another student or tried to pull him out from under the desk."

Mrs. Jackson jumped into the conversation and stated, "Jared has never been in a regular classroom. I don't think we know how he would react. Also, Jared does not have any male African American role models in this school. He would behave more appropriately if he were around more children who were African American. As you know, he rarely even sees his father."

Mrs. Sumner supported her daughter by saying, "As his grandmother, I see Jared every day. He is not a bad child. He just needs to be around more normal kids. If he could go to his home school, he could walk with other neighborhood kids. Ms. Leiter is right. Jared should be placed in a regular second-grade classroom in his home school."

Ms. Boyne, who increasingly felt a loss of control in the meeting, looked at Mrs. Jackson and said, "Mrs. Jackson, you and I have talked in the past. You have been very supportive of Jared's placement here in the BD class. I'm wondering what happened to change your mind."

Mrs. Jackson responded, "My mother feels that this program is not right for Jared, and I agree. She went to a meeting in which Ms. Leiter presented a workshop on including children who have special needs in regular classes. After the meeting, my mother talked to Ms. Leiter, and she said it is Jared's right to be placed in a regular classroom in his home school. She even said she would help us fight the school district to make sure Jared's rights are observed. When you called to arrange this meeting, I was getting ready to call you to arrange a meeting."

Ms. Boyne, again trying to gain control, stated, "I noticed that Jared is currently due for his three-year reevaluation. It could be that Jared has changed since his last evaluation. I suggest that we consider Jared's placement after the reevaluation is completed. Then we can base our decisions on the most recent data. We might want to consider having a psychiatric evaluation in addition to the other components of the evaluation. We would put this decision on hold until the evaluation is completed."

Ms. Leiter indignantly stated, "I do not think it necessary to conduct an evaluation just to observe Jared's right to be placed in the regular classroom. What do you think, Mrs. Jackson?"

Mrs. Jackson, feeling uncomfortable, said, "If Jared needs to be tested, let's do it first. Then we may know what's wrong with him."

Ms. Leiter reluctantly agreed with her client, "Okay, we'll agree to the evaluation, as long as it doesn't take forever to complete."

Ms. Boyne added, "We'll conduct it as quickly as possible. However, we will have to contract with a psychiatrist for an evaluation, and I don't know when this evaluation can be scheduled. We have used a psychiatrist at a teaching hospital in the city. I can make contact with him tomorrow."

The meeting ended without more discussion and on a positive note.

Three weeks later, the evaluation was completed and an evaluation conference was held. Mrs. Jackson, Mrs. Summer, the psychiatrist, and all school staff were present. The advocate, Ms. Leiter, was not present, and neither the parent nor the grandparent mentioned her name. The evaluation revealed a very disturbing profile. Jared displayed some very disruptive behaviors (rolling on the floor, hiding under the desk, making noises) with the psychiatrist, and he suggested that Jared might be experiencing posttraumatic stress syndrome. He recommended placement in a private day treatment school for students with behavior problems. He strongly recommended therapy for Jared. Other data confirmed what the school staff already knew. Jared displayed very serious disruptive behaviors that needed to be addressed in a therapeutic school situation. Mrs. Jackson listened intently and agreed with the school staff. She agreed to visit Heartfield School, a day treatment facility for students with behavior problems.

Two weeks later, a meeting was held to place Jared in Heartfield School. Mrs. Jackson attended the meeting and agreed with the placement.

QUESTIONS

Legal Issues to Consider

1. According to IDEA, does a child with a disability have a right to be placed in general education? Why or why not?

2. According to IDEA, does a child with a disability have a right to be placed in the child's home school? Why or why not?

3. To what extent did the school district follow the LRE doctrine concerning continuum of services?

Other Issues

1. Is it likely that a student's behavior problems would decrease if placed in the general education setting? Why or why not?

2. Is race a valid reason to place students with disabilities in schools with more African Americans? Why or why not?

CHAPTER SEVEN

PARENT PARTICIPATION

CASE 7.1   AMY/PARENTS IN CLASS

CASE 7.2   LANSKY/PARENTAL CONSENT

CASE 7.3   TUNITA/SETTING GOALS

CASE 7.4   KAMI/IMPROPER EVALUATION

CASE 7.5   WASHINGTON/DIVORCED PARENTS

CASE 7.6   ARMSTRONG/DENIAL OF BEHAVIOR

CASE 7.1

AMY/PARENTS IN CLASS

Amy Black began the school year in Mrs. Marion Easton's first-grade class at Dover Elementary School in Maryland. However, midway through the school year, her father, Harry Black, a sergeant in the U.S. Army, was transferred to a base in Virginia. The transfer came as an unpleasant surprise to the Blacks because they had just found the perfect program for Amy at Dover Elementary. Her parents were especially upset because they had worked with school officials prior to her attendance and were especially happy to see Amy in an integrated classroom. Although she was classified as having autism, many of her cognitive skills were average or above average when compared with other peers. Dover had been especially accommodating to Amy: She had been provided with a personal aide, and her classroom was the cornerstone of their new inclusion program.

Through state grant money, the school had taken the initiative to integrate many students who had mild to moderate disabilities into new integrated classrooms. Mrs. Easton's class was viewed as a model program in the district, in part because of her training. Mrs. Easton was certified to teach students in both general education and special education. In the past, she had earned many accolades for her achievements in integrating students with disabilities into general education classes and programs.

When the transfer came, Harry and Ester Black traveled to Greensburg, Virginia, to look for a new house and to view local schools. Because the Greensburg military base was located in a rural section of Virginia, the Blacks were limited in the number of schools for Amy. As the Blacks toured the two school districts in the area, they began to realize that they were limited in their choices. They also began to realize that they were going to have a difficult time getting Amy enrolled in an integrated classroom like her class at Dover.

Within weeks, the Blacks were able to set up and meet with Superintendent Bill Flask and Special Education Director Ginger Gibbon at Amy's new school. At the meeting the Blacks asked about placing Amy in a general education classroom. Mr. Flask told them that no such classes were available because the district couldn't afford to staff a class with both a general education and special education teacher. Ms. Gibbon agreed and elaborated by saying, "This is a little district in the middle of nowhere. We have trouble getting special education teachers to work for us, let alone staffing multiple classes." However, the Blacks were persistent in their request and informed Mr. Flask that he would hear from them again. Over the next few weeks the Blacks made numerous telephone calls and spoke to a number of general education and special education teachers. Eventually, through telephone calls, teachers, parent groups, and even a local congressman, the Blacks were able to influence Mr. Flask's original decision.

By now, the Blacks had reluctantly enrolled Amy in the autistic program, Mrs. Keller's class, at Elmtree Elementary. Having her in a self-contained classroom with other students with autism was the last thing that the Blacks wanted, but they had few options, and they continued pursuing the idea of the school developing an inclusive classroom.

As the weeks progressed, Mrs. Keller began to see the Blacks at the school on a more frequent basis, until the Blacks were at the school daily. Each day the Blacks would arrive at the classroom door with one excuse or another of why they were there. The Blacks were simply being protective and were curious about how Amy was functioning in her new classroom.

One day when Mrs. Black was at the school, she noticed Amy's file on Mrs. Keller's desk. She saw how thick it was and became curious to know what was in her daughter's file. When she asked Mrs. Keller if she could look at her daughter's file, Mrs. Keller refused and told her that it contained only "school stuff, like old IEPs and school records."

The next day Ms. Gibbon received a phone call from Mrs. Black requesting to examine Amy's file. Ms. Gibbon agreed, but she would have to come to the school and Mrs. Black would have to have Ms. Gibbon present. The next day Mrs. Black arrived and was escorted by Ms. Gibbon, and both reviewed Amy's records. As Mrs. Black reviewed her daughter's records, she was surprised to see so much information about Amy's behavior. Mrs. Black was angry when she read about some of the incident reports from Amy's present and past teachers, and she also saw comments about her and her husband in the file. It seemed that Ms. Gibbon and Mrs. Keller had been recording each incident that involved Amy's parents. Soon Mrs. Black was reading references such as "nuisance, pest, and bothering," all to describe the Blacks' classroom visits. There were also notes in the file from Ms. Gibbon and Mrs. Keller that told of how the Blacks were exerting "undue pressure" on school administrators to develop a special class for Amy. All of these harsh anecdotes worried Mrs. Black because she felt it created an unfair picture of them as parents.

In the meantime, under mounting pressure from all parties, both Mr. Flask and Ms. Gibbon finally decided to allow Amy in a general education classroom on a trial basis. At last, the Blacks received the phone call that they had wanted. In their conversation with Mr. Flask, he informed them that Amy would be enrolled in Mr. Samuel Yetter's first-grade class for six weeks and she would have a part-time aide. (The district could not find anyone to work as a full-time aide.) Although all of this was fine, the Blacks were concerned that

Mr. Yetter's attitude toward Amy might be biased by the information in Amy's records. The Blacks graciously thanked Mr. Flask, but then they asked to have any information not related to Amy's education removed from her file. Mr. Flask told them that he would consider their request and would get back to them at a later time. He never did.

Within a week, Amy began school and was an active member of Mr. Yetter's class. The other children in the class slowly warmed up to Amy even though some of her behaviors were not age-appropriate. For example, when Any felt pressured, she flapped her arms, rocked back and forth, and screamed. The first week was rough on Mr. Yetter. Almost on a daily basis, Mr. Yetter had to personally deal with Amy's inappropriate outbursts. Amy's loud screeches and screams were, to say the least, disruptive to the other students in the class. During those times when his part-time aide was not present, Mr. Yetter was quite busy teaching the other 23 students and assisting Amy with her specially designed worksheets. Mr. Yetter also began to see the Blacks frequently showing up at his classroom door. Within weeks, the usually businesslike atmosphere of the classroom became chaotic, filled with incidents of yelling (Mr. Yetter's) and frustration (Amy's). Mr. Yetter also had to deal with daily visits from Amy's parents. It soon became apparent that Amy's trial period would be ending in disaster. In addition, the otherwise altruistic, friendly children began to distance themselves from Amy as her behavior worsened and they found that they could not befriend her.

Mr. Flask, too, was besieged with phone calls from parents of other children from the class and from Amy's parents. The other parents were concerned about Amy's disruptive behavior. On the other hand, Amy's parents called to request about removing so-called erroneous information from Amy's file. As a way to avoid the Blacks, Mr. Flask began to ignore their phone calls, and his secretary became very adept at developing creative excuses to explain why Mr. Flask could not take their calls.

Four weeks later, Mr. Yetter called Ms. Gibbon and told her that he "couldn't take it anymore." Amy had to be removed from the regular classroom. He told her that "the other children in the class are suffering," and he "had been receiving a lot of phone calls from angry parents."

Immediately after their conversation, Ms. Gibbon phoned Mr. Flask to inform him of Mr. Yetter's conversation. Within a few days, Mr. Flask, Ms. Gibbon, Mr. Yetter, and Mrs. Keller were at a meeting to inform the Blacks that Amy had to return to Mrs. Keller's self-contained classroom. Of course, the Blacks viewed Amy's progress differently. They argued that the district had not provided Amy with the proper support—a part-time instead of a full-time aide—and had not given Amy a chance to adjust to her new environment. They claimed that Amy needed the full six weeks to get acclimated to her new environment, and they also argued that Amy had established some new friendships with other students in the class. They pointed out that three of her classmates came to her birthday party and that she was slowly making academic progress. They also argued that they would come into Amy's class to serve as part-time aides to help Amy adjust to her new environment. When Mr. Yetter vehemently disagreed, the Blacks shot back that they "had a right to be in the classroom because (they) had rights to participate in Amy's education." Ms. Gibbon disagreed and told the Blacks that they were not permitted in the classroom.

Angry and disappointed, the Blacks left the meeting. As they walked out the door, they vowed to the school staff that "you haven't heard the last of this."

QUESTIONS

Legal Issues to Consider

1. What factors should be used in making a decision about Amy's placement?

2. Was the district justified in returning Amy to Mrs. Keller's self-contained special classroom? Why or why not?

3. What is meant by *parent participation,* and did Amy's parents have the right to show up in the classroom or to serve as part-time aides?

Other Issues

1. What parts of Amy's records do the Blacks have a right to expunge?

2. Do children with severe disabilities have a right to be integrated in the regular classroom? Do adults with severe disabilities have a right to be integrated in the community?

━━━━━━   CASE 7.2   ━━━━━━

LANSKY/PARENTAL CONSENT

Lansky Reski currently attends Petersburg Elementary School in a small city in southern Florida. Lansky's parents, Ricci and Karla, are from Cuba and are not U.S. citizens. However, Lansky was born in a local hospital, making him a U.S. citizen. Growing up in the small city of Gergardez, Florida, Lansky learned to speak English, but the primary language in his home and community was Spanish.

While Lansky was in second grade his teacher suspected late in the year that his slow progress might be attributed to a disability. Initially she made and documented four different interventions that she used with Lansky in an attempt to improve his academic progress. When the interventions failed, she referred him for a full evaluation. However, due to the end of the school year and lack of funding for a summer program, a decision was made to continue his evaluation once the fall semester began.

Now Lansky is in third grade, and the final portion of his evaluation was recently completed. Mrs. Garner, the district's assistant director of special education, informed the parents and all others involved in the assessment about an upcoming meeting to discuss Lansky's test results.

Ricci and Karla knew that their son was having trouble in school, but they assumed that his problems were a result of his lack of knowledge of the English language. They liked his teachers at Petersburg Elementary and felt comfortable that their son was finally meeting and making friends with other children his age. In second grade, when a letter came informing them that Lansky needed testing, they thought that it was simply part of the school process, and they did not sign or return the consent form to school. When the second request came from the school, his parents again dismissed it.

When Mrs. Garner called and told them the next year that Lansky's test results indicated that he might need special education services, they were surprised.

"When did you test Lansky, and why didn't you tell us?" Karla asked in a mix of Spanish and English.

"We did tell you that he was being tested," Mrs. Garner replied. "Besides, the testing is complete, and it looks like Lansky really needs our (special education) help."

On the day of the meeting, Mrs. Garner prepared everyone to meet Lansky's parents by explaining their limited understanding of the English language. Despite her explanation, no interpreter was present. As Ricci entered the school, he could see that the conference room was full of people sitting around a table. Upon entering the conference room and seeing all of the school officials, Ricci suddenly became self-conscious and very nervous. Before him sat Mrs. Lucy Garner; Mr. Harry Hyde, the school psychologist; Ms. Anita Peterson, the LD teacher; Mrs. Soni Lee, the speech pathologist; and Mr. Frank Lucini, the ESL teacher. With all eyes on him, he stammered as he spoke his name and introduced himself. As the meeting proceeded, Ricci had a difficult time understanding what was occurring, but he did not ask questions. When Mr. Hyde reviewed Lansky's psychological testing, Ricci was quiet and listened carefully, trying to interpret into his native Spanish. Mr. Hyde explained that according to his report, Lansky qualified for special education services under the label of mild mental retardation.

"Mental retardation?" Ricci asked, "What does this mean?"

"Well, it means that Lansky learns more slowly than other children," Mr. Hyde explained.

"My son is not stupid!" Ricci angrily shot back.

"No one said he was stupid," Mr. Hyde quickly responded, apparently flustered by Ricci's response. "It means that Lansky will receive special help in a different school, Mountain Road Elementary," Mr. Hyde further explained.

By now, Ricci was beginning to look worried about his son's future as he said, "My son likes where he is now. We don't want to change his school. He has many friends, and he will be scared at new school."

"Oh, don't worry Ricci, Lansky will make many new friends.

"No, no. I don't want Lansky to move. You can give him help here at Petersburg."

Lucy then tried to explain. "Ricci, the only teachers in the mental retardation program are at Mountain Road Elementary. Why don't you take a look at the program?"

"No. You need to test again," said Ricci, referring to his test results. By now the meeting was nearing completion, but there was no resolution about what would happen to Lansky.

"Ricci, we need to schedule another meeting to discuss Lansky's placement. Why don't you take a copy of the results home and think about what we talked about," Lucy urged.

With that, everyone left the room except Ricci, who sat in his chair, stunned by what had just happened.

Because of the small size of the school district, only two options were available to Ricci. It was either Lansky's placement at Mountain Road Elementary, a special school only for students with disabilities, or a residential facility about 30 minutes away. Ricci was worried because Petersburg Elementary was only five minutes away, but Mountain Road Elementary was about 25 minutes away and located on the other side of town.

QUESTIONS

Legal Issues to Consider

1. According to IDEA, how should a school district gain parent permission for an initial evaluation? Did the school district in this case meet this standard?

2. Was the school district justified in placing Lansky at Mountain Road Elementary? Why or why not?

3. Should an interpreter have been present for the evaluation meeting? Why or why not?

Other Issues

1. Was it appropriate for the general education teacher to refer Lansky for an evaluation? Why or why not?

2. What are some issues in evaluating students whose first language is not English?

CASE 7.3

TUNITA/SETTING GOALS

Tunita Washington works at the local Huligan's Restaurant busing tables and washing dishes. Tunita, a teenager with moderate mental retardation, has worked at Huligan's for the past three years. Now 20 years old, in one year Tunita will be *aging out* and will no longer receive special education services. Despite her age, Tunita still needs a lot of structure. In her current position at Huligan's Restaurant, she needs a job coach to work closely with her and constant supervision. For example, on one recent afternoon she told a customer to "kiss off" when he asked her to clean up a spill. In addition, this position is only part-time. As a result, she typically is in school during the morning hours and then boards the bus to Huligan's.

Tunita's mother, Kersha Noles, has often woken up in the middle of the night worried that her daughter will have problems adjusting to a world without school. Kersha knows that Tunita must be kept busy and active or she will throw a tantrum or get into trouble by another means. Kersha has considered trying to find adult activities in the local community— Larksville—but she can never find activities that would be appropriate for someone like Tunita. Because Kersha works full-time, she knows that once Tunita stops attending school Kersha will have to hire a full-time tutor/living assistant to help her.

Coincidentally at about this time, Kersha hears of a postschool program in another part of the state, Merhsville, that arranges for young adults like Tunita to participate in activities and travel on educational trips. This daily program provides supervision of young adults with disabilities and even has a weekend component that these adults can participate in for a small fee. This particular program, paid for by two participating school districts, is free to former students of the two districts. After a short visit to Merhsville, Kersha comes back to town charged with a mission: to get a similar program started in Larksville.

"Hello, Mrs. Madison," Kersha begins, "I would like to discuss the possibility of starting a postschool program in our Larksville."

Caught off guard, Mrs. Madison, the superintendent of the local district, responds by asking, "I'm sorry, I missed what you said."

Kersha then goes on to describe the Merhsville program. Throughout her description of the program, Kersha hears nothing but silence on the other end of the line. Finally, after her three-minute monologue of Merhsville, Kersha asks, "So, what do you think?"

Mrs. Madison politely but succinctly says, "Kersha, your program sounds wonderful, but our district could never afford to fund such a program."

"But, but…" Kersha stumbles for her next words.

"Look Kersha, if you can find a way to fund such a program, I'll be happy to consider it," Mrs. Madison replies. With that statement, their conversation ends.

Kersha, wise in the way of legal wrangling, decides to call the school to schedule an IEP meeting to make changes in Tunita's individualized transition plan (ITP). At this meeting, Kersha plans to write goals and objectives that seek to get Tunita involved in community activities. Kersha thinks that this will force the district to develop a program. When Tunita's teacher, Betty Dobson, finds out what Kersha is trying to do, she decides to schedule the IEP meeting at times that she knows Kersha cannot attend. Her supervisor, Barbara Walters, likes the idea but cannot condone Betty's actions. After three different attempts (documented by the district) to set up a meeting, Mrs. Dobson reluctantly agrees to schedule an evening meeting, only after Kersha threatens to take her and her supervisor to due process.

Once the meeting is set, Kersha gathers information about leisure-time skills and decides to include these as part of Tunita's ITP. Armed with new goals and objectives and information about community transition programs, Kersha walks into the school's conference room confident that she can persuade school officials to make changes in Tunita's ITP. Instead, Kersha finds that the ITP members are prepared to do their best to oppose any of Kersha's ideas. The meeting begins with Mrs. Dobson reading each of Tunita's goals and objectives and providing a rationale of why each is appropriate. This continues until she reads through Tunita's entire ITP. When Kersha states that she wants to add some new objectives, she is rebutted by team members, who say that the current goals and objectives are appropriate and that Kersha's ideas are not possible in their small, financially strapped district. Kersha leaves the meeting uncertain what her next step will be, but she vows that they will hear from her again.

QUESTIONS

Legal Issues to Consider

1. What are Kersha's rights concerning input into her child's ITP?

2. What can Kersha do if she feels that Tunita's ITP needs to be changed but the school district refuses?

3. Did the district provide appropriate education to Tunita?

Other Issues

1. What other laws are available that will provide rights to Tunita once she leaves school?

2. Should society provide additional schooling beyond age 21? Why or why not?

■■■■■ **CASE 7.4** ■■■■■

KAMI/IMPROPER EVALUATION

Kami has always had trouble with most subjects in school. Although she has excelled in nonacademic subjects such as physical education and music, she always has performed poorly in language arts, particularly in reading. When her problems first became evident to her first-grade teacher, Mrs. Xander, and Kami's parents, Molly and Philbert Gardner, it was suggested that her parents could read to her and provide her with extra practice on school subjects to boost her faltering grades. Despite their assistance, it soon became apparent that Kami might have to be retained. In May of that year, following a brief meeting with her teacher, the Gardners made the decision to retain her but place her with a different first-grade teacher, Mrs. Emily Sootherby.

When fall arrived, the Gardners noticed that Kami had lost many of the skills that she had learned. As Kami progressed in first grade (for the second time), initially she performed well because learning most of the skills was redundant for her. However, within weeks her teacher noticed that she was slowly falling behind. Mrs. Sootherby knew that she would have to refer Kami for an educational evaluation.

The psychologist assigned to Kami's evaluation was Mr. Jonny Holsteadler, a neighbor of the Gardners. Mr. Holsteadler knew Kami through their interactions as neighbors, even though he didn't particularly like her. His disdain for the little girl came about through a disagreement that he had with Kami's parents. In spite of his negative feelings toward the Gardners, Mr. Holsteadler knew he had to provide a fair evaluation of Kami. Over the next two weeks, Mr. Holsteadler assessed Kami and diagnosed her disability as borderline mental retardation. Prior to his evaluation, he sought and obtained permission to have her evaluated; however, her parents did not realize that the Mr. Holsteadler who was doing the testing was the same one as their neighbor.

Because of an increase in the number of evaluations during this particular time of the year, it took district personnel two months to notify the Gardners and set up an MDT/IEP meeting. In attendance at the meeting were Mr. Holsteadler; Mrs. Sootherby; Frank Gunderson, the principal; Shannon O'Fay, the supervisor of special education; and Grant Humphrey, the EMR teacher. When the parents finally made it to the meeting, they were dismayed to find out that Kami had been evaluated and were upset with the diagnosis of mental retardation. They could accept a diagnosis of learning disability, but not retardation. "Kami is definitely not retarded," Mr. Gardner remarked. "What does this mean in terms of Kami remaining in her current class?"

Mrs. Sootherby spoke up, "It means that Kami will receive a more specialized education in Mr. Grant Humprehy's EMR classroom, and we have an individualized education program ready for your signature, if you want to sign it."

"Kami's not moving out of your class, and I won't sign a thing," Mr. Gardner responded.

"We want her to remain in your class, Mrs. Sootherby," Mrs. Gardner pleaded.

"Holsteadler, you're a good-for-nothing SOB, and I wouldn't trust what you had to say if it saved my life," an exasperated Mr. Gardner yelled.

"Now, let's try to remain calm," Mr. Gunderson stated in a firm, resolute voice. It was too late. Upset, the Gardners walked out of the room, refusing to accept the diagnosis and refusing to sign the IEP.

Two weeks later, Mr. Gunderson and Mrs. O'Fay received a letter from the Gardners requesting that Kami remain in Mrs. Sootherby's classroom and that they hire a full-time aide to work with her. In requesting an aide for Kami, they admitted that Kami needed help learning; therefore, they also asked for a second psychological evaluation by a different psychologist and, if needed, a new IEP developed by an independent psychologist chosen by the Gardners.

QUESTIONS

Legal Issues to Consider

1. Do the parents have a right to a second evaluation?

2. Should the school provide a full-time aide to assist Kami in Mrs. Sootherby's classroom?

Other Issues

1. What obligation does the psychologist have to disclose his dislike for Kami?

2. What effect could the assessor's rapport with Kami have on her test scores?

▬▬▬▬ CASE 7.5 ▬▬▬▬

WASHINGTON/DIVORCED PARENTS

"Thelma Sosa?" the voice began.

"Yes," responded Thelma.

The voice continued, "I'm Naomi Everett, Washington's mother.... I just received your letter asking me to show up at his next IEP meeting."

"Oh, yes, go on," Thelma said, sensing that there was some problem.

"Well, I just wanted to know who would be there," Naomi continued.

"Well, let's see, on my list I have you, me, Mr. Dan Klauster (Washington's teacher), Mrs. Janie Penstone (the school's principal), and Mr. Harry Phelps (the speech pathologist)," Thelma said.

"Oh. Okay. Thanks. I'll see you then," a relieved Naomi remarked. As Naomi hung up the phone, she clutched it close to her chest and thought, *Good, that SOB won't be there.*

Two weeks earlier, Washington's father, Jefferson Sosa, had called Naomi and left a message on her answering machine informing her that he had heard about Washington's IEP meeting and that he intended to be at it. *If I see that SOB Jefferson at the meeting, I'll walk out,* she thought. Unknown to either Naomi or Thelma, the school secretary, who was responsible for setting up meetings, had mistakenly sent Jefferson a copy of a letter notifying him of the meeting. She had found his address from the state educational records office, which had kept detailed records on Jefferson.

Jefferson and Naomi had been married for several years until Jefferson decided one night that he couldn't take it any longer. On that fateful night three years ago, he walked out of the house and never came back.

It was only the recent phone message that had alerted Naomi to the possibility that Jefferson was still alive. Before that, Naomi and Washington had not heard from Jefferson. They had assumed he was gone forever, and Naomi wished him dead. For weeks after he left, Washington blamed his mother for the failed marriage, accusing her of "pushing his Daddy out of the house." Previously identified with emotional disturbance, Washington had a number of emotional and psychological problems, and his father's absence only made his life worse.

Washington, now 16, vividly remembered the night his father left and would tell his sad story to whoever would listen. Meanwhile, Naomi was left to provide for herself and Washington. First, they went on food stamps until she could get a job. Now living in federally supported housing, Naomi curses the day her husband left. In the "good old days," as she likes to call them, they lived in the suburbs and enjoyed a very affluent life. She tried to track down Jefferson in an attempt to collect child support, but she was unable to find him. In those days, Jefferson never agreed that Washington needed special education and would constantly comment to Naomi, "Washington just needs to toughen up." He would also tell her that she babied Washington and it was her fault that he had problems.

With each passing day, Naomi became more anxious in anticipation of the IEP meeting. The night before the meeting, Naomi broke the news to Washington that she had recently heard from his father. Washington's eyes widened in anticipation as he asked her a million questions: "Will he be coming home?" "When will we see him again?" "Where is he living?" "Is he okay?" "Did he ask about me?"

With each question, Naomi's anger increased. "He walked out on us!" she yelled. "He is worthless. He abandoned us. Don't you understand what happened?" an exhausted Naomi asked Washington.

Washington only looked down, saddened by her comments, and said, "But Momma, he's my Daddy."

The next afternoon, Naomi took off work early and arrived at the school. Walking in the building, she scanned the parking lot looking for any sign of her ex. Once inside, the secretary directed her to the conference room where the meeting was to be held. Inside the room, all were present as expected and no Jefferson. After introductions, Thelma began by saying, "Okay. Everyone is here. Let's begin by discussing Washington's progress, and then let's talk about his new IEP objectives." Just then, Jefferson walked in the door.

"Excuse me, can I help you?" Thelma asked.

"Oh there's my lovely wife," Jefferson responded, looking at Naomi.

"That's ex-wife to you," replied a bitter Naomi.

"Oh," Thelma chimed in, looking rather surprised. "Well, well…" she stammered, trying to compose herself.

"I don't want him in this meeting," Naomi demanded.

Uh, let's see what to do, Thelma thought. "Are you the legal father?" asked Thelma.

"You bet your ass I am," Jefferson shot back.

Turning to Naomi, Thelma spoke. "Naomi, I'm afraid he has as much right to be here as you do."

Naomi's bottom jaw dropped. For the next 10 minutes, Naomi explained to the IEP members how Jefferson had abandoned her and that she had not received any support from him. Jefferson sat quietly and did not defend himself. When Naomi was finished explaining, he told the IEP team that he wanted the entire IEP changed and he wanted Washington placed in an LD classroom. Shaking her head in amazement, Thelma interrupted him in midsentence saying, "Hold on. Until I can figure out what to do, this meeting will be postponed."

QUESTIONS

Legal Issues to Consider

1. Does Washington's father have a legal right to be at Washington's IEP meeting?

2. If he has a legal right to be a full participant in the IEP process, based on what information would he have a right to request that Washington be moved into an LD classroom?

3. If the natural parents lose their rights to participate in the child's education, what must the state do to make certain that the child's rights are well protected?

Other Issues

1. How do foster parents differ from surrogate parents in terms of representing the child at MDT and IEP meetings?

2. In your own state, who can be a surrogate parent, and how does the state train someone to be a surrogate parent for a child with a disability?

■■■■■■■ **CASE 7.6** ■■■■■■■

ARMSTRONG/DENIAL OF BEHAVIOR

"I hate this crap," Armstrong said as he worked on his math.

"Armstrong, watch your mouth or you'll lose recess," remarked Mrs. Tina Haus.

"I just don't know why I have to read this stuff. It doesn't even make sense," Armstrong replied as he read his science textbook.

"Armstrong, you'll soon be in Mr. Neva Hassen's (BD) class, and there you can complain as much as you want to. Until then, shut your mouth," responded Mrs. Haus, trying not to get angry.

"Yeah, well my parents say I have to stay here, and there ain't nothin' you can do about it," said Armstrong as a smirk emerged on his face.

Mrs. Haus did not respond; instead, she smiled at him and told herself that today's meeting was the answer to her prayers. Besides, she had assurances from Mrs. Calli Osmond (the principal) that she would finally get him out of her class. It was nothing personal, but Armstrong was so disruptive that Mrs. Haus had had to spend an inordinate amount of time working on his behavior. Now, drained and worried about the progress of her other 24 students, she had all but given up on him.

The strain of having him in her class had come at a price. During the past few months, Armstrong had been involved in many incidents and altercations in her class. In her mind, he was a loud, disrespectful student who could never be helped. Through her careful documentation of her attempts to amend his behaviors, she now had enough evidence to finally get a formal evaluation and move him out of her class. Armstrong was not only a problem for her, but also for other students and their parents, who frequently complained about him. His formal evaluation had only came about after he yelled profanities at Mrs. Osmond. If not for Mrs. Osmond's go-ahead, Mrs. Haus would still be documenting different interventions.

It was now 3:30 P.M., "D day" as Mrs. Haus liked to call it, and Mrs. Haus seemed to have a skip in her step as she entered Mrs. Osmond's office for the MDT meeting. When she entered, she said hello to Armstrong's parents, Ellis and Petrina Kawolski, and Mrs. Osmond. As everyone waited nervously for other MDT members to arrive, Mrs. Osmond tried to ease the tension in the room by cracking a joke. Finally, Mike Wagman (the psychologist) walked in with his test results under his arm, followed by Hank Crossman (the special education director), who brought in Armstrong's records, a file 3 inches thick.

"Okay. Everyone's here, let's start. First, I would like to have Mr. Wagman report the results of his formal evaluation. Mike, tell us what you found," said Mrs. Osmond, happy that the meeting could finally begin.

"What I found was that Armstrong performed average on the IQ test that I gave him, slightly below average in achievement, and below average on the behavior measures," Mr. Wagman explained. He then went into a 10-minute, detailed discussion about each of the measures and their findings. As he explained this information to Armstrong's parents, Ellis and Petrina Kawolski began to make counterpoints for each of Armstrong's weaknesses.

"Oh, his behavior is like that of any child his age. Besides, a lot of kids don't like school," said Ellis in opposition to Mr. Wagman's scoring of Armstrong's inappropriate classroom behaviors. These counterpoints continued as the Kawolskis tried to explain away his low achievement, lack of motivation, and inappropriate behaviors.

"But, Mr. and Mrs. Kawolski, Armstrong needs help. I feel that there are academic, as well as behavioral, issues here we need to deal with, and I think that we could begin to resolve these issues in Mr. Neva Hassen's BD classroom," Mr. Wagman replied, trying to send home the point that Armstrong needed individual attention.

"I think all he needs is a kick in his butt," Mr. Kawolski angrily replied.

Just then, Mr. Crossman stepped in and said, "Look, we know that this is a lot to digest. Why don't you folks go home and we'll meet in 2 weeks to discuss Armstrong's IEP."

As Mrs. Kawolski left the room, she said that at the next meeting they would be bringing their attorney to get Armstrong out of this mess.

Less than one week later, Armstrong was again in trouble in school. This time, he hit his teacher and was now being threatened with a one-month suspension. He was sent home and told not to return to school for one month or until a different decision was made at his MDT/IEP meeting, which had already been scheduled for one week later.

When the day of the meeting finally arrived, the Kawolskis were fully prepared to fight the BD classification. At the meeting, the Kawolskis and their attorney, Cooper Wolfgang, met with the same MDT members. When the meeting began, the Kawolskis told the team that they would agree to an LD classification, but never a BD one, and they wanted their son to begin LD services immediately.

"Well, we really don't believe that he is LD, and we think that this latest incident really is more indicative of a BD label," Mr. Crossman pointed out.

"Then, we'll seek an independent evaluation, and we want you folks (the district) to pay," retorted Mr. Kawolski, with his attorney shaking his head in agreement.

"Well, if he is going to be classified LD, he will have to be out of school for his monthlong expulsion," Mr. Crossman added, "because an LD child would never commit such an act, only children with behavior or emotional problems."

"That's not true," Mr. Wolfgang said, pointing out another teacher-hitting case in the state in which the child was LD.

"Oh," replied Mr. Crossman, unaware of the case. "Well, nevertheless, he will have to finish out his one-month expulsion because it would set a bad trend for our district," Mr. Crossman continued.

Without reaching agreement, all parties argued for another 10 minutes before they agreed to continue the meeting at a later date. Days later, Mr. Crossman received a letter from Mr. Wolfgang requesting that Armstrong be permitted to begin school immediately in an LD classroom and that all references to a BD label, including any information about inappropriate behavior (e.g., incident reports, anecdotal records, etc.) be expunged from his records.

QUESTIONS

Legal Issues to Consider

1. When a child with a disability is being suspended for longer than 10 days, or more than 10 cumulative days, what should the district personnel do?

2. Can the parents request that information from a child's records be expunged? What happens if the school refuses to expunge information from a child's records?

3. Guns and drugs are two reasons for expulsion from school. How does IDEA address these issues concerning students with disabilities?

Other Issues

1. How can a school ensure that other students are safe when a student with emotional disturbance presents dangerous behavior?

CHAPTER EIGHT

DUE PROCESS

CASE 8.1 JAMES/EXPULSION

CASE 8.2 BOBBY/DISCIPLINE

CASE 8.3 ANN/TUITION REIMBURSEMENT

CASE 8.4 LUKE/STAY PUT

CASE 8.5 SUSAN/PARENT INPUT

CASE 8.6 LORI/INDIVIDUALIZED IEP

CASE 8.1

JAMES/EXPULSION

James Otero was a 17-year-old student at Cedar High School. He had received special education services since first grade and was labeled learning disabled and hearing impaired, because he had a slight hearing loss in his right ear. His parents were both professional persons in the community who were very involved with James and his education.

James had always been well behaved in school and was successfully progressing toward graduation from high school. He spent half of his school day in special education classes and the other half in general education vocational-education classes. James was projected to graduate from high school in three weeks.

In May, James was caught by the assistant principal possessing marijuana. He admitted having the marijuana for his own personal use. He was promptly suspended from school for 10 days, and his parents were told that he would have an expulsion hearing. The school district had a policy that included strict consequences for anyone possessing drugs on school grounds. If James were expelled from school, he would automatically lose academic credit and would not graduate from high school.

James' parents immediately secured the services of an attorney, who also happened to be a friend of the family. A due process hearing was filed by the parents' attorney. At the hearing, the family and the school district were represented by attorneys, and many witnesses were present. They included the parents; a telephone testimony from the parents' private evaluator; the special education administrator; the high school principal; the assistant high school principal; the hall monitor, who discovered the marijuana; three high school special education teachers; and the school psychologist. An impartial due process hearing officer conducted the hearing. As the hearing began, a court reporter recorded verbatim the entire hearing. After both attorneys presented opening statements, the witnesses were called to testify. Part of the testimony included the direct examination of the special education teacher by the school district's attorney. The testimony, in part, focused on the IEP conference to determine the relationship, if any, between James' misbehavior and his disability.

The school district's attorney began the questioning by asking, "And you feel the IEP of May 6 is appropriate for James?"

The special education teacher, Kalimah Muhammad, responded, "Definitely."

The school district's attorney, Mr. Borsick, continued, "Okay. You were in attendance at the multidisciplinary conference on May 31?"

Ms. Muhammad said, "Yes. I was."

Mr. Borsick asked, "Can you briefly explain to us what happened at that meeting?"

Ms. Muhammad confidently answered, "Well, we first reviewed the disciplinary incident that had occurred. And then we began to discuss the relationship between the behavior and the disability. In doing that, we reviewed the most-recent evaluation with our psychologist and James' IEP. We also reviewed information that Ms. Bay, our hearing-impaired consultant, could bring to us because she has knowledge of the student. We reviewed information about James' progress in school from his special education teachers. We also considered an outside evaluation that was given to us at the meeting by the parents and their attorney. In fact, I recall that it was a rather lengthy packet, and we recessed for about 30 minutes so that everyone could read the input. This information was then considered. Ultimately, it was the consensus of the team that the behavior of bringing marijuana to school was not related to James' disability."

Mr. Borsick responded by saying, "Thank you."

After this witness completed testifying by direct examination, the parents' attorney was able to cross-examine the witness.

The parents' attorney, Ms. Sims, began the questioning by stating, "Now, in developing these IEPs, we don't just do it in a flash-picture-type mechanism in which we just look at what's occurred in the last couple of days. I assume the reason we maintain these large files on this student is so that, even though you weren't here when James was, say, in the third grade, those records would be available to you?"

Ms. Muhammad responded, "The records are always available to the team. As you know, we are required to reevaluate a student every three years. And the intent behind that requirement suggests to me that we need to base educational decisions on the most recent evaluation."

The parent's attorney continued, "Okay. But in reaching those decisions, you don't totally disregard the past eight years of experience with that child, do you?"

Ms. Muhammad stated, "I'm not sure what you mean by totally disregard."

Ms. Sims, looking angry, said, "I mean totally disregard. You look at that stuff, don't you?"

Ms. Muhammad said, "Sure."

Ms. Sims asked, "You consider it, don't you?"

Ms. Muhammad answered, "Sure. It's part of the history, but…"

The parents' attorney interrupted abruptly "And part of the history is what helps you develop an individual education program for this student, isn't it?"

Ms. Muhammad again tried to answer, "We base our decisions primarily on the most-recent information and…"

The parents' attorney again interrupted and sounded angry when she said, "I understand what you base your decisions on. The question is whether it's proper to base your decisions on that. Now, my question is, I'm trying to determine what you *do* base your decisions, on and I'm asking you very simply. Do you go back and look at, for example, the third-grade IEP?"

Ms. Muhammad said, "No."

Ms. Sims continued, "And see how he would progress from that and from the utilization of that program?"

The special education teacher continued, "We do not at the age of 17 go back to a third-grade IEP to plan. No. We don't."

After 14 hours of testimony and a short dinner break, the attorneys presented closing statements.

The school district's attorney, Mr. Borsick, began by stating the district's position: "It is our position, and I think the testimony and the records in this case bear that out, that this district has appropriately identified this student's disabling condition. We have had extensive testimony today about the psychological evaluations and critiques of both the district evaluations and private evaluations and the differences between those evaluations. It is our position that evaluations by the district have been appropriate in nature and degree…. There has not been any indication that the educational placements of this student have been inappropriate. On the contrary, we have heard that the district has conducted itself correctly with regard to providing an appropriate program and placement…. What has brought this case about is the disciplinary incident—not the evaluations, not the program or placement—but the disciplinary incident. Were it not for the facts that James has been suspended and the district has moved to convene expulsion proceedings, we wouldn't be here today…. The district held a multidisciplinary conference and determined that James' behavior was not symptomatic of his disability…. We cannot let the existence of a disability be a cloak or shield for illegal activity, including the possession of drugs on school grounds. And that's what you're dealing with here today. Special education should not be misused to cover for the possession of drugs on school grounds. The parents would like you to believe that James did not understand that bringing drugs on school grounds was illegal…. The district can, and I emphasize can, expel a student when there is no direct substantial relationship between the disability and the behavior."

The parents' attorney, Ms. Sims, stated her position. "This district is in a hostile and adversarial position to James and his parents. The simplest of questions would frequently require 10 to 12 attempts to get a simple yes or no answer because they did not want to do anything that might help the parents keep their child in school. The room reeked of that hostility… You're being asked to determine, based on the testimony of the people from the district, that the behavior on that day in May is not related to his disabilities. That's an interesting position to take for a district that doesn't recognize the disability. And they do not. There was not one witness who said that James has an auditory processing deficit. And so, no, I would not expect them to come in here and say it's related to it because they don't even recognize it…. The question is not, as the school district's attorney framed it, about whether they made a reasonable effort to get James to understand these rules. That's not the standard. The standard is: Did they get James to understand the rules? It is the opinion of a private psychologist who has dealt with James over a period of many years since his grade-school days that James could not possibly understand the school handbook…. In conclusion, I would suggest that this district did at one time, but no longer does, appropriately identify James' disability…. I would further posit that this district stretches your credulity when they tell you they can't figure out a way to educate James short of throwing him out of school.... When you read the record, Mr. Hearing Officer, you will find that James does have an auditory processing deficit and that the deficit does relate to the behavior in question. You will also see that the district is failing this child in not providing an adequate educational program for him and trying to remove him from school during his senior year."

The hearing officer concluded the hearing by stating, "My closing statement will be more brief. The hearing officer's decision will address oral testimony and written evidence. The decision will contain orders related to all issues. The district is responsible for the official written record of this hearing. After completing the decision, all material will be returned, and I will have no further contact with the parties about this matter. The written findings of fact and decision will be made by certified mail within 10 days of the close of the hearing. The requesting party and the respondent will receive copies of the decision, as well as the state board of education. The decision will be binding upon the parties unless the decision is appealed. The decision will completely detail the procedures for appeal. This hearing is concluded."

QUESTIONS

Legal Issues to Consider

1. Describe the rights of both parties during a due process hearing. Were those rights observed in this case?

2. Parents have two additional rights during a due process hearing. Describe these additional rights and how these rights were displayed in this case.

3. According to IDEA, what does the term *impartial* mean when used to describe the hearing officer?

4. Under what circumstances can a party request an impartial due process hearing?

5. Why was this hearing initiated?

Other Issues

1. It has been said that due process is the legal expression of fairness. What does this mean in terms of special education?

2. How do citizens have due process in society?

━━━━━ **CASE 8.2** ━━━━━

BOBBY/DISCIPLINE

Gary Erickson quickly went through the mail that was on his desk. He had been out of the office for three days at a due process hearing in which he represented a school district in a case involving discipline. The district contacted him because he had developed, over a period of 20 years, an excellent reputation for defending school districts in due process hearings and court cases involving students with disabilities. He felt confident about his defense of the school district in this case. However, he was too much of a realist to assume that the district would prevail. One just never knew until the judgement was received.

Two weeks later, Gary received the outcome of the hearing. The school district did not prevail on any of the issues. He felt that the ruling was unfair and advised the school district to appeal the ruling to the federal district court. In preparing the appeal, Gary carefully reviewed the written transcript of the due process hearing. During the hearing, a court reporter had carefully recorded in verbatim all dialogue. This transcript would not only help him prepare the appeal, but it would also become part of the record forwarded to the judge. Gary got out his note pad and began to carefully review the transcript. The transcript included the following dialogue. As he read the transcript, he could almost visualize the hearing.

Mr. Haley began the hearing: "This due process hearing will come to order to consider the case of Bobby Sessions. The primary issues in this case are:

1. Whether the student has a behavior disorder
2. The nature and degree of the disability
3. Whether the student's rights were observed when a change was made to the student's IEP in a meeting on October 17
4. Whether the previous placement and the placement proposed by the school district is appropriate
5. Whether the student's disability is related to a disciplinary incident that occurred on October 30
6. Whether the school district properly considered an outside report on Bobby provided by his parent

"This hearing will be conducted in a fair and impartial manner. The parties shall have the right to question witnesses. The parties have been advised of their rights.

"We will try to conclude this hearing today. It has the potential to be a rather lengthy one; however, that doesn't always pan out. If, in fact, it cannot be concluded today, we will decide at that time how we'll proceed.

"Are there any other questions before we begin the proceedings? Okay. We are ready for opening statements from the district and then from the parent."

Gary Erickson said: "My name is Gary Erickson. I'm an attorney representing the school district in this case. The parent has asked for a due process hearing in this matter on several issues, and I'll just briefly outline our position on them.

"First of all, it is the district's position that it has appropriately identified the disabling condition of Bobby Sessions and has determined an appropriate program eligibility for the student. The records will reflect that the student was in a behavior disorder resource program, cross-categorical in nature. The district is proposing a change in placement due to a pattern of violent behavior displayed by Bobby, most recently directed toward a staff member. The district is proposing a change to a day treatment facility for students with behavior disorders. It's the district's position that the IEP that has been determined for this student is appropriate and is in the least restrictive environment. Furthermore, the student has had several evaluations, and it's our position that those evaluations were appropriate in nature and degree.

"It appears that this hearing has been generated in part because of a disciplinary incident involving this student, as well as a history of violent behavior. Recently, the student hit a physical education teacher with his fist. Hitting school staff is a violation of school policy, and Bobby admitted that he knew this was wrong.

"The staff will testify today that the school has a policy in its handbook that says hitting a staff member is prohibited and that there are certain disciplinary consequences to a violation of that policy. The staff will testify about how students are informed of that policy and, specifically, instances in which Bobby Sessions was informed of that policy.

"With regard to the issue of linkage—that is, whether or not the behavior is symptomatic of a disabling condition—it is our position that hitting a teacher is symptomatic of this student's disabling condition. The IEP conference participants made that determination. We would ask the hearing officer to uphold that finding and allow the district to place Bobby in an appropriate setting—a day treatment facility for children with behavior disorders."

Ms. Cable, the parents' attorney, stated her position: "My name is Katherine Cable and I am an attorney representing the parents and Bobby Sessions.

"This student has received an inappropriate special education program from this school district. An IEP meeting was held on October 17, and a decision was made to place Bobby in two regular classes. The evidence will show that the decision was based only on parent and student request. The federal law says that the right to a free and appropriate public education belongs to the child, not to the parent. The school district made a serious error when it agreed to place Bobby in regular classes even when the IEP team felt it was not appropriate. In addition, the IEP team did not consider an independent report from the student's counselor that clearly stated that Bobby was extremely sensitive to touch due to his adoption and possible prior abuse by his natural parents. If the IEP team had made an individually based decision using *all* current information, this situation—hitting a teacher—would not have occurred. In addition, the IEP did not adequately address Bobby's behavior problems. This child should not be punished for behavior resulting from an inappropriate IEP and placement. This district should be ordered to conduct an IEP meeting using all available data and to place Bobby back in the junior high school. The district should not be allowed to remove Bobby to a day treatment facility for students with behavior disorders. It should place him in the least restrictive environment in his home school."

After three hours of testimony, Ms. White, one of Bobby's special education teachers, was called to testify. Mr. Erickson, school district attorney, led the direct examination. After approximately one hour, Ms. Cable, parents' attorney, led a cross-examination of Ms. White. The cross-examination consisted of heated questions and answers between Ms. Cable and Ms. White.

Ms. Cable asked, "Now, Ms. White, you are Bobby's special education English teacher, aren't you?"

Ms. White answered, "Yes, I am. I have had Bobby in my English class for two years."

Ms. Cable continued, "Were you in attendance at the IEP meeting of October 17?"

Ms. White said, "Yes, I was."

Ms. Cable asked, "Do you have the IEP of October 17 in front of you?"

Looking at the IEP, Ms. White answered, "Yes, I do."

Ms. Cable asked, "Will you please turn to page 4 of the IEP and read it?"

Ms. White read the IEP: "Placement—It is recommended that Bobby be placed in two additional regular classes, science and social studies. This is against the recommendation of the school staff due to Bobby's inappropriate behavior. The recommendation is made based on the mother's request. Mrs. Sessions insists that Bobby will function better in the regular classroom."

Ms. Cable asked, "Ms. White, did you agree with this recommendation?"

Ms. White looked uncomfortable as she answered, "Well, not really, but it was the best decision at the time. Bobby wanted to be placed in regular classes, and his mother was very supportive of the change. We decided that if Bobby didn't do well he could be moved back to special education classes."

Ms. Cable confidently said, "So, you made a decision based on what Bobby and his mother requested, not on what was in his best interest."

Ms. White said, "Well, that wasn't really the intent and…"

Ms. Cable cut her off by continuing, "I can see what you did, Ms. White. Now, you indicated that you thought that Bobby was experiencing behavior problems. Did you write on Bobby's IEP any type of behavior management plan?"

Ms. White tried to answer, "Well, no, but we discussed his behavior and…"

Again Ms. Cable cut into Ms. White's answer and continued, "I asked you, did you write on Bobby's IEP any type of behavior management plan?"

Ms. White said, "We didn't write anything on his IEP, but we did discuss Bobby's behavior problems."

Ms. Cable asked, "Were you aware, Ms. White, that Bobby was adopted and that he was sensitive to anyone touching him?"

Ms. White answered, "I knew that he was adopted, but I never witnessed any problem with touch. In fact, I often give my students a pat on the back, and Bobby didn't indicate any problem with touch."

Ms. Cable looked at her notes and asked, "Ms. White, were you aware of this document dated September 1 from Bobby's private counselor addressing issues about his adoption, especially that he was very sensitive to touch?"

Ms. White said, "No, I don't think I've ever seen that report before."

Ms. Cable continued, "This report was sent to the school on September 5. Are you saying it was never considered by the IEP team in making a decision about Bobby's placement in the October 17 meeting?"

Ms. White looked upset as she said, "I said that I have not seen the report, Ms. Cable."

Ms. Cable asked, "If you have not seen the report, I wonder who has seen the report. If the IEP team had seen the report, would you have placed Bobby in two additional regular classes?"

Ms. White answered, "I'm not sure."

Ms. Cable forcefully continued, "And if the report were considered, is it possible that Bobby never would have been in a position to hit a teacher?"

Ms. White said, "I don't know."

Ms. Cable looked at the hearing officer as she said, "What has happened here is that the IEP was changed because of a parent request. The IEP was based on partial information, not the most important and recent information sent by Bobby's private counselor. If this information, which was provided to the school district, had been considered at the October 17 meeting, Bobby would not have hit the teacher. Bobby hit the teacher because you did not provide an appropriate IEP for Bobby. Don't you agree with this, Ms. White?"

Ms. White looked very upset, and her eyes had tears in them as she stated, "We just did the best we could."

Ms. Cable coldly stated, "If that's the best you can do, then you should not be involved in teaching children with disabilities, Ms. White."

Gary Erickson put down the transcript and pad of paper. He thought, *Why does it have to be so hard emotionally on a teacher to testify at a due process hearing?* He sat for a minute thinking, then continued reading the transcript.

QUESTIONS

Legal Issues to Consider

1. What was the primary issue that prompted the due process hearing? How did the school district respond to this incident in terms of a change in placement? From the evidence given, was this an appropriate response?

2. The parents' attorney stated that Bobby was placed in two regular classes simply because of the parents' request. Was this appropriate? Why or why not?

3. The parents' attorney alleged that the school district did not consider an outside report on Bobby. What is the school district's responsibility to consider the report?

Other Issues

1. As a teacher, how would you feel about being questioned in the same manner as the teacher in this case?

2. How can you, as a teacher, prepare to become a witness in a due process hearing case?

◼◼◼◼ CASE 8.3 ◼◼◼◼

ANN/TUITION REIMBURSEMENT

An impartial due process hearing was held November 30 at 10:35 A.M. on behalf of Ann Spencer. The hearing was continued to Wednesday, December 6, and again to Monday, December 18, when both parties submitted their closing statements. The hearing was requested by Mrs. Spencer, Ann's mother. The issues presented to the hearing officer were:

1. Did the school district substantially verify Ann's educational needs?
2. Were Ann's special education placement and related services appropriate to her identified educational needs?
3. Were Ann's rights fully observed relative to identification, evaluation, and placement procedures?
4. Is the family entitled to receive reimbursement for tuition paid to a private high school?

Mrs. Spencer's position was stated by her advocate, Mrs. Wilson. She said that Ann was mistreated by the school district, which tolerated and perpetrated semiliteracy on the part of the students and incompetence on the part of the learning disability teaching staff. In addition, the school district failed to permit inspection of school records on site, failed to obtain parental consent before placing Ann full-time in a special education class, and failed to integrate Ann in nondisabled classrooms to the maximum extent possible. Therefore, Mrs. Wilson requested on behalf of her client that the school district reimburse Mrs. Spencer for the tuition she is paying for Ann to attend a private school.

The school district's position, as stated by Mr. Garrett, attorney, was that the IEP developed for Ann was reasonably calculated to provide her an educational benefit in the public school setting and fulfilled her fundamental right to education in the least restrictive environment.

Ann's background was summarized by the special education administrator, Dr. Craft. Ann is 14 years old and currently attends a private high school. She began her school career in Afton School as a kindergarten student. After an unsuccessful year in first grade, she repeated first grade. Ann was identified as a student with learning disabilities in second grade. Throughout her school years, she received the following services.

Second grade—LD services 200 minutes per week

Third grade—LD services 200 minutes per week

Fourth grade—LD services 200 minutes per week

Fifth grade—LD services 200 minutes per week; social work consultation 10 minutes per month

Sixth grade—LD services 300 minutes per week; social work services 20 minutes per month

Seventh grade—LD services 400 minutes per week

Eighth grade—LD services 1,300 minutes per week; social work services 30 minutes per week

Mrs. Spencer did not want Ann to receive self-contained LD services or social work services in eighth grade. However, she was in attendance at the conference to discuss the change, and she was notified of the increase in LD services.

At the end of Ann's eighth-grade year, an annual review was conducted to plan her transition to high school. Mrs. Spencer did not attend the conference because she had requested a due process hearing four days before the annual review. At the meeting, an IEP was developed for Ann in high school.

After the due process hearing request was made, Mrs. Spencer went to Ann's school to review her school records. Mrs. Spencer was told that the records were not on site at the school and that they had been transferred to the school district's central office because of the request for a due process hearing. Mrs. Spencer did not request a review of the records at the central office.

Before to the due process hearing, Mrs. Spencer and the school district's representatives agreed to mediation. The mediation resulted in an agreement that called for the school district to reconvene an IEP meeting within two weeks to address a transition plan for high school. The meeting, according to testimony from school staff, was scheduled for one week later. The school district did not send a formal notice of the meeting to Mrs. Spencer because the date and time were discussed in the mediation.

The meeting was held one week later, and Mrs. Spencer was not present. She claimed that she was not notified of the date and time of the meeting. At the meeting, high school transition was again discussed, and Ann's proposed IEP for high school was reviewed.

In September, Ann did not return to the public high school. Instead, Mrs. Spencer enrolled her in a local private high school, where she was in attendance until the time of the due process hearing in December.

The due process hearing officer ruled on the case within 10 days after the hearing. The ruling, in written form, stated the following:

1. All parties are in agreement that Ann has needs that require special education intervention. Three evaluations have been completed on Ann during her school career, and all

have been appropriate in nature and degree. All parties agree that Ann has learning disabilities, and her diagnostic profile has been substantially verified by the evaluations.

2. The school district offered appropriate special education services through her eighth-grade year. The proposed IEP for ninth grade was reasonably calculated to provide educational benefit.

3. Ann's rights were fully observed. The parent contended that she was not able to inspect Ann's school records on site. This was true, but it was common practice for the school to transfer school records to the central office when a due process hearing was requested. Mrs. Spencer was told she could review the records at the central office and she did not do so.

   Mrs. Spencer indicated that she did not give permission for Ann to receive increased LD services in eighth grade. However, she was present at the meeting in which the change was discussed and received notice of the change. Also, at that time, Mrs. Spencer did not request a due process hearing.

   Mrs. Spencer claimed that she was not notified of the IEP meeting to discuss Ann's transition to high school after the mediation. The school district stated, and the hearing officer agrees, that the meeting was agreed upon as part of the mediation and that further formal notification was not necessary.

4. The hearing officer believes that Ann received special education services in the least restrictive environment. During her school years, the school district was careful to keep Ann in the regular education environment, and it was a gradual process to increase special education services. It was after six school years that a decision was made to place her in a self-contained special education environment.

5. Receipt of a request for an impartial due process hearing causes the student to remain in his or her current educational placement, unless a mutual agreement is reached between the parent and school district, until the conflict is resolved. There was no evidence that an IEP conference was held to determine that Ann's educational needs could not be met in the public school setting. There was also no evidence that, by mutual agreement, Ann was to be placed in a private school setting until the conflict was resolved. Therefore, reimbursement of tuition is denied.

QUESTIONS

Legal Issues to Consider

1. Did Mrs. Spencer have to give permission for Ann to receive increased LD services in eighth grade? Why or why not?

2. Describe the case law that requires that an IEP be reasonably calculated to confer educational benefit.

3. Why did the hearing officer deny tuition reimbursement for the private school to the parent?

Other Issues

1. What is mediation? Why might mediation be useful prior to a due process hearing?

2. In what areas does our society use mediation?

LUKE/STAY PUT

The setting of the teachers' meeting is the library. It is a large room filled with bookshelves in half of the room. In the center of the room are enough tables and chairs to seat about 75 people. It is 2:45 P.M. and students in the junior high school have left for the day. Teachers begin filing into the room for the after-school meeting. The superintendent, special education administrator, and building principal stand, waiting for all staff to arrive. As soon as about 30 teachers are seated, the meeting begins.

The principal began the meeting by saying, "Okay. I think all teachers are here. We'll go ahead and begin the meeting now. Mr. Rand, our superintendent, asked to meet with us today to discuss the incident with a special education student last week. Some of you have shared your concerns, and we are here today to address those concerns. Mr. Rand, would you like to speak first?"

Mr. Rand walked to the front of the room and said, "Thank you for the opportunity to talk with you. Before I ask for questions, I'd like to review this situation and the district's response. Last week, some of you dealt with a difficult situation. An eighth-grade student hit the physical education teacher in the gym during class. First of all, I want you to know that this kind of violent misbehavior will not be tolerated by the school district. The building principal immediately dealt with the situation by contacting the student's parent. The student was suspended from school for the maximum amount, 10 days. As you know, the student was a special education student, specifically, behavior disordered. Therefore, an IEP conference was held during his suspension to determine whether the student's behavior was related to his disability. The school staff at the conference found that the behavior was related to the disability. The student's IEP was changed to place the student in an out-of-district day treatment facility for students with behavior disorders. Two days later, the student's parent filed for a due process hearing. This means that the student must return to his current placement until the due process hearing decision is rendered. We requested an injunction to prohibit the student from returning to school until the due process hearing was concluded, but this request was denied by the hearing officer. Therefore, this student must return to his current placement at the end of his 10-day suspension. Special education federal law prohibits us from doing anything else. We want to support you as teachers and will do everything possible to ensure that this situation does not occur again. Now, does anyone have questions?

Ms. King, English teacher, stood up and stated in an angry voice, "Are you telling us there is a double standard for special education students? This special education student can hit a teacher and return to school after 10 days' suspension? If any nonspecial education student hit a teacher, he would have been suspended 10 days and probably expelled by the school board."

Mr. Rand answered, "I don't know if double standard is the right word, but there are two laws dealing with students. The federal law covering special education protects the rights of these students."

Ms. King got red-faced as she said in a loud voice, "Who is going to protect the rights of teachers? Why isn't this student being considered for expulsion like any other student who engages in violent behavior directed toward a teacher?"

Mr. Lock, special education administrator, stood up and said in a calm voice, "Perhaps I can answer this question. After the incident occurred and the student was suspended for 10 days, an IEP conference was held. As Mr. Rand stated, it was determined that the student's disability was related to the behavior of hitting a teacher. Therefore, the district cannot expel the student. If the student's behavior is related to his disability, a student cannot be expelled."

Mr. Weiss, math teacher, stated in a reasonable tone of voice, "I still don't understand why this student has to return to school. You said his placement was changed to an out-of-district day treatment facility for BD students. Why can't he be placed there? What kind of message will that send to the other students? They will see that a student can hit a teacher and return to school."

Mr. Rand replied "The law states that if a parent disagrees with the placement change—that is, the move to the out-of-district day treatment facility—the parent can ask for a due process hearing. While this is going on, the student has to return to his original placement. We have no choice in this matter."

The physical education teacher, Mr. Wallace, stated, "I am the person who was hit by this student. I had no idea that this student was in special education. I treated him like everyone else in the class. Then he turns around and hits me in the face with his fist. And now you tell me that I have to take him back in my PE class? I can tell you right now that I refuse to take this student back in my class!"

Ms. King said, "I have this student in my fourth-hour English class. I am afraid of him. If he hit one teacher, what will prevent him from hitting me?"

Mr. Lock answered, "We don't think this will happen, given the student's history. However, should the student pose a threat, it will be dealt with immediately. We will do everything possible to protect every teacher's safety."

Ms. King asked, "Why won't a hearing officer remove the student? You stated that the hearing officer could grant an injunction preventing the student from returning to school."

Mr. Rand answered, "A hearing officer has the authority to grant an injunction. The school district attorneys have reviewed the case, and we requested an injunction. The hearing officer denied the injunction because the student has no other violent episodes in his school history."

Mr. Weiss stated, "That's not good enough. It's hard for me to believe that any hearing officer would return a student to school who had just hit a teacher."

The superintendent again answered, "I know that some of you don't agree with everything the district has done in this case. Please be assured that we are pursuing this case aggressively and that we do not believe the student should be allowed to return to this school. However, we are operating under special education laws, and we don't have any choice but to return the student to school, at least until the due process hearing is completed. We will do everything possible to convince the hearing officer that the student should be placed in another facility."

Ms. King asked, "Just when will this due process hearing occur?"

"A final decision must be rendered not more that 45 days after the hearing was requested. The hearing was requested last week," stated Mr. Lock.

"So this student could be in my English class the rest of the semester," Ms. King said. "What do I do if he poses a threat?"

Mr. Lock stated emphatically, "Just because the student has to return to your class does not mean he can do anything he wishes. If he endangers you, other students, or himself, we will deal with him as we normally would with any other student. In other words, you will be protected."

As the meeting ended, teachers walked out of the library. Some were visibly upset and stayed to talk to the administrators. Others were quiet. The next week, Luke returned to school. He was moved to another PE teacher's class during the same hour so that the teacher he hit would not have him in class. The teachers tried to be fair to Luke, but he aggravated the situation by making statements to teachers such as, "My mom has an attorney. You can't do anything to me." One day, about a week after Luke returned to school, a teacher requested that Luke take his hat off in the building, which was a standard school rule. Luke responded by cursing at the teacher and running away. The principal suspended Luke for one day. The tension in the building among the teachers was considerable.

Two weeks after the teachers' meeting, the due process hearing was scheduled. The parent's attorney forwarded a settlement offer to the school district's attorneys. The offer requested that Luke be placed in a residential facility for students with behavior disorders at school-district expense. If the school district would agree to the offer, the due process hearing would not be held and Luke would immediately be placed. After considering the offer, the school district decided to accept the offer. Luke was placed in a residential facility three weeks later at school-district expense.

QUESTIONS

Legal Issues to Consider

1. What is the primary issue of due process in this scenario?

2. On what basis could the school district have pursued an injunction to remove the child from school pending the outcome of the due process hearing?

3. Why was the school district unable to expel the student?

4. The PE teacher stated that he had no idea the student was in special education. If this is true, will there be a legal concern? If so, what will the concern be?

5. What were the issues of LRE in the settlement offer?

Other Issues

1. Is there a double standard between general education and special education in terms of discipline? If so, describe the standards.

2. How would you have responded in the meeting if you were the teacher that Luke hit?

3. If a person hits someone in the community, what will happen? How are these consequences different from the school scenario?

■■■■■■   **CASE 8.5**   ■■■■■■

SUSAN/PARENT INPUT

Susan Suresh, a 4-year-old girl diagnosed with multisystems developmental disorder, was the subject of an impartial due process hearing against the local school district. Mr. and

Mrs. Suresh, Susan's parents, requested the hearing in a letter (Figure 8.5.1) addressed to the district special education administrator.

FIGURE 8.5.1   A Letter to the Special Education Administrator

```
May 20

Ms. Middleton, Special Education Administrator
Lakeview School District
Parkview Town, USA


Dear Ms. Middleton:

    As provided for under the Individuals With Disabilities
Education Act and State Law, we are requesting the
opportunity to select an impartial due process hearing
officer to conduct a due process hearing on behalf of our
daughter, Susan Suresh, whose birth date is August 14.
    The hearing is requested to resolve differences over the
following:

    1. We are requesting a one-to-one aide for Susan.
    2. The school district's violation of due process for not
       filing a request for the hearing within the required
       timeline.
    3. The school district's failure to provide occupational
       therapy during the summer session.
    4. The school district's failure to provide parental input
       into the IEP for the evaluation and selection of goals.

    We would be interested in mediation to help resolve the
disagreement, but we wish to pursue the due process hearing
at the same time. Please contact us at 433-1711 if you have
any questions or desire further information.

Sincerely,


John and Carol Suresh
```

BACKGROUND

Susan was diagnosed with multisystems developmental disorder when she was 2 years old. At 2½, Susan's parents consulted a nationally known expert in multisystems developmental disorder, Dr. Blackboro, in a neighboring state. Dr. Blackboro saw Susan three times. He indicated in his report that Susan had a tendency to stay within herself in an autistic-like state. When in this state, Susan was unable to process any cognitive thought. He stated that Susan must be brought out of this state and connected to the world outside of herself. Human contact was the only way to bring Susan out of herself and keep her involved in the real world. When involved in the world outside of herself, Susan could benefit from stimuli around her. Children afflicted with this type of disorder had a relatively small window of opportunity to reach the outside world. Relationships and connections with the outside world must be made before the child is 7 years old or they may not be made at all.

Dr. Blackboro recommended that the parents take Susan to a local expert for follow-up treatment. Susan began seeing the local expert on a weekly basis. She also saw a private speech and language therapist.

CHRONOLOGY OF EVENTS LEADING TO THE HEARING

When she was 3 years old, Susan was placed by the school district in an early childhood class-room for children with disabilities. The program had five students with a teacher and an aide, and it met two and a half hours per day. Susan continued in this program for the full school year. At the end of the first year, an IEP meeting was held. At the meeting, the parents re-quested a one-to-one aide for the next school year and some form of transition to summer school to assist Susan because of her difficulty in forming relationships. The school district personnel attending the conference rejected the parents' request. It was stated that Susan re-ceived considerable individual attention during the school day. In fact, she was involved in group activity only 10 to 20 minutes each day, and the remainder of the school day was indi-vidualized attention. Susan received this attention from the teacher, the aide, and a speech and language therapist. School staff concluded that Susan should continue in the current program and receive a summer school program for 10 weeks. Although the parents were unhappy that their request had been denied, they were in agreement that Susan was making progress.

During the summer session, Susan's early childhood teacher was her teacher. The school district contracted with a local hospital to provide occupational therapy. On the first day of summer school, the occupational therapist quit. The school district immediately began a search for a replacement. However, it was 7 weeks before an occupational thera-pist was located. Susan only received therapy for one week during the summer.

In August, when Susan was 4 years old, she continued to attend the early childhood class. However, her parents were upset about some last-minute changes in the program. Two weeks before school began, the parents were notified by letter that Susan's class was being relocated to another school building within the district due to changing and increas-ing enrollments. In addition, the early childhood teacher did not begin the school year be-cause she was on maternity leave. A long-term substitute taught Susan's class until December. At the annual review in May, Susan's parents disputed the district's evaluation of her annual goals. The parents felt that they should have direct input into how Susan's goals were evaluated and the selection of new goals. The special education administrator stated that the school district personnel would make these decisions.

Immediately after the annual review, the parents requested mediation services and a due process hearing. The special education administrator immediately requested a mediator but did not submit the request for a due process hearing until August. When the parents contacted the administrator in August to inquire about the status of the due process hearing, it was discovered that the request had been misplaced. After this contact, the school district requested a due process hearing. Mediation failed to help the parents and school district reach an agreement, and a due process hearing was held in September. During the due process proceedings, Susan returned to her early childhood class.

At the conclusion of the due process hearing, the hearing officer sent a written order to the parents and school district. The order included the following:

1. The school district's placement of Susan in the early childhood classroom without a one-to-one aide is affirmed. Evidence and testimony indicated that Susan receives considerable individual attention during the school day and that she is receiving educational benefit from the program the school district has planned and implemented.
2. The school district failed to meet the timeline for submission of the request for a due process hearing. Evidence and testimony clearly indicated that the request for due process was made in May and not acted upon by the school district until August. The school district admitted misplacing the request.
3. The school district failed to provide the amount of occupational therapy indicated in Susan's IEP during the summer session. Even though this was due to a circumstance beyond the school district's control, the school district shall provide an additional amount of occupational therapy during the next school year to make up for the lost occupational therapy during the summer.
4. The school district failed to allow the parents input into Susan's IEP in terms of the evaluation methods for goals and the selection of goals. The school district shall convene an IEP within 30 days of this order and afford the parents input into the development of the IEP.

QUESTIONS

Legal Issues to Consider

1. Describe the legal errors made by the school district and their basis in IDEA.

2. The hearing officer indicated that Susan was receiving educational benefit from her educational program. What was the basis in case law for affirming Susan's placement in the early childhood classroom?

3. What was the legal basis for returning Susan to her original placement during the pendency of due process hearing proceedings?

Other Issues

1. Was it fair for the hearing officer to direct the school district to provide makeup occupational therapy when the circumstances of the therapist leaving were beyond the district's control?

2. Should the parents receive reimbursement for any legal expenses incurred? Why or why not?

▬▬▬   CASE 8.6   ▬▬▬

LORI/INDIVIDUALIZED IEP

Lori was a 17-year-old girl who attended Central High School, a high school of about 2,000 students. Lori had received learning disabilities assistance for the past six years. In February, Lori's parents requested an impartial due process hearing because they felt Lori's special education program was not appropriate.

Lori was placed in a special education class for English. She participated in general education classes for science, social studies, and math. At the end of the first semester, Lori was failing three of four academic classes. Lori was only passing her special education English class.

Lori's parents engaged the assistance of a local attorney specializing in parent advocacy for children with disabilities. The due process hearing was held on March 30. One of the witnesses called by the parents' attorney was Ms. Bolen, Lori's special education teacher for English. Ms. Bolen was also responsible for writing Lori's IEP. Part of the direct examination of Ms. Bolen by the parents' attorney, Mr. Blackman, follows:

Mr. Blackman began the questioning by asking, "Ms. Bolen, would you please state your full name, your relationship with Lori, and your qualifications to teach students?"

Ms. Bolen answered, "Yes. My name is Susan Bolen, and I am Lori's English teacher in special education. I was also responsible for writing Lori's IEP for this school year. I met with the parents last spring to formulate the IEP. I have been a special education teacher at Central High School for the past five years. I have a bachelor's degree in special education, and I am certified to teach students with learning disabilities."

Mr. Blackman continued, "Now, you stated that you wrote Lori's IEP last spring. Were you responsible for notifying the parents of the IEP meeting on May 15?"

Ms. Bolen answered, "No, I wasn't. The special education office usually sends out letters to notify parents of the IEP meetings."

Mr. Blackman continued, "So, you were not aware that the parents were not notified of the IEP meeting of May 15?"

Ms. Bolen said, "No, I wasn't. I do remember that the parents did not attend the meeting, but that isn't unusual. Many parents are unable to attend IEP meetings during the day."

Mr. Blackman asked, "Ms. Bolen, were you involved in the decision to place Lori in special education English and general education math, social studies, and science for the eleventh grade?"

Ms. Bolen stated, "I was."

Mr. Blackman asked, "Were you aware that Lori had difficulty in science and social studies in ninth and tenth grades and that she was placed in special education for these classes?"

Ms. Bolen thought for a moment and said, "I remember discussing that."

Mr. Blackman continued, "Then why was she placed in general education classes in social studies and science in high school?"

Ms. Bolen answered confidently, "All of our students in special education at the eleventh grade level take general education classes in science and social studies. We have two really good teachers in these areas, and our students do well in those classes. Lori was no exception. We felt that she would do well in those classes."

Mr. Blackman asked, "So Lori was placed in general education classes in social studies and science because all students in special education take those classes?"

Ms. Bolen said, "Well, sort of. We also felt that she would be successful."

Mr. Blackman continued by asking, "Now, when were you made aware that Lori was failing those classes in high school?"

Ms. Bolen answered, "No one actually told me. I just noticed that Lori was feeling down after report cards had been sent out, and I asked her what was wrong. She told me that she failed three classes—math, social studies, and science."

Mr. Blackman asked, "So you found out in January that Lori had failed three classes in general education. Did you at any time during the semester ask Lori how she was doing in her regular education classes?"

Ms. Bolen answered, "No, I assumed she would tell me if she was having difficulty."

Mr. Bolen continued, "Did you at any time during the semester check Lori's progress in the three general education classes?"

Again, Ms. Bolen confidently answered, "No, I felt it was the student's responsibility to tell me if she was having difficulty in any class."

Mr. Blackman asked, "Lori was obviously having difficulty in the regular classes. Did you at any time during the semester talk with Lori's general education teachers about Lori's progress in those classes?"

She again said, "No, I didn't."

Mr. Blackman asked, "Did you write this goal on Lori's IEP: Lori will pass all regular classes'?"

Ms. Bolen looked at the IEP as she answered, "Yes, I did."

Mr. Blackman asked, "What exactly did you do to assist Lori in meeting this goal?"

Ms. Bolen explained, "Well, I usually write this for all of my students. I expect the students to tell me if they're failing any classes. If they talk to me, I provide tutoring for them."

Mr. Blackman followed up by asking, "Did you provide tutoring for Lori?"

Ms. Bolen said, "No, she never talked to me about failing her classes."

Mr. Blackman continued with another line of questioning, "Okay. Let's go back to Lori's IEP written on May 15. Can you point out to me where transition services for Lori were discussed and where services for transition are listed on the IEP?"

Ms. Bolen said, "It wasn't exactly written on the IEP, but we did talk about what Lori wanted to do after high school."

Mr. Blackman asked, "Did you write an individualized transition plan for Lori?"

Ms. Bolen answered, "We usually just discuss what the student wants to do after high school and place the student in vocational classes, if needed."

Mr. Blackman said, "So you did not write an individualized transition plan for Lori. Now, on the IEP of May 15, I see a goal that reads, 'Lori will improve math skills.' Special education services written on the IEP state that Lori will be placed in English and math classes. Yet, Lori failed a general education math class. How was Lori placed in a general education math class when her IEP states that she should be placed in a special education math class?"

Ms. Bolen thought for a moment, then answered, "As I recall, we did place her in special education math, but we changed the class to general education in September when her mother called to request the change."

Mr. Blackman asked, "When you changed the IEP in September, was an IEP meeting held?"

Ms. Bolen answered, "No, that wasn't necessary. I just talked to Lori's mother over the telephone. She wanted Lori in the regular class because she felt the special education class was too easy. So I just changed her schedule."

Mr. Blackman looked surprised when he said, "You're telling me that you didn't think it was necessary to change Lori's IEP when special education services were changed?"

Ms. Bolen said, "Because Lori's mother requested the change, I didn't think it was necessary."

Mr. Blackman asked, "On Lori's tenth-grade IEP, which was reviewed at the May 15 meeting, where on that IEP does it indicate Lori's progress on her goals?"

Ms. Bolen looked at the IEP as she answered, "I remember that we talked about Lori's progress, but I don't remember writing anything on her tenth-grade IEP."

Mr. Blackman said, "So you did not review Lori's progress on her tenth-grade IEP."

Ms. Bolen, looking frustrated, said, "I didn't say that. I said I think we talked about her progress."

Mr. Blackman stated, "There is nothing on the tenth-grade IEP that indicated Lori's progress on her goals. If you talked about her progress, it's not indicated on the IEP."

After several other witnesses testified, the hearing concluded. Two weeks later, the school district was ordered to reconvene an IEP meeting and write a new IEP for Lori.

QUESTIONS

Legal Issues to Consider

1. Was Lori's IEP individualized? How do you know?

2. Why might Lori's IEP be inappropriate?

3. What legal rights concerning due process did Lori's parents exercise in this scenario?

Other Issues

1. What could you as a special education teacher have done to fix Lori's IEP?

2. Do you think Lori's IEP was inappropriate? Why or why not?

CHAPTER NINE

CONFIDENTIALITY AND PRIVACY

CASE 9.1   DARRELL/PERSONAL NOTES

CASE 9.2   JEFF/IMPROPER DISCLOSURE

CASE 9.3   KEVIN/DELAYED RECORDS

CASE 9.4   JOHN/WITHHOLDING INFORMATION

CASE 9.5   DEAN/INVASION OF PRIVACY

CASE 9.6   CARLOS/FALSIFYING DOCUMENTS

CASE 9.1

DARRELL/PERSONAL NOTES

As director of special education, I was requested to attend Darrell's IEP meeting on Thursday at 3:00 P.M. I didn't think this conference was going to be anything unusual. I was often requested to attend conferences in which there might be potential conflict. I was always well prepared for conferences like this. I reviewed Darrell's file before the conference. It indicated that Darrell was a third-grade African American student in the elementary BD classroom. Darrell had been placed in this self-contained special classroom beginning in kindergarten. Before this class, he was placed in the cross-categorical early childhood special education program for two years. Darrell lived with his mother, older sister, and grandmother. Darrell rarely saw his father. His grandmother was a particularly strong influence on Darrell and his mother. She was also a prominent member of the community and worked in the library as an aide at the local high school. She was often involved in city committees and groups concerned with diversity in the community. Darrell's mother worked on a construction crew as a laborer and sometimes was gone for three weeks at a time, working on projects out of town. Darrell's grandmother indicated that the mother (her daughter) had been drug addicted when Darrell was born. During the past five years or so, Darrell's mother had been free of drugs. When Darrell's mother was working out of town, his grandmother assumed the parental responsibilities.

In the past few months, the teacher and special education supervisor had informed me that Darrell's behavior was deteriorating. Darrell had always been a challenge, but there were some significant changes lately in his behavior at school. In the mornings, Darrell barked like a dog and hid under the teacher's desk until the teacher pulled him out. At lunch recess, he had been involved in some conflict with other children, often arguing and hitting others. Two weeks ago, Darrell had become frustrated in the classroom, ripped the aide's blouse, and pulled a necklace from her neck. He also had kicked the teacher in the shin on another occasion when angry. The incidence of violent behavior was becoming more frequent and more serious. When these episodes occurred, the teacher attempted to contact Darrell's mother. When she was available, Darrell's mother was very supportive of the teacher, and she came to the school for numerous meetings. Often, though, Darrell's mother was unavailable, and the teacher had to contact Darrell's grandmother, who was somewhat critical of the teacher's actions. The grandmother always came to the school when called and took Darrell home for a day or two as a cooling-off period and as punishment.

After many attempts to help Darrell change, the teacher finally called me. She suggested that Darrell might need to be placed in a day treatment facility for children with BD. She indicated that Darrell's mother was very supportive of a change in placement so that he could receive intensive therapy. A meeting to discuss this placement and IEP change was arranged, and this was the meeting I was now attending.

The meeting was held in a conference room at the elementary school and was to begin at 3:10 P.M. As I walked into the room, the staff were sitting in a circle. Staff included the teacher, Mrs. Nesbitt; the BD crisis interventionist, Mr. Brown; and the special education supervisor, Mrs. Rule. The principal, Mr. August, walked in and said that he had another meeting and would be unable to attend. At 3:25 P.M., we were wondering if Mrs. King, Darrell's mother, had forgotten the meeting. At 3:35, Mrs. King walked into the meeting with her mother, Mrs. White, and two other unknown persons. They identified themselves as Mrs. Liner, an advocate, and Mr. Jones, the advocate's assistant. I recognized the advocate, Mrs. Liner, as a prominent statewide promoter of total inclusion for all children with disabilities. Following is part of the dialogue that occurred at the meeting.

I began the meeting by stating, "Thank you for attending this conference. We are here to discuss Darrell's progress in the behavior disorders classroom and to consider changes in his IEP. Mrs. Rule, our special education supervisor, will take notes of this conference and give all of you a copy at the conclusion of the conference. Mrs. Nesbitt, would you please review Darrell's progress?" As Mrs. Nesbitt began to talk, I pulled out my yellow legal pad and began to take personal notes.

Mrs. Nesbitt looked at Darrell's mother as she said, "Mrs. King, you and I have talked frequently, and you have been very supportive of Darrell in this program. I have had Darrell in my classroom for the past 3½ years. He has made minimal progress, especially lately in terms of his behavior. As you know, recently he has been demonstrating some violent behavior. He kicked me, tore the aide's blouse, and tore a necklace from the aide's neck. This seems to occur when Darrell becomes angry. He also is displaying this behavior out on the playground with other children. Almost every day he is involved in a fight with another child. Even on the school bus, he is throwing books and hitting children. I am very concerned about Darrell. I know that you have also expressed concern about Darrell's behavior at home."

As Mrs. Nesbitt talked, I continued to jot down notes on my yellow pad. Mrs. King sat quietly and looked at the floor.

Mrs. White abruptly entered the conversation by stating, "I know why Darrell isn't doing well. It's because he's in a classroom of students with behavior problems and in a school that isn't his home school. If he were in his home school in the regular classroom, he would do better. Why, he has no African American role models here! At his home school, there are lots of African American students." As she spoke, Mrs. King sat silently and said nothing.

Mrs. Liner stated in a strong voice, "As an advocate, I can tell you that it is Darrell's right to be placed in the regular classroom in his home school. You have to move him there if the parent makes a request to have him moved. I am representing the parent, and I am making that request on the parent's behalf."

Mrs. White nodded her head, and Mrs. King said nothing. I continued to take notes on my yellow pad. The special education supervisor took notes also. At the end of the conference, the following dialogue occurred.

To summarize the meeting, I stated, "Okay. I think we all agree that Darrell should be reevaluated because it has been 2½ years since his last evaluation. In this evaluation, we will include a psychiatric assessment. I will contact a major teaching hospital in the city and find an appropriate psychiatrist to conduct the assessment. We will complete the evaluation as quickly as possible. As soon as the evaluation is completed, we will reconvene this meeting. We can then base our decisions on the recent evaluation. Are there any questions?" No one answered.

"Mrs. Rule, you have been taking notes for this conference. Would you please give everyone a copy of the notes?" Mrs. Rule gave all participants a copy of the notes.

Mrs. Liner looked at me and stated, "Wait a minute. You have been taking notes of this conference. I want a copy of your notes."

Surprised, I said, "These notes are my own personal notes, and I don't intend to share them with anyone."

Mrs. Liner said again, "I demand a copy of your notes."

I was feeling irritated when I said, "I do not have to give my personal notes to you. They will not be shared with anyone."

Mrs. Liner continued, "You have to give me a copy. This is a formal request for the notes, and I assure you this will become an issue at a later date."

After the parent, grandparent, and advocates left the meeting, all school staff expressed surprise at the discussion. I wondered if I was correct in stating that I didn't have to give the advocate a copy of my notes.

Darrell was evaluated by the psychiatrist, who confirmed that Darrell was exhibiting serious emotional problems. At the second meeting to discuss the results of the reevaluation, Mrs. King attended. The advocates and Mrs. White, the grandmother, did not attend. Mrs. King readily agreed with a change in placement to the day treatment program for children with BD.

QUESTIONS

Legal Issues to Consider

1. Were the director of special education's personal notes considered part of the school record? Why or why not?

2. Did the parent have the right to bring an advocate and another relative to the meeting? Why or why not?

3. Was the advocate correct in stating that the child had a right to be placed in a regular classroom in his home school? Why or why not?

Other Issues

1. Why is it a good idea to be cautious about what you write about a child?

2. Could the notes that the special education director wrote have been requested by a judge in a court of law?

━━━━━ **CASE 9.2** ━━━━━

JEFF/IMPROPER DISCLOSURE

Mrs. Baker stood in the teacher's lounge as she talked with five other teachers. She was clearly frustrated and upset.

She stated, "I've been a first-grade teacher for 20 years, and this is the worst class I've ever had! It's October and the entire class cannot go into the lunch room without a behavior problem. Just today, Jeff, who is labeled behavior disordered, pushed Andy, who fell into a table and hurt himself. Then Jeff kicked Andy! My lunch is disrupted every day by these children. I tell you, Jeff should be in a special education class, and he would be if this district were assertive about his placement. I was told that Jeff was labeled and placed in a BD classroom last year in another school district. When he moved to this district, his mother didn't want him in BD, so this district said they would try him in regular first grade. Well, I have 26 students, which is far too many, and I cannot address these BD needs in my class!"

Mrs. Helfner, another teacher, responded, "I know just what you mean. It seems like we're being asked to work with more severe students with larger class sizes. This school district has always been known for its excellence and its small class sizes. Professional, high-income families have always made up the majority of this community. Now the board of education is trying to increase class sizes. You certainly should not have to take a violent child in first grade who is labeled BD."

Mrs. Baker sighed and said, "I just don't know what to do. I've tried everything. I can't teach these children with so many children and behavior problems in the classroom!"

Mrs. Baker received considerable support from the other teachers in the teacher's lounge. She walked out feeling very upset. Now she would have to deal not only with Jeff, who had hurt Andy, but also with Andy's parents.

At the end of the day, Mrs. Baker was working in her room, preparing for the next day, when Andy's father walked into the room.

Mrs. Baker said, "I'm so happy you stopped by, Dr. King. I want to make you aware of a situation that occurred today in the lunchroom. I wasn't there to witness the incident, but the lunchroom supervisor saw everything. Apparently, while standing in line, Jeff pushed Andy and Andy fell into a table. Jeff then kicked Andy. We took Andy to the nurse, and she felt he did not require any medical attention. Jeff's parents were also contacted by the principal."

Dr. King didn't respond, and Mrs. Baker continued. "As I have told you in the past, Jeff is a behavior disordered student. He has no sense of right and wrong and is very violent. In fact, he was in a BD class last year. This year, his family moved to this district, and his mother didn't want him in the BD class, so he is in my class. He is very disruptive and mean to other children. He doesn't even know how to follow any rules. He defies me all day, every day. He really needs some special help. I'm so sorry your child had to be involved in this situation."

Dr. King was clearly upset as he stated, "Well, I'm really upset that this could occur in this school. My son should be protected. I know he didn't do anything to provoke this child. Why would this district allow such a disturbed child like Jeff to be placed in the regular classroom?"

Mrs. Baker responded, "I can assure you, Dr. King, that I have voiced my opinion in a very strong way to the principal and superintendent. You are correct when you say that Jeff is very disturbed. He does not belong here. However, he is allowed to stay because the administration doesn't want to anger Jeff's parents and go through a due process hearing."

Dr. King continued, "Well, there is something very wrong when my son cannot be safe in school. I'll certainly do everything possible to change this situation."

Dr. King walked out of the classroom. Mrs. Baker was very upset. She had never in 20 years felt so discouraged. She knew she was an excellent teacher. All of her children learned to read each year, and very few went into special education. She felt so responsible for her children. She felt so frustrated and discouraged that she didn't seem to have control this year. She was a very structured teacher, and her children always responded to her tight rules and expectations.

Mrs. Baker finished her class preparation and left the room. She went to the local health club and walked furiously for five miles. When she returned home later, she felt somewhat better, although she dreaded the next day.

Meanwhile, that evening Dr. King talked to his wife about what Mrs. Baker had told him about Jeff. Both agreed that something had to be done now. They looked up Jeff's home address in the school directory and got into the car. They drove slowly around Jeff's house a few times and observed Jeff and his father talking to a neighbor in the front yard. Finally, they pulled into the driveway. Jeff's father was outside. Dr. King got out of the car and introduced himself to Mr. Kappel, Jeff's father. Mr. Kappel invited Dr. King inside the house.

Dr. King began by saying, "Mr. Kappel, I'm here to talk to you about your son, Jeff. I understand that Jeff is very disruptive at school, and he pushed and kicked my son, Andy, today at school."

Mr. Kappel was embarrassed as he said, "I know about the incident, and I can assure you that Jeff is being adequately punished. I'm very sorry this happened to Andy."

Dr. King stated, "I understand that Jeff is unable to follow any school rules. If he is going to make it in school, he will have to learn to follow rules."

Mr. Kappel said defensively, "Dr. King, Jeff is able to follow rules."

Dr. King ignored Mr. Kappel's comment and continued, "I also understand that Jeff is labeled behavior disordered and that he should be in a special education class. It sounds like Jeff would do better if he wasn't around the general education students. I have been told that he is very violent with other children. I am very fearful of what he might do to my little Andy."

Mr. Kappel asked, "Who told you this, Dr. King?"

Dr. King answered, "I stopped by Mrs. Baker's room after school to discuss the incident between your son and Andy. Mrs. Baker was very honest with me about Jeff. She cannot teach other children with Jeff in the classroom."

Mr. Kappel ended the conversation by saying, "Dr. King, I will do everything I can to help my son, Jeff. Thank you for your concern."

The next day, Mr. Kappel delivered a letter (Figure 9.2.1) to the principal. The principal immediately contacted Mr. Kappel and arranged a meeting. She then talked to Mrs. Baker about the situation, and Mrs. Baker freely admitted to sharing the information about Jeff with another parent out of anger and frustration. The principal directed Mrs. Baker to stop sharing any information about Jeff or any other student with anyone except someone directly involved in that child's education. The principal then met with Mr. Kappel and assured him that the situation had been resolved and would never occur again.

FIGURE 9.2.1   A Letter to the Principal

```
October 25

Mrs. Collier, Principal
Central Elementary School
Whoville


Dear Mrs. Collier:

    I would like to make an appointment with you to discuss my
son, Jeff. Apparently, Jeff has been involved in some
behavioral problems at school. His teacher, Mrs. Baker, has
made me aware of each disruptive incident, and I have tried to
apply appropriate consequences at home. I certainly do not
condone Jeff's behavior. What I do object to is the lack of
confidentiality and privacy afforded my son's records. These
special education records were shared with you and Mrs. Baker
in a multidisciplinary conference. At that meeting, we all
agreed that Jeff would be placed in Mrs. Baker's classroom. I
understand from another parent, who happened to visit my home
last night, that Mrs. Baker has shared confidential
information about my son. I am appalled! My son does not have
a chance for success in this classroom if other parents are
biased against him by Mrs. Baker sharing confidential special
education information.
    I am available at your convenience to discuss this
situation with you. If we cannot resolve the issue, my only
recourse would be to request a due process hearing to stop the
sharing of confidential information about my son. Thank you
for your consideration. I look forward to hearing from you.

Sincerely,


Daniel Kappel--Parent of Jeff
```

QUESTIONS

Legal Issues to Consider

1. Was the information that Mrs. Baker shared with the other teachers and the parent considered an educational record? How do you know?

2. Was it appropriate for Mrs. Baker to talk about Jeff to other teachers in the teachers' lounge? Why or why not?

3. Was it appropriate for Mrs. Baker to talk about Jeff to another parent (Dr. King)? Why or why not?

4. If Mrs. Baker's analysis of why Jeff was placed in her class was correct—that is, by parent request—was this an appropriate action by the placement team?

Other Issues

1. As a teacher, if you felt as frustrated as Mrs. Baker, what would be an appropriate way to respond?

2. Do you think Dr. King took appropriate action to protect his son by visiting Jeff's father at home? Why or why not?

3. What might be some of the consequences of Dr. King's visit to Jeff's home?

■■■ CASE 9.3 ■■■

KEVIN/DELAYED RECORDS

Mrs. Allen felt upset as she drove to the school district's central office to request and review Kevin's school records. Two days ago, she had received a telephone call from the building principal concerning Kevin's behavior on the bus. She was told that Kevin kicked and cursed the bus driver. The principal told Mrs. Allen that Kevin should stay home the next day as punishment. The principal also indicated that Kevin's teacher would be out of the building at a meeting the day after his punishment day, and his BD class would have a substitute teacher. She indicated that Kevin would be better off at home on that day also because he didn't do well with substitute teachers. The principal stated that the day at home would not count as a suspension from school, simply a "therapy" day. Although Mrs. Allen felt that Kevin needed to be in school, she agreed with the principal and kept Kevin home one day for his poor behavior on the bus and the next day because he was having a substitute teacher.

This was not the first time Kevin had been in trouble in his BD class. He entered the class in first grade because he was inattentive and threw temper tantrums, and his skill level was below average. By this year, fourth grade, Kevin had not made significant progress. He barely knew how to read, and his behavior was becoming more aggressive. When asked to do something he didn't want to do, he threw books, desks, and anything else around him. He didn't have any friends and often was unable to play on the playground at recess because he might hit another child. Lately, his aggression was displayed on the school bus.

The punishment was to be removed from the bus for one day and to ride with his father to school. This seemed more a reward than a punishment for Kevin. When she tried to tell this to the principal, Mrs. Allen's concern was dismissed.

When she arrived at the central office of the school district, Mrs. Allen asked to speak to the special education administrator, Dr. Whitford.

Dr. Whitford walked in the room and said, "Come and sit down, Mrs. Allen. How can I help you?"

Mrs. Allen said, "Dr. Whitford, I am very concerned about Kevin's progress in school. Lately, his behavior has become more aggressive, and he is being sent home more and more. Sitting at home and riding to school with his father certainly isn't helping. Yesterday, the principal told me to keep Kevin at home because his class was going to have a substitute teacher! I don't know what is happening. I'm here today to review Kevin's records and to request a copy of all records."

Dr. Whitford stated, "Well, the record can't be reviewed today, Mrs. Allen. After I gather all of Kevin's records, I'll call you. Also, if you want a copy of the records, I'll have to charge you a fee for each page, and you know how thick Kevin's file is."

Mrs. Allen looked concerned as she said, "I really wanted to see all of Kevin's records today, Dr. Whitford. I don't care what it costs to get a copy of the records; I want a copy."

Dr. Whitford said, "I'll call you as soon as the copies are ready, Mrs. Allen. I need to gather all of the records from the school, and I'll let you know when I receive them."

Mrs. Allen calmed down as she said, "Well, okay. Thank you, Dr. Whitford, I'll look forward to hearing from you."

As she drove home, Mrs. Allen wondered why she couldn't look at her own son's school records on the spot. She didn't realize that she would have to wait for the records to be gathered.

Mrs. Allen patiently waited for Dr. Whitford's telephone call. However, Kevin's behavior began to improve somewhat, and he wasn't being sent home any more due to his disruptive bus and classroom behavior. Mrs. Allen did not forget her request for the records, but she didn't actively pursue contacting Dr. Whitford a second time. Two months after Mrs. Allen's initial request for records, Kevin was suspended from school for five days. Apparently, he was fighting at school. This meant Mrs. Allen had to take a week of her vacation time to stay home with Kevin.

Finally, out of frustration, Mrs. Allen contacted a friend who was also an attorney for advice. The attorney advised Mrs. Allen to obtain Kevin's records immediately so that they could be reviewed. Mrs. Allen again contacted Dr. Whitford to request Kevin's records. Dr. Whitford apologized and said that he had completely forgotten to send the records to Mrs. Allen. He indicated that he would copy and send them by the end of the week. Mrs. Allen finally received Kevin's records two and one-half months after she initially requested them.

Mrs. Allen's attorney reviewed the records and couldn't find any record that Kevin had been suspended from school or the bus. In fact, there were no discipline reports from the bus driver at all. The attorney contacted Dr. Whitford. Dr. Whitford stated that those records were housed in the school building office and that he had forgotten to gather them. Dr. Whitford obtained the school records and sent them to Mrs. Allen's attorney.

In conversing with her attorney, Mrs. Allen indicated that Kevin's BD teacher kept graphs on his behavioral progress. The behavioral graphs had been discussed at Kevin's recent IEP meeting. The attorney stated that the graphs were not in the record. Again the attorney contacted Dr. Whitford. Dr. Whitford stated that the teacher's record had been inadvertently left out of the record. He promptly requested that Kevin's teacher send the record to the attorney. Kevin's teacher, Mrs. Gregory, responded to Dr. Whitford by stating that the behavior graphs were her personal records, and she didn't think she had to send them. The graphs also had many anecdotal comments about Kevin and his behavior. Dr. Whitford told Mrs. Gregory to forward all of her teacher files to the attorney. Reluctantly, Mrs. Gregory complied.

Three months after Mrs. Allen's original request to review and receive a copy of Kevin's records, she finally received all records. Mrs. Allen's attorney filed a request by letter directed to the superintendent for a due process hearing on May 1. The reasons for the request included the following:

1. Failure to place Kevin in an appropriate special education placement.
2. Illegal and inappropriate suspensions from school.
3. Failure to allow the parent to inspect and review all of Kevin's school records in a timely manner.

After the superintendent received the letter, he immediately requested an impartial due process hearing officer. Three weeks later, the hearing was held. The due process hearing required many witnesses, including the building principal, BD teacher, and special education director. All witnesses were questioned about their role in providing records. They were also questioned about suspensions from school and Kevin's progress in the BD classroom. The due process hearing lasted 10 hours.

Two weeks later, Mrs. Allen received the decision from the hearing officer. The hearing decision stated, in part, the following:

1. Kevin shall not be suspended from school more than 10 school days, cumulative. For suspensions up to 10 school days, the school district will afford him all legal rights.
2. The school district did not observe the rights of this child in regard to the request to inspect, copy, and review records. The district will request from the state board of education an in-service workshop for all staff involved in the storage of records on how to store records and how to respond to requests for record review.
3. The school district shall convene an IEP meeting within 10 days of this order to write an appropriate IEP for Kevin. The IEP will address Kevin's aggressive behavior and will include an appropriate behavioral management plan that keeps Kevin in school.

Mrs. Allen was very pleased about the hearing decision. Finally, Kevin would be able to stay in school and receive an appropriate education.

QUESTIONS

Legal Issues to Consider

1. Why was it a problem for the school district to wait two months to send the bulk of Kevin's records to Mrs. Allen?

2. Mrs. Gregory indicated that the behavioral graphs were her personal records, and she didn't have to give them to the parent. Was this true? Why or why not?

3. Was Kevin's "therapy" day at home considered a suspension from school?

4. Was Dr. Whitford correct when he told Mrs. Allen she would be charged a fee for copying Kevin's records? Why or why not?

Other Issues

1. How are records in other areas of society (e.g., credit, banking) maintained and handled with regard to a request to review them?

2. Why is it important to maintain confidentiality and privacy of records?

3. Can you think of situations in which you think records should or should not be shared in a school situation?

<hr>

CASE 9.4

JOHN/WITHHOLDING INFORMATION

Five people gathered around the round table in the conference room to discuss the placement of John, a 15-year-old tenth-grade student. John was identified as behavior disordered and currently was placed in a self-contained BD class at Jefferson High School. The discussion centered around where John would be placed for the next school year. There was some debate among the professionals, not only about his future placement, but also about how much information to share with the receiving high school if John's placement were changed to a less-restrictive environment.

The professionals attending the conference included Ms. Clark, the special education cooperative administrator; Mr. Fox, the cooperative school psychologist; Mr. Darien, the cooperative social worker; Ms. Long, the current BD teacher at Jefferson High School; and Ms. Beach, the BD teacher at Lincoln High School. Ms. Beach was invited to the conference because the special education cooperative included students with disabilities at Lincoln High School, even though it was located in a different school district. Jefferson High School served BD students who needed self-contained placements, and Lincoln High School served BD students who needed resource placements. John's mother, a single parent, had been invited to the conference but did not attend.

Ms. Clark looked at Ms. Long and asked, "Why do you think John is ready to move to a less-restrictive environment at Lincoln High School? We just discussed the fact that he recently threatened to kill another student in your class."

Ms. Long answered, "I really think the threat was an isolated incident. John was very angry that day at the other student, and he just lost control. That degree of anger had not been observed previously in the two years that John has attended this high school. His academic skill level is close to average, and John expresses a desire to graduate from high school. Even though he can become angry, he really has learned to control his anger most of the time. I would like to see John in some general education classes, perhaps industrial arts and art classes."

Ms. Beach sounded skeptical as she said, "I'm not so sure John will succeed at Lincoln High School. The BD students in my program have mild disabilities. They rarely engage in violence. Most of them need encouragement to stay in school and some assistance conforming to rules, such as how to complete homework and how to be accepted by peers. Few of my students have ever been sent to the assistant principal's office for discipline problems."

Ms. Long replied, "That is one reason why I think John might succeed. He does well when he is around appropriate role models. If adults treat John in a fair and matter-of-fact manner, he usually is very responsive. It's when he feels challenged that the anger surfaces."

Ms. Beach said, "That is probably true, and this would be an advantage of my classroom. However, if the assistant principal found out that John threatened to kill another student, I think he would be opposed to John's placement at Lincoln. In fact, he would want me to talk with all of John's teachers to tell them about his disability and past behavior."

Mr. Fox stated, "That just doesn't seem fair. Before John even was given a chance to perform, all of his teachers and the administration would be prejudiced against him."

Mr. Darien asked, "Is there any way we can place John at Lincoln High School on a trial basis and not forward his discipline records? We certainly would make all other records accessible, but we could hold back on the discipline records so that the Lincoln staff wouldn't be prejudiced against him. It's very likely that John would perform well and that the threat was just an isolated incident, as Ms. Long stated."

Ms. Clark answered, "I don't see why not. We don't always forward discipline records when a student transfers from one school in the special education cooperative to another school within the cooperative. As records custodian, I will keep all records in the special education cooperative office but will share only the evaluation and the current IEP."

Ms. Beach agreed, "I am certainly aware of the situation, but I agree, John needs a fresh start in school. I think he may do very well."

Ms. Clark ended the meeting by stating, "Okay, I think we are all in agreement about John's change in placement from BD self-contained at Jefferson High School to BD resource at Lincoln High School. I will notify John's mother of the change, and I think she will be pleased with the change. I will also notify the Lincoln High School office so that they know that John will transfer in the fall."

The group then wrote an IEP for John outlining his special education program at Lincoln High School. All appropriate persons were notified of the change, and Ms. Long talked with John. John agreed to try hard to succeed at the new high school. He also agreed that he would not use violence when he became angry.

During September, John attended school regularly. His schedule included special education classes for English and math and general education classes for woodworking, art, and science. Ms. Beach worked with John in his special education classes and tutored him during his study halls. John seemed to respond to Ms. Beach, and he was beginning to complete work in his classes.

One day in November, John asked to use the restroom during the last 10 minutes of his industrial arts class. The teacher knew that John was a BD student, but because John seemed responsible and had finished his work for the day, he allowed him to leave the room. John did not return to class that day, and the industrial arts teacher reported this to Ms. Beach.

At the end of the school day, a high school senior wanted to use the restroom on the second floor of the school before attending a science club meeting. She screamed and ran from the restroom. Mr. Jackson, the assistant principal, heard the screams and entered the restroom. To his horror, he found a girl lying on the floor crying hysterically. She looked as if she had been beaten around the face, and her clothes were torn. He ran to the next classroom and called the office for help. Five teachers and the principal, Mr. Gore, ran to the restroom. They summoned an ambulance, the police, and the girl's parents.

The girl lying on the floor in the restroom was a 14-year-old freshman. She was taken to the hospital and kept for observation overnight. The police interviewed her and found that she had left study hall that day to use the restroom during the last 15 minutes of the school day. A man was waiting for her in the restroom, and she was beaten and raped. The police interviewed all the teachers and asked for any student with knowledge to come forward. Ms. Beach and the industrial arts teacher talked to the police about John leaving class to use the restroom at about the same time that the girl was raped. The girl who was raped positively identified John as the person who assaulted and raped her. John was immediately arrested and placed in a maximum-security juvenile detention home. He was charged as an adult with assault and rape and ultimately received a lengthy prison sentence.

The high school staff were in shock that something like this could happen at Lincoln High School. The school principal immediately requested all school records on John. To his dismay, he found that John had a history of violent behavior. He was told by the special education cooperative that this information was not routinely shared with a receiving school when a student was transferred to another school within the cooperative. He was also told that persons in attendance at the IEP conference made decisions on where to place students with disabilities and that his BD teacher was in attendance at the conference to place John at Lincoln High School. The principal was furious! If he had known about this violent student, he would never have agreed to his placement at Lincoln High School. He was also very upset that his BD teacher had not informed other teachers and administrators about John and that discipline records were not routinely forwarded to the receiving school by the special education cooperative. If only his teachers had known about this student, they might have been able to prevent this horrible crime!

The board of education for Lincoln High School's district lobbied the state legislature to strengthen the law concerning disclosure of student records for students with disabilities. They also insisted that their local special education cooperative make the building principal aware of all discipline records when a student was transferred within the cooperative.

QUESTIONS

Legal Issues to Consider

1. Did the receiving school have legal access to John's discipline records? Why or why not?

2. Assuming that John's violent behavior was not addressed in his IEP, was his IEP appropriate? Why or why not?

Other Issues

1. Is it morally right to withhold information from general education teachers because, as a special education teacher, you feel it would prejudice the teachers against a particular child? Why or why not?

2. What kind of information should be withheld? What kind of information should be shared?

3. Should the special education teacher and the cooperative be held responsible for creating the circumstances for this crime to occur? Why or why not?

<hr>

CASE 9.5

DEAN/INVASION OF PRIVACY

Dean was labeled behavior disordered and learning disabled in first grade. From the beginning of Dean's school career, he was viewed as different. He displayed inappropriate peer relationships, which usually included extreme teasing and picking on other children, usually girls. Dean was a very bright, verbal child. Most children avoided playing with him because he was viewed as a wimp and a whiner.

Dean lived with his mother, Pam, and her live-in female friend, Donna, who acted as Dean's stepparent. Dean's mother had been divorced from Dean's biological father before Dean was born, and Dean had no contact with him. Pam became involved with Donna when Dean was in third grade. Pam was very honest with Dean about their relationship, and Dean was very accepting of Donna. When Dean was in fourth grade, Donna moved in with Pam and Dean. Both of Dean's parents, Pam and Donna, were very interested in Dean's welfare. They were also very honest with the school staff about their relationship and interest in Dean's education. For example, when Dean's special education teacher arranged an annual review, both Pam and Donna were invited, and both fully participated. They followed through on most suggestions from Dean's teacher to help him improve. One suggestion involved a male role model in Dean's life. Both Pam and Donna readily agreed, and they requested a "Big Brother" for Dean, which helped. During routine reevaluations, both Pam and Donna participated and offered information, both about Dean and their ongoing relationship and its effect on Dean.

Only once in 10 years was Dean upset about his mother's relationship with Donna. When Dean was in sixth grade, Donna moved out of the house because of a conflict with Pam. Dean was very upset about this because he loved Donna. Even when Donna left the home, she continued to see Dean on a regular basis, usually every other Saturday and once during the week. After six months, Pam and Donna reunited, and Donna moved back into the home.

When Dean was in seventh grade, his behavior became more and more bizarre. He began grabbing girls' breasts, and he verbally harassed them. Dean's BD teacher met with Pam and Donna to revise the IEP to include a behavior management plan to monitor Dean and extinguish this inappropriate behavior. Then four seventh-grade girls began to receive prank telephone calls with lewd remarks. The girls were terrified, and the police became involved. The telephone calls were traced to Dean's house. Three times during Dean's seventh grade, bomb threats were called in to the school. Each time, the school was evacuated and searched, but no bomb was found. In addition, four times the fire alarm was falsely pulled.

Each time, the school was evacuated, and the fire department searched the school. All of these incidents were traced to Dean, and he admitted all offenses. The final offense that school year involved an attempted rape of a seventh-grade girl by Dean in the restroom. Dean was suspended from school for 10 days and expelled for the remainder of the school year. His expulsion began December 1 and the school district did not provide any educational services.

It was suggested by the special education administrator that Dean be reevaluated during his expulsion from school. Pam and Donna agreed and signed a consent for evaluation. All necessary components were gathered. Pam and Donna met with the school social worker for a social history update. Dean's vision and hearing were screened. The BD teacher completed an update on Dean's school progress, and the school psychologist evaluated Dean.

A conference was held in January after the evaluation was completed. Pam and Donna attended the meeting, along with all school staff members who had gathered information for the evaluation. In addition, Ms. King, special education administrator, and Mr. Locket, building principal, attended. Ms. King led the conference. All participants agreed that Dean's behavior had progressively deteriorated and that much of his inappropriate behavior centered on violence of a sexual nature directed toward girls. Pam and Donna discussed their relationship and any possible effect it might have on Dean's behavior. The school psychologist summarized his testing by stating that Dean was a very bright, verbal child who seemed fixated on girls. All participants agreed that the only significant change in Dean's life was Donna leaving the home and eventually returning. The school staff agreed that Dean's behavior required a more intense therapeutic environment than the school district could provide. It was recommended that Dean attend a residential treatment facility. Although sad and upset, Pam and Donna agreed to the placement. At the conclusion of the conference, Pam and Donna were given copies of the summary of the meeting and Dean's new IEP.

When Pam and Donna got home, they again reviewed the written meeting summary and new IEP. Pam noted that on the first page of the meeting summary, it was stated that Dean's mother was a lesbian and that Donna was her live-in friend. Although this was true and the school had always been aware of the relationship, Pam was offended that this information was written in the meeting summary. She felt that it violated Dean's privacy and might be misleading to anyone reading the records. Donna agreed and suggested that Pam contact Ms. King, the special education administrator.

The next day, Pam made an appointment to see Ms. King. She explained that she wanted the remarks regarding her lifestyle removed from the record. Ms. King listened intently, taking notes. Ms. King remarked, "Pam, we have freely discussed your lifestyle at this meeting and I think it is appropriate to include this information in the meeting summary. In fact, over the years of working with you, we have always freely discussed your lifestyle and its possible effect on Dean."

Pam stated, "That may be, Ms. King, but it is not appropriate to write this in a report about Dean. If someone other than staff from this school district read this information, it might be misleading. It also invades Dean's privacy."

Ms. King thought for a moment, then said, "Pam, my decision is to keep the information in Dean's record because I feel it is relevant." Two days later, Pam received a letter from Ms. King stating that the information would remain in Dean's school record, but that Pam had the right to request a records hearing to amend the record.

Pam decided to request a records hearing to try to remove the information from the meeting summary. Pam wrote a letter to Ms. King requesting the hearing. Ms. King forwarded the letter to the school district's assistant superintendent, who acted as the records hearing officer. Within 10 days, a hearing was arranged. The hearing officer conducted the records hearing by asking Pam to state her objections to the records, which she easily conveyed. She stated that the information, although accurate, was an invasion of Dean's privacy and the privacy of his family. It was not necessary to share private information about Pam's lifestyle in written format within the meeting summary. The information, when reviewed by Dean's new school, might be misleading. Pam requested that any information concerning her lifestyle be removed from the record. Ms. King was then asked to state why the information should remain in the record. She stated that the information had been freely offered by the parent and that it was discussed at the meeting. She said the information might be relevant to Dean's new school and should be included in the record. The hearing officer listened intently and concluded the hearing by stating that a decision would be made within the next two weeks, and both parties would be informed in writing of the decision.

About 10 days later, Pam received a letter from the hearing officer. The letter stated that he agreed that the information contained in the hearing summary about Pam's lifestyle was an invasion of Dean's privacy and that it might be misleading. The information would be immediately removed from Dean's school record. Pam and Donna were very relieved and pleased that they prevailed in the hearing. Dean was placed in the residential treatment center in August of the same year.

QUESTIONS

Legal Issues to Consider

1. Was it necessary for Pam to sign consent for a reevaluation? Why or why not?

2. Was it legal for the school district to expel Dean, assuming his behavior was found to be related to his disability? How do you know?

3. Under what conditions did Pam have the right to a records hearing?

4. Was the records hearing conducted appropriately? Why or why not?

Other Issues

1. Do you think information about Pam's lifestyle is relevant in this case? Why or why not?

2. At what point should private family information be made part of the educational record of a child?

CASE 9.6

CARLOS/FALSIFYING DOCUMENTS

Mary was a third-year special education teacher at White County High School. The high school was located in a rural area about 15 miles from any large town. The high school itself sat in the middle of corn fields and had approximately 600 students in ninth through twelfth grades. The special education population was 58 students, and it included students with learning disabilities and behavior disorders. Some of the students with BD were transported from the town of Southville, 10 miles to the east. Southville had its own high school, but it had an agreement with the White County School District to transport its BD students to White County High School. In return, Southville High School would serve all mild mentally impaired students. In the past, this was the only way to properly serve these populations appropriately because each school could operate one particular program.

At White County High School, LD and BD students were served in a cross-categorical setting, with four special education teachers. Mary taught special education sections in English and math.

One day, Mr. Bing, the regional special education administrator, came by Mary's room. He said, "Mary, do you have Carlos Rodriguez in your English and math classes?"

Mary answered, "Yes, I do, Mr. Bing. In fact, Carlos has been in my English class for the past three years. This is the first year he has been assigned to my math class."

Mr. Bing continued, "Just yesterday I received a request from Carlos' mother asking for an impartial due process hearing. She thinks he shouldn't be labeled behavior disordered and he should be transferred back to his home school district, Southville. She thinks he has a severe learning disability and could be appropriately served there."

Mary said, "I agree that Carlos has a severe learning disability. He's in tenth grade, and he can't read his own name. I've never seen any child who seems completely unable to read the printed word. However, Carlos also demonstrates behavior problems, perhaps due to his inability to read. He has difficulty getting along with his peers and, if challenged by school staff, will explode in anger."

Mr. Bing said, "The hearing will be scheduled within the next month. I would like for you to testify at the hearing. I will represent the school district, and I will meet with you before the hearing to prepare for the questioning."

Mary looked surprised as she said, "I've never testified at a due process hearing before, but I'll be happy to help in any way possible."

Mr. Bing said, "Thanks, I think your testimony will be helpful. I'll call you when the hearing is arranged."

Carlos was a difficult student, but Mary rarely had problems with him in class, probably because she did not verbally challenge him. In fact, Carlos was eager to please Mary and felt safe in her class. Carlos and Mary had talked on occasion about Carlos' inability to read. Mary offered to arrange an individual tutorial program in reading for Carlos, but to date, Carlos had declined to participate. In English class, Carlos' assignments were adapted, and most work was completed orally or with a peer helper. Carlos could barely read his name and could not write the entire alphabet. When asked to write his name and address, he had to copy from an identification card he carried in his wallet. Carlos could not go into a fast food restaurant to order food because he could not read the menu. He was extremely sensitive about his inability to read. When in a situation in which he was required to read something, he usually made jokes or became loud and aggressive, probably to cover for his inability to read. Carlos had average ability verbally, and one would not suspect his severe reading disability. He could complete simple math problems in his head and on paper, but if reading were required, he needed assistance. Overall, the goal was for Carlos to gain life skills and to be able to hold a job, take care of his personal needs, and live independently.

Two weeks later, Mary received notice that the hearing had been scheduled. Mr. Bing met with Mary and one other witness—the work–study teacher—to prepare them for questioning. They rehearsed questions and discussed the strategy that would be used to demonstrate that Carlos' current program was appropriate.

Two days before the hearing, Mary received a telephone call from Mr. Bing concerning the hearing.

Mr. Bing said, "Mary, I've just discovered that there is no IEP for Carlos for the current school year. I have IEPs for the previous 10 years, but this one is missing. Do you know if one was written last spring?"

Mary answered, "I think one was written, but I haven't seen it."

Mr. Bing stated anxiously, "The hearing is two days away. We will lose this hearing if we don't have a current IEP. I would like for you to write one today. Would you be willing to do this?"

Mary hesitated, then said, "I guess I could write it for you. We have an in-service meeting this afternoon. Instead of attending the meeting, I can write the IEP."

Mr. Bing said, "Thank you. I'll tell your principal to excuse you from the meeting. I'll pick up the IEP around 3:00 P.M. Is that okay?"

Mary answered, "I think I can finish it by then."

That afternoon, Mary gathered blank IEP forms and began constructing an IEP for Carlos. She wrote the amount of time in special education to match Carlos' schedule and created goals and objectives. The goals and objectives centered around life-skills development and functional reading skills. Mary left the date of the IEP blank and placed only her name on the line for participants. At exactly 3:00 P.M., Mr. Bing came into Mary's room and got the IEP. He promptly made copies and sent one to Carlos' attorney in overnight mail.

Two days later, the due process hearing was held. An attorney represented Carlos and his mother. For an expert witness, the attorney had arranged for an independent evaluation by a professor at the local university. Mr. Bing represented the school district. His witnesses included Mary, as Carlos' English and math teacher, and Mr. Rome, Carlos' work–study teacher. The school superintendent sat silently and listened to the proceedings. The hearing officer conducted the hearing in a formal manner, and a court reporter recorded the proceedings. Mr. Bing began with an opening statement, and then Carlos' attorney gave an opening statement. School witnesses were brought to the front of the room one at a time and questioned, first by Mr. Bing, then by Carlos' attorney, then again by Mr. Bing. Part of the testimony and questioning included the following:

> Mr. Bing asked Mary, "Mary, would you please state your name and certification to teach in special education?"
>
> Mary answered, "My name is Mary Smith. I am certified to teach learning disabilities and behavior disorders from kindergarten through twelfth grade. I have a master's degree in remedial reading and also am certified to teach elementary education. I have taught five years, with the past three years at White County High School."
>
> Mr. Bing continued, "Please tell us about Carlos' IEP and his involvement in your classes. You do have Carlos for English and math classes?"
>
> "Yes, I do. Carlos has been in my English class for the past three years and has been in my math class this year. Carlos' IEP focuses on basic living skills and functional reading. He is unable to read anything. In fact, he cannot write the alphabet. Most of his instruction

is adapted to allow for oral answers, and he receives individual assistance when reading is required. Because he is 16 years old, I try to build on his verbal strengths. Carlos has had some behavior difficulties, mostly outside of the classroom. He has been involved in several fights with other students resulting in suspension from school. In class, he tries hard and does not have significant behavior problems."

Carlos' attorney then questioned Mary by asking, "I just received this IEP yesterday, and it does not have a date of when it was written. First of all, I want the record to reflect the lateness of receipt of the IEP document. Second, Mary, when was this IEP written?"

Mary said, "It was written for this school year."

The attorney asked, "Why is there no date on the IEP?"

Mary again said, "I don't know. It was written for this school year."

The attorney asked, "Why didn't I receive a copy of this IEP earlier?"

Uncomfortable, Mary said, "I don't know. It isn't my responsibility to mail out copies of IEPs. The secretary in the special education office mails them to parents. I don't know why you didn't receive the IEP."

The questioning continued with Mary and ended after about one and one-half hours. All witnesses were questioned, and the hearing was brought to a conclusion at the end of the day. Mr. Bing felt that the hearing went very well, and he thanked Mary and Mr. Rome for their participation in the hearing.

On the way home, Mary felt both good and bad. She had answered tough questions in a confident and straightforward manner, and this made her feel great. However, she was uncomfortable about the questions concerning Carlos' IEP. She did not lie when asked when the IEP was written, but she did not tell the whole truth, either.

Two weeks later, Mr. Bing stopped by Mary's classroom. He told her the school district had prevailed in Carlos' due process hearing. The hearing officer had agreed that Carlos had a behavior disorder and learning disability. He stated that Carlos' placement at White County High School was appropriate and met his special needs. He stated that Carlos' home school district could not provide an appropriate program for Carlos given his behavior disorder. Mr. Bing was very upbeat and again thanked Mary for her participation in the hearing. He said without her testimony the school district would not have prevailed.

QUESTIONS

Legal Issues to Consider

1. Was it legal for Mary to create an IEP document in the manner requested by Mr. Bing? Why or why not?

2. Was it legal for Mr. Bing to forward a document to the parent's attorney two days before a due process hearing?

3. Was Carlos' placement appropriate? Why or why not?

Other Issues

1. Should you, as a teacher, do something you know is improper if requested by your superior? How should you handle a situation like the one in this case?

2. If you were a probationary or first-year teacher, would you change your answer?

3. If the IEP had not been not created before the due process hearing, would the outcome of this hearing have changed? Why or why not?

CHAPTER TEN

STUDENT MISCONDUCT

CASE 10.1   DONNIE/BRINGING A GUN

CASE 10.2   ANDY/IMPULSIVE BEHAVIOR

CASE 10.3   KATIE/MARIJUANA CIGARETTE

CASE 10.4   MIKE/VIOLENT THREATS

CASE 10.5   TIM/TEACHER AND PARENT REBELLION

CASE 10.6   MARIO/EXPULSION PROCEEDING

CASE 10.1

DONNIE/BRINGING A GUN

Mr. Cook, assistant principal for Whitford High School, was making his usual rounds during lunch in September. As he walked down a hallway, many students were making their way to the cafeteria for lunch. Students were placing books in lockers, standing around in groups talking and laughing, and walking in the crowded hallway. As he approached a group of lockers at the end of the corridor, he noticed Donnie Sommers opening his locker. When Donnie saw Mr. Cook, he had a scared look on his face and quickly threw something in his locker. Donnie then stood in front of the locker, apparently hiding something. Mr. Cook thought that there was something suspicious and stopped. He said, "Hi, Donnie, I haven't seen you lately. How are you?"

Donnie stared at the floor with his hair covering his eyes and said in an angry tone, "Man, just leave me alone, I don't want to talk to you. Get out of here."

Mr. Cook responded, "Wait a minute, Donnie. I was just walking down the hall. By the way, what do you have in that locker that you don't want me to see?"

"Just get out of here or I'll call the cops. I didn't do nothing wrong."

At this point, Mr. Cook noticed a glint of metal in the bottom of the locker. He said, "Donnie, what is that?"

Donnie moved away from the locker, and it was apparent that he had thrown a gun into his locker. Mr. Cook quickly picked up the gun and said, "Come with me, Donnie."

Donnie followed Mr. Cook to the office, where the police and his mother were called. Mr. Cook talked to Donnie about the gun. Apparently, some older boys were threatening

Donnie. To protect himself, he had brought the gun, which he had taken from his uncle. Donnie stated that the gun was unloaded and that he intended to scare the other boys, not hurt them.

The police and Donnie's mother arrived at about the same time. Mr. Cook had already informed Mr. Dixon, the principal, and both administrators talked to Mrs. Sommers first. They presented her with a letter that stated that Donnie would be suspended from school for 10 days, then placed in an interim alternative educational setting for 45 days. They asked Mrs. Sommers to sign a consent form for district personnel to conduct a functional behavioral assessment. They also asked Mrs. Sommers to come back to the school in a week to discuss Donnie's special education placement and the evaluation. Mrs. Sommers was very upset, but she agreed. The police completed a report after talking with both Donnie and Mr. Cook. They then arrested Donnie. Donnie left with the police, and Mrs. Sommers followed them to the police station.

The next week, an IEP meeting was held. Participants included Mr. Cook; Mrs. Sommers; Mr. Dixon; Dr. Miller, special education administrator; and Ms. Johnson, Donnie's special education teacher.

Dr. Miller began the meeting by stating, "We are here today to review Donnie's IEP and placement in light of the incident of bringing a gun to school. We will also be making a determination of whether Donnie's behavior of bringing a gun to school is related to his disability. In making this judgement, we will not only consider Donnie's IEP, but also his most-recent evaluation, including the functional behavioral evaluation and observations of him in school. We will determine an appropriate placement for Donnie in an alternative setting for 45 days. In addition, we will carefully discuss Donnie's behavior and develop a behavior management plan. This is a very serious situation involving the safety of all students in this school."

Ms. Johnson continued, "As you know, Donnie is labeled behavior disordered. He was placed in a self-contained setting in fifth grade. This is his first year at the high school. His most-recent evaluation, including the functional behavioral evaluation, indicates that Donnie is a bright child and very capable academically. He has on several occasions been involved in fights at school. He has also threatened other students. Most of this behavior occurs in unstructured situations such as the cafeteria. In the classroom, Donnie is mostly cooperative, although at times he argues with other students. Donnie seems to have a very poor ability to relate to his peer group. He doesn't seem to know how to make friends and will often argue and fight to resolve differences."

Dr. Miller asked, "Mrs. Sommers, I know you have been very supportive of Donnie and his education. Would you like to tell us your observations?"

Mrs. Sommers said, "I'm so angry at Donnie for doing such a stupid thing. He knows how dangerous guns can be. I've noticed that Donnie has been more distant with me since last year sometime. Before, we could at least talk. Now, he barely speaks to me. He sits in his room and watches TV. When I say something to him, he gets really angry. I think he needs help."

The team continued to discuss Donnie's IEP, placement, and behavior. They decided that Donnie would be placed in the school district's alternative school for 45 days after he served the 10-day suspension. The team also developed a very strict behavior management plan that included frequent rewards and consequences. Donnie was also to be monitored at all times so he would have no unstructured time. The team determined that the behavior of bringing a gun to school was a manifestation of Donnie's disability. Donnie's IEP was revised, and it was determined that another IEP meeting would be held after one month to consider future placement. Mrs. Sommers, although upset and discouraged, agreed to the placement change.

Because of this incident, the local newspaper carried a series of stories on school violence, and many parents expressed concern about guns in school and school safety in general. The board of education employed an off-duty policeman to patrol the hallways during school hours. Students, parents, and community members were very concerned. Most persons expressed anger and disbelief that the student involved in bringing the gun to school was still receiving an education, even in another setting. Many people wrote letters to the editor of the local newspaper expressing concern.

After a month, another IEP meeting was held. The participants were the same, with the addition of Ms. White, Donnie's new teacher at the alternative school.

Dr. Miller began the meeting by stating, "At our last meeting, we determined that Donnie would attend the school district's alternative school for 45 days. We also determined that his behavior of bringing a gun to school was related to his disability. We revised his IEP to include a behavior management plan. Today, we will evaluate Donnie's IEP and placement and determine future placement."

Mr. Dixon, who generally listened in meetings like this, stated, "I can say that bringing a gun to school has disrupted the education of many students and alarmed many parents and community members. Although I understand that this student has special education needs, I will not agree to him returning to this high school under any circumstances."

Dr. Miller said, "We understand your position, Mr. Dixon, and we will consider your input. The decision here will be made based on the needs of this student."

Ms. White, the alternative-school teacher, said, "I've only known Donnie for about a month, but I can say that his placement at the alternative school seems to be helping. At first, Donnie was angry about being monitored all the time, but in time, I think he began to feel safe and secure. He has been cooperating for the most part, and he has not been involved in any fights. It is apparent, however, that Donnie needs direct instruction and help in learning to control his anger and get along with other students. He still argues and threatens others. Donnie also seems to be developing a positive relationship with his therapist, who works with him on a daily basis."

Mrs. Sommers stated, "I feel really bad about what has happened to Donnie. I also feel that he really needed help. He does seem happier and is willing to go to school every day. I only hope he gets probation when his case goes before the judge."

After further input, Dr. Miller said, "It seems that Donnie is beginning to progress in the alternative school. I propose that we make a change in placement so that he can continue there beyond the 45 days."

Mrs. Sommers asked, "Does that mean he can't ever go to the regular high school?"

Dr. Miller answered, "We will continue to review Donnie's IEP every year to monitor his progress. If, at some time, we think he can succeed at the regular high school, he will be placed there."

Mr. Dixon responded, "I agree to placing Donnie at the alternative school, but I will not ever agree to his return to the regular high school."

Dr. Miller concluded the meeting by stating, "We have consensus on changing Donnie's placement to the alternative school. Mrs. Sommers, you may wish to share this information with the judge when Donnie goes to court. Perhaps it might help."

Donnie's IEP was changed, and he continued placement at the alternative school. He never returned to the regular high school, and he graduated after completion of high school at the alternative school.

QUESTIONS

Legal Issues to Consider

1. On what legal basis was the IEP team able to place the child in an alternative placement?

2. What would have occurred if the parent had not agreed with the alternative placement?

3. Could this student have been expelled from school (i.e., removed from school for a lengthy period of time)?

Other Issues

1. Why does there seem to be an increase in violence in schools?

2. Is it fair to have two standards of behavior for students—one for students with disabilities and one for general education students? Why or why not?

3. Should all students with disabilities continue to receive an education, no matter what behavior they display? Why or why not?

4. Should there be a point at which a student with a disability is taken out of school permanently for displaying dangerous behavior? What type of behaviors would cross that threshold?

CASE 10.2

ANDY/IMPULSIVE BEHAVIOR

Mrs. Sherwood angrily stormed into the principal's office at noon. "I need to see Mr. Ames right now!" she barked at the secretary.

"Go right in, Mrs. Sherwood," said the secretary.

Mrs. Sherwood stomped into the principal's office, where Mr. Ames was seated behind his desk. He motioned for her to sit in a chair opposite his desk. She stood and glared at Mr. Ames.

"I don't know where to begin. I am so upset! I was just walking down the hallway to my sixth-hour class. The hallway was crowded with students. Out of nowhere, a special education student came flying down the hall. He ran into me as hard as he could, practically knocking me over! My books and papers scattered. I yelled at him to stop, and he looked at me and cursed. Then he continued running down the hall. I have *never* been hit by a student in my 30 years as a teacher here. I am shocked and upset that this could happen. I have never been a big supporter of special education, but this makes me think that these students should not be in this building. You can't let this student get away with hitting a teacher! This district has a strict policy on violence. Why, if one student had done that to another student, he would at least be suspended! Certainly, because a teacher was involved, serious consequences should be applied."

"The first thing we need to find out is who the student is, Mrs. Sherwood," said Mr. Ames.

"The students who helped me pick up my books said the student is Andy Meng, a student in Mrs. Gilford's special education class. They said he's a seventh-grader."

"I will immediately call the student to my office, Mrs. Sherwood. I can assure you I will get to the bottom of this. Would you write a short summary for me detailing what happened?"

"I will have it to you by 3:30 today, Mr. Ames."

Mrs. Sherwood left the office, and Mr. Ames checked his computer's discipline file to see if Andy Meng had any discipline record. There was no record. He then walked to Mrs. Gilford's classroom.

Mr. Ames stood at the doorway and said, "Mrs. Gilford, may I see you for a minute?"

Mrs. Gilford came out into the hallway after directing the teaching assistant to continue the lesson.

Mr. Ames continued, "Mrs. Gilford, do you have a student named Andy Meng in your class?"

Mrs. Gilford looked surprised and said, "Why, yes, I do. In fact, he just came back from lunch. Do you need to see him? What happened?"

Mr. Ames explained, "Mrs. Sherwood just came to my office and said that Andy hit her, knocking her books on the floor, as she was walking down the hall. Apparently, he was running down the hallway. When she confronted him, he cursed at her and kept running."

"Wow, I've never had any trouble with Andy before," said Mrs. Gilford.

"Well, I need to see him now," said Mr. Ames, "and you may as well come with me, Mrs. Gilford, because Andy's a special education student."

Andy was escorted to the office by Mr. Ames and Mrs. Gilford. When confronted with the situation as described by Mrs. Sherwood, Andy simply sat quietly.

"Well, Andy, what do you have to say? Did you hit Mrs. Sherwood?" asked Mr. Ames.

"I...I was just running to stay away from those bigger guys. They were teasing me and said that I acted like a baby. I...I guess I did run into her."

"Andy, did you curse at her?" asked Mrs. Gilford.

"Well, I don't know. I think I might have said something. I didn't know she was a teacher," he quietly said.

"Andy, she told you to stop, and you kept running. I think you know better than that," said Mrs. Gilford.

Mr. Ames said, "We have no choice but to suspend you from school for 10 days, Andy. I will also ask for an expulsion hearing, as this involved hitting a teacher. We'll call your mother to come and pick you up from school now."

Andy's mother came to school within an hour. Mr. Ames and Mrs. Gilford discussed the incident with her, and she was upset and shocked that Andy would hit a teacher. Mrs. Gilford requested consent from Andy's mother to conduct a functional behavioral assessment. She signed the form, then took Andy home.

Mr. Ames informed the superintendent of the incident and contacted Mr. Phillips, the special education administrator. Mr. Phillips suggested that an IEP meeting would need to be arranged to discuss the relation of the behavior and Andy's disability.

"Mr. Phillips, related or not, I cannot allow teachers in my school to get hit just walking down the hall. It will be my recommendation that Andy be expelled. I have to support my teacher," said Mr. Ames.

The next week, an IEP meeting was scheduled to discuss the incident. The participants included Mrs. Sherwood, Mr. Ames, Mr. Phillips, Mrs. Gilford, Mrs. Meng, and Mr. Charles, the school psychologist. The discussion was long, and tempers flared. The school psychologist reviewed the most recent evaluation of Andy, including the results of the functional behavioral evaluation. Andy was labeled mildly mentally handicapped, with an IQ of 65. He had been known to be impulsive and was very social with his peers. Sometimes, Andy behaved in an immature manner, and he was known as a pest, although most students liked him. He would do almost anything to please his peers and the adults around him. He had been in a self-contained special education classroom since preschool.

Mr. Phillips asked, "Mr. Charles, do you think that Andy understood what he did was wrong?"

Mr. Charles answered, "Based on the most recent evaluation, I don't think Andy always knows right from wrong, due to his limited intellectual capacity."

Mr. Phillips continued, "Do you think Andy could have controlled this behavior?"

Mr. Charles answered, "Andy is very impulsive and is a follower. I don't think he could have controlled this behavior."

Mrs. Sherwood cut in, "Wait a minute. Are you saying that, as a teacher, I should excuse a student hitting me?"

Mr. Phillips said, "No, Mrs. Sherwood, but we must look at the individual involved and the circumstances."

Mrs. Gilford supported Mr. Charles' assessment with her classroom observations. Andy was basically a compliant child, but he was impulsive. He functioned far below average in basic academic skills. Andy's adaptive behavior skills were also below average.

Mrs. Sherwood stated, "We cannot allow this child back into this school. What kind of example would that set for other students? I think he should be expelled."

Mrs. Meng, who had been quiet up to this point, said, "I do not think Andy should be expelled. He made a mistake and has been suspended for 10 days. That is enough. He needs to return to school."

After a lengthy discussion, it was determined by consensus that Andy's disability was directly related to the behavior in the hallway. Mrs. Sherwood did not agree with the decision, and Mr. Ames reluctantly agreed with the consensus.

The IEP team then revised Andy's IEP to include a behavior management plan. The plan involved removing Andy from the hallway during lunch and providing an escort to and from the cafeteria when students were not in the hallway. Overall, Andy would spend almost all of his school day within the classroom. After a period of time, Andy would gradually be integrated back into the unstructured times during the school day. Mrs. Meng agreed with the plan.

Mrs. Sherwood did not agree with the decision or plan. She discussed her situation with the teacher's union representative and was told she had no further recourse.

QUESTIONS

Legal Issues to Consider

1. According to IDEA and the information given, did the IEP team make an appropriate manifestation-determination decision? Why or why not?

2. Could the school district have expelled the student? Why or why not?

3. Why couldn't the school district place the child in an interim alternative educational setting for 45 days?

Other Issues

1. Is it appropriate for a child in special education to hit a teacher and return to school after a 10-day suspension?

2. If the student had not been labeled special education, what would have occurred?

3. Why do we have dual standards in disciplining students in special education and general education?

■■■■■■■ CASE 10.3 ■■■■■■■

KATIE/MARIJUANA CIGARETTE

Mrs. Shea got ready to go to school in the morning on Wednesday, November 18. She had cried for two days. Then she had become angry, especially at her daughter, Katie, who was a tenth-grade student at the high school where she was a counselor. She felt guilty about yelling at Katie, but it was Katie's poor choice that had placed them in this terrible situation now. At this time, Mrs. Shea felt despair and even embarrassment.

Mrs. Shea had been an excellent school counselor at the high school for 20 years. She had counseled many children and families about drugs. She was very vocal in her opposition of the strict zero-tolerance policy the school district had toward drugs at school. She felt that students needed therapeutic intervention, not expulsion, when drugs were involved at school.

Mrs. Shea would never in her wildest dreams have thought that her only daughter would be caught with marijuana at school. Katie was such a well-behaved child. Even though she had been identified as learning disabled, she had always had friends and was even popular with other students at school. Her friends were not known drug users. Katie only attended one special education class in math, and no one thought anything of her inclusion in the special education program. Katie had never been in trouble at school. Reports at IEP meetings always indicated that Katie was a well-adjusted, well-liked, and responsible student. She even talked about attending the local community college after graduation.

Now Mrs. Shea was faced with the very real prospect that Katie would be expelled from school. The school district had about 20 cases a year in which students were caught with drugs at school. Without exception, the students were expelled from school for one year. How could Mrs. Shea face this IEP meeting today? The outcome would be an indication of what would happen to Katie. As a parent, she felt angry, yet protective of her daughter.

Mrs. Shea walked into the IEP meeting with Katie at 8:15 that morning. Other participants included Mrs. Jenkins, special education administrator; Mrs. Quinn, high school principal; Mr. Gleason, Katie's special education teacher; and Mr. Thornton, school psychologist. Mrs. Jenkins began the meeting by introducing everyone, even though Mrs. Shea knew all of the participants.

"Mrs. Shea and Katie, the reason we are here today is to discuss Katie's behavior of bringing marijuana to school and to determine if the behavior is related to Katie's disability. We will begin by reviewing the behavior incident."

The high school principal, Mrs. Quinn, reviewed the incident. Apparently, a teacher overheard Katie talking to a friend at her locker about having marijuana in her pocket. The teacher asked Katie to empty her pockets, and one marijuana cigarette was in her pocket. Katie was then taken to the principal's office. The police were contacted, Katie's mother was called, and Katie was suspended for 10 school days. Katie told the principal that someone gave her the marijuana and told her to give it to another student. She denied using marijuana.

Mrs. Quinn concluded by saying, "I have to say that Katie has never received a referral to my office for discipline reasons. In fact, she has always been a polite and considerate student."

Mr. Thornton then reviewed Katie's most recent evaluation. "Katie is a bright student, as we know. She has historically had difficulty with math. She was identified as learning disabled with a disability in math in fifth grade. Since that time, she has received assistance from the special education teacher in math."

Mr. Gleason continued, "Katie has done well in the high school setting. She has earned all credits toward graduation. Most of her grades have been Cs, with an occasional B. In my math class, Katie struggles but always tries hard. She completes all assignments and asks questions when she doesn't understand. I have never had a behavior problem with Katie in class."

Mrs. Jenkins asked, "Do you think that Katie understood that having marijuana at school was against school policy?"

Everyone sat silently. After a minute, Mr. Thornton said, "Based on the evaluation, it appears that Katie has the ability to understand what is right and wrong."

The other team members nodded.

Mrs. Jenkins then asked, "Do you think that Katie could control her behavior?"

Again, the team was silent. Finally, Mr. Gleason said, "Katie seems able to control her behavior in school because she has never had a behavior problem before."

Mrs. Jenkins said, "Then we have consensus that Katie's disability is not related to her behavior of bringing marijuana to school?"

No one said anything. Finally, they nodded in agreement.

Mrs. Jenkins then turned to Mrs. Shea and said, "It appears that the team agrees that Katie understood that her behavior was wrong and that she has the ability to control her behavior. The team doesn't think her behavior is related in any way to her disability. Do you have anything to add?"

Mrs. Shea sighed, "I have known everyone in this room for 20 years, and I know you understand how difficult this is for me. Of course Katie understands right from wrong and can control her behavior. She made a poor choice and a terrible mistake one time. Is that a reason to move to expel her from school? Katie has agreed to attend counseling with me on a weekly basis so that we can get to the bottom of how this could happen. I can assure you that this will never happen again."

Mrs. Jenkins said, "Mrs. Shea, it is beyond the scope of this meeting to determine what will happen to Katie. At this time, our determination will be forwarded to the superintendent. That determination is that Katie's behavior is not related to her disability and that the district can discipline Katie as it would any other student. The superintendent will arrange for an expulsion hearing. The results of both this meeting and the expulsion hearing will be given to the board of education, which will make a final decision on expulsion. However, as you know, the school policy is very strict regarding drugs at school."

As they left the meeting, both Katie and Mrs. Shea knew what would happen. On the way home Katie turned to Mrs. Shea with tears in her eyes and said, "I'm really sorry, Mom."

As she predicted, the expulsion hearing recommended that Katie be expelled for having drugs at school, as the school policy stated. Two days later, the board of education, in closed session at a regular meeting, discussed the situation.

At the meeting, the board members were divided. Three members knew Mrs. Shea personally. They said that it wasn't right to expel Katie because she had never been in any trouble before and she would be attending counseling sessions with her mother. Three other members thought the opposite. They said it wasn't fair to have a strict policy and not use it consistently. Yes, they felt sorry for the family, but if they were soft this time, why shouldn't they be next time? Anyway, they felt it was important to send a strong message to the student body and the community that drugs were not acceptable under any circumstances. The seventh member listened to both sides and finally agreed that Katie, like any other student, should be expelled.

Mrs. Shea was contacted immediately after the meeting. She was told that Katie would be expelled from school for one year. She was also told that it was not the school district's responsibility to provide any education during that time. Katie would be encouraged to reenroll in school in one year.

QUESTIONS

Legal Issues to Consider

1. What other action could the school district have taken regarding the student's placement after the suspension?

2. How closely did the school district follow IDEA procedures in regard to the manifestation determination at the IEP meeting held after the incident?

3. Was it proper to expel the student with no education? Why or why not?

Other Issues

1. Should different consequences be applied to different situations in the case of drugs at school? In other words, should Katie be treated in the same manner as a gang member who was labeled BD and had a history of behavior difficulties? Why or why not?

2. What kinds of situations would warrant a deviation from the strict drug policy?

CASE 10.4

MIKE/VIOLENT THREATS

Seven persons sat around the crowded conference table in the office adjacent to the principal's office. The room was warm, and the tension was great. Mrs. Morris, Mike's mother, sat at one end of the table. She looked angry as she glanced around the room and at the floor. Next to Mrs. Morris sat Mike. Mike, a biracial 17-year-old boy, sat stretched out in his seat staring at the table. Other members of the team sat around the table with papers and folders in front of them.

Mrs. Miller, special education administrator, began the meeting by saying, "We are here today to discuss a serious behavior incident involving Mike and one of his special education teachers, Mrs. Steinberg. Before we begin, let's start by introducing ourselves."

All staff members introduced themselves to the parent. Mrs. Morris quietly acknowledged each person. Staff members included Mr. Peterson, high school principal; Mrs. Steinberg, Mike's special education English teacher; Mrs. Christenson, school psychologist; Mrs. Bond, special education teacher from a local, private, day treatment program; and Mrs. Miller. As participants spoke, Mike didn't make eye contact with anyone.

Mrs. Miller continued in a businesslike manner, "Our purposes today are to discuss the behavior incident so that we clearly understand what happened, to review the most-recent evaluation of Mike, to review his IEP, and to determine if Mike's behavior is a manifestation of his disability. Last, we will discuss any needed changes in his IEP."

Mrs. Morris blurted out loudly in an angry voice, "I will not allow you to expel Mike. You have always been out to get him ever since he came back to this high school from that special school. And another thing, Mike will *not* go back to that special school."

Mrs. Miller calmly continued, "Thank you for expressing your feelings, Mrs. Morris. We will continue by reviewing the recent behavior incident."

Mrs. Steinberg stated, "I can describe what happened. Last week, in English class, Mike came in late. I asked him why he was late, and he cursed. I told him I would have to mark him tardy. Then he got up and came toward me. He looked very angry. He looked right at me and said, 'I ought to kill you. In fact, you better watch yourself. One way or another, I'm going to get you. You'll be sorry.' I have never had a problem with Mike in class before. The way he looked at me was scary. Other students were in the room. I backed off, and Mike sat down. Another student went to the office to get the assistant principal. When he arrived, Mike was taken to the office."

Mr. Peterson stated, "This was a serious incident. We do not take threats to harm someone lightly. Mike was immediately suspended. His mother came to pick him up from school, and the police were notified. Mike is no longer on probation, so we could not notify his probation officer."

Mrs. Morris angrily said to Mrs. Miller, "What they *didn't* tell you is that Mike didn't mean what he said. Mike always threatens, but he is never serious. If you kick everyone out in this school for threatening someone, you won't have many students left. Also, I had to leave work that day to pick Mike up here, and if that happens again, I'll get fired."

Mr. Peterson responded, "We have no way of knowing if a threat to harm someone is real or not. However, we make the assumption that if a threat is made, the student may act on the threat, and we must protect the staff member."

Mrs. Miller asked, "Mike, do you have anything to add?"

Mike shook his head.

Mrs. Miller said, "We now will review Mike's recent evaluation."

Mrs. Christenson stated, "Mike was reevaluated during the past school year. His school history indicates that he was originally eligible for behavior disorders services in the third grade. Apparently, his behavior deteriorated in seventh grade. The record states that Mike was stealing and was violent toward other children and staff members. In eighth grade, Mike was placed in a private, day treatment school, The Education Therapy Center. He attended that school until last year, when he was moved back to this high school. In addition to the three-year reevaluation, a functional behavioral evaluation was conducted. The results indicate that Mike sometimes is angry and verbally threatening and that there isn't a consistent pattern in why he becomes angry. Most incidents occur outside of the classroom. In the classroom, he usually is quiet."

Mrs. Bond added, "If I may add, I was Mike's teacher at The Education Therapy Center. Mike made good progress during the time he was at the school. We only had one incident with Mike and that was when he brought an unloaded gun to school. We also suspected that he was involved in gangs. After that incident, in which the police and probation officer were involved, Mike made a turnaround. He attended school regularly and became a positive role model."

Mrs. Christenson continued, "Thank you, Mrs. Bond. Mike's evaluation indicated that he has above-average ability and achieves in an average range in all academic areas. Mike continued eligibility as behavior disordered due to his violent behavior. In addition, it is noted that Mike continues to be involved in gangs and possibly drugs."

Mrs. Miller stated, "Mike's IEP for this school year states that he is placed in two special education classes, English and social studies. He is placed in the regular vocational program for welding and metalworking. His behavior management program indicates that Mike is to be monitored on a weekly basis and receive tutoring in his subjects as needed. His goals and objectives indicate that he will not be involved in any discipline incident resulting in removal from the classroom this year. Mrs. Steinberg, can you elaborate?"

Mrs. Steinberg stated, "Mike passed all classes first semester with Cs. In my class, he was usually quiet and respectful. On occasion, I have overheard Mike and other students discussing drugs, and I stopped the discussion. One time I intercepted a note from Mike to another student in class. The note was written in a code, and I always thought that it might have been gang-related. Mike always completed the work in class. However, he rarely completed homework. His other teachers reported that he was quiet and polite. He was an average student academically. Up to this point, there have been no discipline referrals on Mike."

Mrs. Miller asked, "In your opinion, was Mike's IEP appropriate?"

Mrs. Steinberg answered, "Up to this point, I think it was appropriate. However, now I'm beginning to wonder if more is happening behaviorally than I thought. I wonder about Mike's ability to become violent."

Mrs. Miller asked, "Mrs. Christenson, based on Mike's recent evaluation, do you think that Mike understood his behavior and could control the behavior?"

Mrs. Christenson answered, "Yes, I think that Mike understood his behavior during this incident. However, I do not believe that Mike could control his behavior. He has a long history of violence and inability to control the violence."

Other team members nodded in agreement.

Mrs. Miller concluded, "Then it is the consensus of this team that Mike's behavior of threatening a teacher is a manifestation of his disability of behavior disorder."

Other team members again nodded in agreement.

Mrs. Miller asked, "Do we need to revisit Mike's IEP and revise it in any way?"

Mrs. Steinberg said, "I definitely think that Mike needs more help. He cannot go around threatening teachers. I think that we need to revise Mike's placement and return him to the day treatment school. He can receive regular therapy, both individually and in a group. Mike is a threat to other staff members and perhaps other students."

Mrs. Bond said, "We would be happy to return Mike to our day treatment facility. Mike certainly would benefit from intensive therapy."

Mrs. Morris said in a loud voice, "Mike will *not* go to that school. I will ask for a hearing to keep him here. He has served his suspension and paid his dues. He needs to come back to this high school."

Mrs. Miller said, "How do other team members feel?"

Other team members stated they felt that Mike should be placed in the day treatment facility.

Mrs. Miller continued, "It appears that the team thinks that Mike's needs can best be met at the day treatment facility. Mrs. Morris, in 10 days, Mike will return to the day treatment facility. Here is a copy of the revised IEP and a notice of the placement change. I will also review with you your parent's rights." Mrs. Miller then reviewed the parent's rights and gave Mrs. Morris a copy of the rights.

Mrs. Morris stood up and said, "I can assure you that Mike will not attend that day treatment facility. I will contact my attorney and will file for a due process hearing."

The meeting ended with Mrs. Morris and Mike leaving abruptly. After the meeting, Mrs. Miller met with the staff regarding *stay put*. If Mike's mother requested a due process hearing, Mike would have to return to his original placement. The only recourse would be to request an injunction from the due process hearing officer to keep Mike out of school until the dispute was settled. The high school staff did not want Mike to return and requested an injunction, if necessary.

Two days later, a letter requesting the due process hearing was received. The due process hearing officer was quickly assigned. The school district attorney requested an injunction to keep Mike out of school during the dispute due to the physical threat against the teacher. The hearing officer denied the injunction. He reasoned that the student was not likely to cause injury simply because he made one threat. Before this incident, the student had not been engaged in a serious discipline incident for more than two years. He also stated that the school district had proposed no steps to reduce the likelihood to harm and that the current IEP apparently was not appropriate because the district proposed to change the placement. In addition, the school district did not propose an interim alternative educational setting that would allow the student to continue to progress in the general education setting (vocational classes) as well as continue to receive IEP services.

School district personnel were very upset. An expedited hearing was requested, but 10 days after the incident, Mike was scheduled to return to school. The teachers were very upset that Mike was allowed to return to school, given the nature of the threat to the staff member. On the eleventh day after the suspension, Mike did not return to school. One week later, the hearing officer notified the school district that Mike had dropped out of school, and the request for a due process hearing was withdrawn.

QUESTIONS

Legal Issues to Consider

1. Did the school district follow correct procedures in conducting the IEP meeting? How do you know?

2. What is *stay put* and why was it used?

3. What are the required elements for determining that a student with a disability is dangerous?

Other Issues

1. As a teacher, how would you feel if a student threatened you and was allowed to return to your class?

2. Does a verbal threat constitute a dangerous situation? Why or why not?

3. What do you think should happen to a student who engages in the type of behavior described?

CASE 10.5

TIM/TEACHER AND PARENT REBELLION

It was a beautiful Saturday morning as 15 parents filed into Mrs. Lemmons' home for a hastily arranged parents' meeting. Mrs. Lemmons and another parent, Mrs. Cullen, had contacted all parents in the first-grade class, except Tim's mother, to attend the meeting. The message to the parents was that there was a serious behavior problem concerning a dangerous child in Mrs. Bush's classroom that parents needed to discuss. The parents were seated in Mrs. Lemmons' living room, some sitting on the floor. After exchanging greetings and introductions, Mrs. Lemmons began the meeting.

"I appreciate all of you coming on such short notice. We have a common problem in the first-grade classroom this year, and our children are getting shortchanged. This year, we have a child who is classified as behavior disordered in the classroom. The child, Tim, has his own special aide, Mrs. Jackson. The teacher, Mrs. Bush, told me that she doesn't think she can teach effectively with Tim in her classroom. Mrs. Bush said this child lies, steals, and, worst of all, physically harms other children. Mrs. Bush said Tim is very disturbed and shouldn't be allowed in first grade. She said he was placed in her classroom against her will and, even with an aide, cannot achieve and behave. I know firsthand how Tim behaves. I volunteer one day a week to assist in the classroom, and what I observed was awful! One day Tim started screaming and threw his books on the floor. The books hit a nearby child, and the disturbance caused the entire class to become distracted. Mrs. Bush ordered the aide to remove the child from the classroom. She did so physically, with the child hitting and screaming. I was appalled, and I think we should do something!"

Mrs. Cullen stated, "I agree completely. My son, Chris, came home the other day with a bruise on his neck. When I asked him how this happened, he said that Tim pushed him in the cafeteria. I am very upset that such a dangerous child is allowed in the school. Surely, there is a place for children who are so disturbed."

The other parents nodded in agreement as Mrs. Richards added, "I also volunteer in the classroom and have witnessed some very disturbing behavior from Tim. First grade is so important, and the teacher seems to be spending all of her time disciplining Tim. I want my son to learn to read, and I don't want him to witness this kind of violent behavior. I am also afraid of who might get hurt the next time Tim lashes out when he's angry."

The parents began to talk all at once, telling what they had observed and what their children had told them about Tim.

Mrs. Frey, who hadn't said anything up to this point, spoke up. "I really understand your concerns, but what about Tim? Doesn't he have a right to be in the classroom as a student with a disability? I'm a special education teacher, and I know that Tim must have an IEP that supports his placement in the first-grade room. I wonder if Mrs. Bush needs more help and support. I'm also a little uncomfortable talking about someone else's child. I don't see Tim's mother here."

Mrs. Cullen responded, "I don't think any child has the right to be in a classroom when the majority of children can't learn because of his presence. Kids in special education seem to have more rights than anyone. Why doesn't my child have the right to learn? He doesn't have these super rights because he's only average. Just who is going to protect the rights of a child who is average?"

Mrs. Lemmons suggested, "I think we need to start a petition to have this child removed from the first-grade classroom. If the majority of us sign it, I will present it to the principal."

The majority of parents agreed and signed the petition. The petition stated that Tim should be removed to another placement because of the harmful effect he was having on other children in the class, both educationally and physically. Mrs. Frey did not sign the petition and left the meeting feeling helpless.

Two days later, Mrs. Lemmons brought the petition to Mrs. Lefton, the school principal. Mrs. Lefton discussed the situation with Mrs. Lemmons and said she would look into the matter. After Mrs. Lemmons left the office, Mrs. Lefton walked down the hallway to see Mrs. Bush. She showed Mrs. Bush the petition.

Mrs. Bush stated, "I think they have a good point. I can't teach children to read when I have one child in my room who is continually disturbing and hurting others. The aide is helpful, but I am the person responsible for these children, and I can't teach effectively with Tim in my room."

"Mrs. Bush, I completely understand. Starting tomorrow, I want you to send Tim and his aide to my office for the entire day. Please send assignments with the aide, and she can work with Tim. We will keep Tim out of your classroom until I can contact the special education administrator and arrange some kind of meeting to get Tim removed permanently from your room."

After talking to Mrs. Bush, Mrs. Lefton immediately contacted Mr. King, the special education administrator, and explained the situation. Mr. King suggested an IEP meeting the following week. He said he would contact the parent and other participants.

Two weeks after Tim was removed from Mrs. Bush's classroom, the meeting was held. Mr. King chaired the meeting, and the following persons attended: Mrs. Singleton, Tim's mother; Mrs. Bush; Mrs. Lefton; Mrs. Jackson, Tim's aide; and Mr. Emerson, the special education teacher-consultant. The participants introduced themselves, and Mr. King began the meeting.

"I received a telephone call from Mrs. Lefton recently, and she indicated that Tim was having a great deal of difficulty in Mrs. Bush's classroom. Mrs. Lefton, would you tell us your concerns?"

"I certainly will. First of all, Tim has been removed from Mrs. Bush's classroom pending this meeting. I just couldn't continue allowing him to disturb the entire class and to continually hit and hurt other children. Second, I received a petition signed by 15 of the 20 parents of students in Mrs. Bush's classroom. The petition demands that Tim be permanently removed from the room because of his continual disturbance. I think Mrs. Bush can better tell you what has been happening on a day-to-day basis."

Mrs. Bush stated, "Tim doesn't belong in my room. Even with Mrs. Jackson, his aide, in the room, he hits other children and pushes, kicks, and pinches when he is upset. It seems that Tim is always upset! He doesn't listen well, and I find myself spending an inordinate amount of time with him. The other children are suffering. Children with behavior problems as severe as Tim's do not belong in the regular classroom."

Mr. Emerson said, "I have talked with Mrs. Bush on a regular basis, and I did not have any indication that Tim was a problem. I know he has had some difficulty, but each time we worked out another plan, and it seemed to work."

Mrs. Bush responded, "The reason I didn't talk to you is that every time I do, you come up with another plan for me to try. I've tried everything at this point, and I'm tired of making special accommodations for Tim. In fact, I'm not going to make any more. Tim needs to be placed in a special class."

Mrs. Singleton, who had been silent up to this point, stated, "I am very upset that Tim would be taken out of his classroom without my permission. However, I can tell you that any placement is preferable to this classroom, where he is obviously not welcome by the teacher or any of the other parents. Tim is unhappy here. Yesterday, he came home crying because all of the other students had been invited to someone's birthday party over the weekend and Tim was the only child not invited. I will agree to another placement, but not because I think he can't do well in a regular first-grade classroom. I will agree to a special class because at least he will be welcome and will receive the individual attention and support he deserves."

The school participants breathed a silent sigh of relief. The team then revised Tim's IEP and placed him in the primary class for behavior disorders. Tim never returned to Mrs. Bush's classroom.

QUESTIONS

Legal Issues to Consider

1. Was it proper for Mrs. Bush to talk to a parent other than Mrs. Singleton about Tim? Why or why not?

2. Was it proper for Mrs. Lefton to unilaterally remove Tim from Mrs. Bush's classroom for two weeks to work in another room with the aide? Why or why not?

3. Legally, can parents of general education students insist that a child with a disability be removed from a particular classroom?

Other Issues

1. Should a child with a disability have more rights than nondisabled children? Why or why not? Try to think of specific examples.

2. What might happen if a general education teacher refuses to make accommodations for a student with a disability?

3. As a parent, what would you have said at the parents' meeting at Mrs. Lemmons' house?

━━━━━━━━ **CASE 10.6** ━━━━━━━━

MARIO/EXPULSION PROCEEDING

The IEP meeting occurred at 3:00 P.M. on Thursday in the library conference room at West Junior High School. Seven persons attended the meeting: Mr. Jones, the principal; Mrs. Schneider, the hall monitor; Mr. Winkler, the special education administrator; Mr. Peterson, the special education teacher; Mr. Johnson, the school psychologist; and Mr. and Mrs. Clark, Mario's parents. Although Mario was invited to attend the meeting, Mr. and Mrs. Clark decided that he should not attend.

Mr. Winkler began the meeting by asking the participants to introduce themselves. He then said, "I appreciate all of you attending this meeting on such short notice. The reason we are here today involves a serious behavioral incident involving marijuana. Mario was caught with a bag of marijuana by the hall monitor last Friday during lunch. We'll discuss what happened, then determine whether Mario's behavior is related to his disability. This information will be presented in the expulsion hearing. As you know, the school district's policy states that students possessing drugs will be considered for expulsion by the board of education. Let's begin by discussing the incident involving Mario. Mrs. Schneider, would you please tell us what happened last week?"

"Yes. I was walking down the hallway during my routine supervision during the lunch periods. As I passed a cluster of lockers, I noticed a group of boys standing around a locker. As I looked more closely, I saw Mario place a clear plastic bag in his pocket. The boys quickly scattered as I walked up to Mario. I then asked him to empty his pockets. I think he knew he was caught. He handed me the bag, and it appeared to be marijuana. I told Mario to come with me to the office. He came with me without incident."

Mr. Winkler said, "Thank you, Mr. Jones, you dealt with Mario in the office. Would you tell us what happened next?"

"Mrs. Schneider brought Mario to my office with the purported marijuana. I asked Mario what was in the bag, and he stated that it was marijuana. I asked him why he had it at school, and he just shrugged his shoulders. I told Mario this was a very serious incident and the police would be contacted immediately, along with his parents. He asked me if he would be expelled, and I told him this was a possibility. I contacted the police and Mario's parents. The police field-tested the substance, and it tested to be marijuana. They arrested Mario and took him to the police station. Mario's parents were given a letter stating that Mario would be suspended for 10 days and that an expulsion hearing would be held. After they left, I contacted you, Mr. Winkler, to arrange this meeting, because I knew that Mario was in special education and we would need some kind of meeting."

Mr. Winkler continued, "Mr. and Mrs. Clark, do you have anything to add?"

Mrs. Clark said, "I am very upset and disappointed in Mario's behavior. We have worked so hard with him in and out of school. Last year, he began to hang around a rough group of kids, and I suspected that drugs were involved. Other than that, I don't have anything to add."

Mr. Winkler then asked Mr. Peterson, Mario's teacher, to discuss Mario's IEP and current program. He said, "I have Mario in three classes this year: English, math, and tutoring during study hall. He is in the regular classroom for social studies, science, PE, and industrial arts. Mario is a student who always seems to be around other kids who are known to use drugs. In class, though, he is quiet and polite. He always completes assignments and often asks for help during study hall. At this time, he is passing all of his classes in special and general education. To my knowledge, he's never been sent to the office for any discipline problems. However, he is definitely hanging around a group of students known to be involved with drugs. Mario's IEP goals and objectives focus on developing academic skills in reading and math. There are no behavior-oriented goals or objectives, nor was there any reason to address social and emotional areas. Mario seems to be a student with mild learning disabilities whose needs have been met with some direct intervention in special education. Overall, up to this incident, Mario seemed to be progressing adequately."

The psychologist, Mr. Johnson, continued, "Mario was last evaluated a year ago, in sixth grade. The evaluation suggests that Mario has average ability, with weaknesses noted in the academic areas of reading and math. Mario functions at the fifth-grade level in both of those areas. Socially, Mario seems somewhat impulsive and appears to be a follower. The evaluation team decided that he would continue eligibility for learning disabilities, with a resource placement most appropriate to meet his needs."

Mr. Winkler said, "We need to determine if Mario's behavior of having marijuana at school is a manifestation of his learning disability. Does anyone have an opinion, given the information we have just discussed?"

Mr. Jones spoke up in a strong voice. "Mario is labeled learning disabled. He knew what he did was wrong. He even asked if he was going to be expelled. I don't think there is any relationship between Mario's behavior and his disability. He should be treated like anyone else caught with drugs at school. There should not be special considerations for Mario, because he's learning disabled, not behavior disordered."

Mr. Johnson stated, "Based on the evaluation, Mario appears to understand right from wrong. However, he is impulsive and a follower, and this may have influenced him in this incident."

Mr. Peterson continued, "I completely disagree. Mario is only eligible for learning disabilities and has only academic deficits. What Mr. Jones said is true. Mario just has learning problems. Sure, he's a little impulsive and a follower, but aren't all seventh-grade students this way to some extent?"

Mr. Winkler said to the parents, "Do you agree?"

Mr. Clark said, "Mario definitely knows that what he did was wrong. This had nothing to do with his learning disability."

Mr. Winkler said, "It seems that the majority of school staff, with support from the parents, thinks that Mario's behavior is not related to his learning disability. This information will be relayed to the school staff at the expulsion hearing and to the board of education to assist them in making a decision regarding expulsion. This means that Mario will be treated just like any child who brought marijuana to school. Mr. and Mrs. Clark, it might be in Mario's best interest not to send him back to school until we know the outcome of the expulsion decision by the board of education."

The parents reluctantly agreed, even though Mario's letter of suspension indicated that the 10-day suspension would end in two days. The expulsion hearing was four days away, and the board of education would make its decision in six days. That meant Mario would be suspended a total of 14 days. The parents felt it was better to cooperate with the school district rather than argue about a few extra days at home. They were hopeful that the board of education would be more lenient if they fully cooperated.

The expulsion hearing was held. The school district personnel—Mrs. Schneider and Mr. Jones—presented what had happened on the day Mario was caught with the marijuana. Mr. and Mrs. Clark and Mario were afforded an opportunity to respond. Mrs. Clark again stated that what Mario did was wrong. Mr. Clark stated that the family would be willing to obtain counseling if Mario were allowed to continue in school. A summary of the recent IEP meeting was reviewed by Mr. Winkler. He stated that Mario's behavior was not a manifestation of his disability.

Two days later, the board of education held a special meeting to consider matters of student discipline. The board went into executive session to discuss Mario's case. Each board member read carefully through information provided to them by the superintendent, Mr. Rand. The information included a summary of the expulsion hearing, the IEP meeting, and statements from Mrs. Schneider and Mr. Peterson about the incident. They also reviewed a summary of Mario's progress in school and his disciplinary record. The board members stated their opinions about what should happen.

One board member said, "I feel sad about this case because the parents are willing to get help for Mario, but we cannot allow drugs in our schools. Our policy states that we have a zero tolerance to drugs in school."

Another member agreed, "Yes, that's right. We have discussed 25 cases concerning drugs since last year, and in every case we have voted to expel the student from school."

A third member continued, "This student is in special education, but the information presented to us states that there is no relationship between his disability and the behavior of bringing marijuana to school. Does that mean we can expel him?"

Mr. Rand, the superintendent, responded, "Yes, that is correct. If there is no relationship, you can expel the student."

In 45 minutes, the board of education unanimously agreed that Mario should be expelled from school for the remainder of the school year. The board of education, in an open session, voted unanimously to expel a student for the remainder of the school year for possessing drugs at school. After the meeting, Mr. Rand notified Mr. and Mrs. Clark of the board's decision by telephone. The parents decided that they would try to enroll Mario in a private school.

QUESTIONS

Legal Issues to Consider

1. What errors were made in the IEP meeting when the behavioral incident was discussed?

2. What other discipline action could the school district have immediately taken, along with suspension from school?

3. The special education administrator told the parents at the IEP meeting not to send Mario back to school until a decision was made on his possible expulsion. Was this appropriate? Why or why not?

4. Was the school district able to legally expel Mario without providing services? Why or why not?

Other Issues

1. Do you think Mario's behavior was a manifestation of his learning disability? Why or why not?

2. Is it possible that students with learning disabilities can engage in misbehaviors that are manifestations of their disabilities? Why or why not?

3. If there is no relationship between a student's behavior and disability, should the school district be able to expel the student without providing services? Why or why not?

4. In the community and in our society, should there be provisions for a manifestation determination to be made in criminal cases? Why or why not?

■ ■ ■ ■ ■

CHAPTER ELEVEN

COMPLIANCE TECHNIQUES

CASE 11.1   JANIS/INADEQUATE BUILDING
CASE 11.2   LISA/GRADUATION FEARS
CASE 11.3   MICHAEL/SEXUAL MISCONDUCT
CASE 11.4   KRISTEN/ESSENTIAL THERAPY
CASE 11.5   JANET/IDENTIFICATION OF PROBLEMS
CASE 11.6   GABRIEL/VOCATIONAL TRAINING

■■■■■■■ **CASE 11.1** ■■■■■■■

JANIS/INADEQUATE BUILDING

Janis was a 16-year-old student at Wildwood Junior High School. It was the end of the school year, and Janis was ready to be transitioned into a high school setting. Janis was diagnosed with Down syndrome, including multiple cardiac-vascular anomalies. The school district found her eligible for a self-contained physically handicapped and educable mentally handicapped program with related services from the itinerant teacher of the partially sighted and the itinerant teacher of the hearing impaired, as well as consultative nursing. Resource placement was not an appropriate option because Janis required placement in an air-conditioned building that was accessible. If Janis had to walk more than 100 feet, she became fatigued. On long walks, she was confined to a wheelchair. Mrs. Vaughn, Janis's mother, was very supportive and involved in her education. Janis had been placed in a special education classroom since the age of 3. Overall, Mrs. Vaughn had been pleased with the quality of Janis's education, and she attended all special education meetings to discuss Janis's IEP and evaluations.

On the day of Janis's IEP and annual review meeting, Mrs. Vaughn received a telephone call from her friend Maggie.

Maggie excitedly stated, "Do you know the new special school you've been looking into for Janis? I think it's called Our Lady of Snows School. It's going to open in August. I just saw an article in the newspaper about the school. It sure looks great."

Mrs. Vaughn replied, "Yes, I saw the article today, and I'm going to contact them. I think this would be a better school for Janis. The classes are smaller, and it looks like the school is on one floor and has air-conditioning."

Maggie stated, "I'm so glad you're going to look into the new school. I know it will be costly in tuition, but Janis will be very happy there."

Mrs. Vaughn said, "Yes, I think she would like this private school. It's close to home, and, frankly, I've had some misgivings about Janis attending a regular high school. I'm afraid she won't be in the sheltered environment she needs."

The conversation ended, and Mrs. Vaughn got ready to attend Janis's IEP meeting. On the way to the meeting, she stopped at the new private school. She was able to talk to the school's director, Mrs. Stevens. Mrs. Stevens was enthusiastic about the possibility of having Janis attend the new school. Mrs. Vaughn made an appointment to bring Janis for a visit during the summer and promised to forward Janis's school records.

At the IEP meeting, the team discussed Janis's progress. The year before, Janis would have been eligible to move to the high school, but Mrs. Vaughn requested that Janis be allowed to attend the junior high school one additional year. The team agreed, and Janis turned 16 in eighth grade. After discussing Janis's progress, which was described by her teacher as "excellent," the team began to discuss Janis's IEP for ninth grade.

Mrs. Park, Janis's junior high teacher stated, "Janis will need to be in a building that is air-conditioned and accessible. She can't walk very far without becoming fatigued. Are both high schools air-conditioned?"

Mrs. Walsh, special education administrator, answered, "The closest high school to Janis's home, Williams High School, has no air-conditioning and no elevator. The other high school, Lawson High School, is air-conditioned in the newer section of the building and in the cafeteria, which is in the older section of the building. It would make sense to consider Lawson High School for Janis."

Mrs. Vaughn said, "I know where Lawson High School is located. The students get off of the buses at the front of the building, and Janis would have to walk a long distance in a non-air-conditioned hallway to the new section of the building. I think this would be too far for her on a regular basis. She probably would have to be in a wheelchair to move to her classroom daily."

Mrs. Walsh said, "We probably could make some accommodations, Mrs. Vaughn."

Mrs. Vaughn cut in stating, "Well, I don't think either of those options are very good for Janis. I have been made aware of a new private school, Our Lady of Snows. It is specifically designed for students with severe disabilities just like Janis. I think Janis will be attending this school in the fall, so there is no need to continue with this meeting. I would, however, like to request that Janis's school records be forwarded to the director of this school."

The meeting ended without drafting an IEP for Janis. Mrs. Vaughn signed a record release form so that Janis's school records could be forwarded to Our Lady of Snows School.

For the next three years, Janis attended Our Lady of Snows School. Mrs. Vaughn was pleased with Janis's progress, and she was appointed to the school's board of directors.

After three years, Mrs. Vaughn became aware that the public high school close to her home, Williams High School, was going to be fully air-conditioned and would have an elevator installed. The renovation would be completed in August, just before school began. Mrs. Vaughn began thinking about transferring Janis to the public high school because, at 19, Janis would only be able to attend school two more years, until she was 21. Mrs. Vaughn thought that the public high school could offer Janis some job training skills, something that had not been possible at the private school. At the beginning of August, Mrs. Vaughn contacted Mrs. Walsh, the special education administrator. Mrs. Walsh said she would arrange an IEP meeting for Janis at Williams High School. Mrs. Vaughn agreed and the meeting was arranged. Janis's IEP meeting was held and her IEP was planned. Services included the many related services that were previously required and transition services. The transition services included a functional skills curriculum with community integration. Mrs. Vaughn was pleased with the program, and, after two years, Janis was eligible to graduate from high school because she was now 21.

Mrs. Vaughn allowed Janis to graduate from high school, but she was unhappy that Janis did not have specific competitive job skills. In May, the year of graduation, Mrs. Vaughn requested an impartial due process hearing. Mrs. Vaughn requested three years of compensatory education at school-district expense because the district allegedly had not offered an appropriate education during the three years when Janis attended the private school.

The due process hearing was held in July, with attorneys representing both the parent and school district. Mrs. Vaughn, on the witness stand, stated that Janis was denied FAPE when she graduated from the junior high school. Janis had a severe congenital heart condition that caused her to be at risk physically if not in an air-conditioned environment and in an accessible building. Therefore, no high school program discussed at the annual review conference five years previous had been appropriate for Janis, given her need for an air-conditioned learning environment and an elevator. Williams High School lacked air-conditioning and an elevator, and Lawson High School was only partially air-conditioned. At Lawson, Janis would have been sentenced to a wheelchair because of the great distance between the bus departure point at the front of the building and the classroom located in the new section of the building. Mrs. Vaughn asserted that she was forced to find an appropriate private placement for Janis. Therefore, Janis was enrolled in Our Lady of Snows private school, which met Janis's physical requirements for controlled temperature and accessibility. Mrs. Vaughn stated that she had no choice but to place her daughter at the private school because the school district was unable to accommodate her daughter in a school that met her needs. Mrs. Vaughn ended the testimony by stating that the school district was legally required to compensate Janis for the three years of total denial of FAPE.

The school district's position was stated by Mrs. Walsh. She said that Mrs. Vaughn had taken no action to protest until five years after the junior-high annual review conference. Even though Janis had attended her last two years at the public high school, Mrs. Vaughn had not protested the current or previous placement. Mrs. Walsh maintained that the two high schools were discussed with Mrs. Vaughn at the end of Janis's junior-high education, but Mrs. Vaughn had learned of the new private school, looked into that possibility, and placed her in that facility. Mrs. Walsh said that Janis was 21 and was allowed to complete her high school education at Williams High School. She also stated that Mrs. Vaughn was given written information about her parental rights, including the right to request a due process hearing, many times. She knew or should have known what action she could have taken to notify the school district that Janis was not offered a school placement to meet her needs. Mrs. Walsh stated that accommodations could have been provided five years ago at one of the high schools, but Mrs. Vaughn was only interested in the private school. Mrs. Vaughn rejected the offer to place Janis at Lawson High School, which did have air-conditioning in some areas. Mrs. Walsh stated that Janis was provided with FAPE before her graduation from the junior high school and during her placement the past two years at Williams High School. Mrs. Walsh ended her testimony by stating that it was Mrs. Vaughn's definite decision to place

Janis at the private school. They would have worked further on accommodations for Janis, but they felt that Mrs. Vaughn had made up her mind about the private facility.

Ten days after the due process hearing, Mrs. Vaughn received the hearing officer's order by certified mail. The order stated, in part, that, "The school district shall not provide three years of compensatory education for Janis."

QUESTIONS

Legal Issues to Consider

1. What was the hearing officer's rationale for not ordering compensatory education?

2. Under what circumstances would the parent have been eligible to receive tuition reimbursement for the private school placement?

3. If the school district had not provided an appropriate education for Janis in junior high, would this have changed the outcome of this case? Why or why not?

Other Issues

1. If a child requires air-conditioning for health reasons, should a school district be required to provide the service, even at considerable expense? Why or why not?

━━━━━━━━━ **CASE 11.2** ━━━━━━━━━

LISA/GRADUATION FEARS

"I'm so happy that Lisa's IEP meeting could be rescheduled for this afternoon so that both of us can attend," said Mrs. Layton.

"Yes, I always like to attend every meeting on Lisa. I don't think we've missed any in the past 10 years," said Mr. Layton.

It was quiet, and Mr. Layton continued reading the newspaper as he always did in the morning before work. Mrs. Layton drank her coffee and reminisced about Lisa, their only daughter. She thought about how Lisa was a delightful child, even as a baby. Even though it was discovered she had a seizure disorder as a toddler, Lisa adjusted well to the medications and frequent seizures. In kindergarten and first grade, although the seizures were becoming less frequent, Lisa struggled in school in reading, math, spelling, and writing. Everything was so difficult for her! Mrs. Layton remembered that they had been so grateful when Lisa's second-grade teacher suggested a referral for possible special education services. The evaluation revealed that Lisa had borderline intellectual capabilities and below-average skill development in all academic areas. It was quite a shock to learn of Lisa's intellectual capabilities. Mrs. Layton remembered emphatically stating that Lisa was at least average intelligence. Based on the evaluation and parent input, Lisa was eligible for learning disabilities assistance, and she had been placed in a self-contained classroom. She vaguely remembered something stated about Lisa needing a speech and language evaluation, but that the LD classroom would meet Lisa's speech and language needs. For Lisa, school went well after she was placed in special education.

Mrs. Layton remembered when Lisa had brain surgery. It was the most frightening thing that ever had happened to her family. She remembered sitting in the hospital waiting room worried about Lisa living through the surgery. Thank goodness the surgery was successful! Even though the recovery was long and difficult, at least Lisa had fewer seizures. She hadn't experienced a seizure in about five years.

Mr. Layton continued to read the newspaper, and Mrs. Layton's thoughts about her daughter continued. After the brain surgery in fourth grade, Lisa's physicians suggested that Lisa have a speech and language evaluation in the hospital to determine if the surgery had affected her speech and language skills. The evaluation was conducted and shared with the school district. The school district held a meeting to consider the results before Lisa returned to school after surgery. At the meeting, it was stated that, although Lisa had a need for special help in speech and language, the LD teacher was addressing those needs appropriately in the special classroom.

Mrs. Layton remembered that Lisa was not evaluated by the school district again until sixth grade. The evaluation confirmed Lisa's borderline intellectual capabilities and below-average academic skills. Lisa remained in a self-contained LD program throughout her school career. She seemed happy and progressed. Her physical condition improved greatly after the surgery, and she rarely had seizures, although she continued to take medication.

"Did you know that Lisa could graduate from high school next year?" asked Mrs. Layton.

"Of course she could. She's 17 years old now," said Mr. Layton.

"Do you think she's ready to graduate? I mean, do you think she's mature enough to be successful in the real world?" asked Mrs. Layton.

"I'm not sure. I can't visualize Lisa working in a job and living by herself," said Mr. Layton.

"Maybe we should talk to her teachers today at the meeting about working with Lisa on job skills and independent living skills," suggested Mrs. Layton.

"Good idea," said Mr. Layton. "Now, I have to get to work early, and I'll meet you at Lisa's IEP meeting this afternoon."

Mr. Layton left the house, and Mrs. Layton completed her regular housework chores during the day.

At Lisa's IEP meeting that afternoon, Mr. and Mrs. Layton arrived early and met Lisa in the conference room. The school psychologist, Mrs. Merl, attended the meeting, as did Mrs. Nance, Lisa's special education teacher. The meeting began by reviewing Lisa's progress.

Mrs. Nance stated, "Lisa has done quite well this year. She passed all of her special education classes with Bs and Cs. She has improved her reading and writing skills. She can now write a three-paragraph story with minimal prompts. She can compute three-digit-by-two-digit multiplication at about 80 percent accuracy. She has earned all of her credits toward graduation. Lisa tries hard and seems to have some close friends at school."

Mrs. Merl said, "Lisa is completing her junior year in high school. She will be eligible for graduation at the end of next year."

Mrs. Layton said, "We're a little concerned about Lisa graduating next year. It seems that her program here has only focused on academic skills. She really has had no job-related skills or independent living skills. I'm not sure what Lisa will do when she graduates without some job skills."

The team discussed Lisa's transition program and decided that Lisa should be enrolled in the special education work–study program. Lisa's IEP reflected a functional skills curriculum instead of an academic curriculum. Even though some changes were made, the Laytons left the meeting with some uneasiness.

The truth was that Mrs. Layton was terrified of Lisa graduating next year, and she panicked. She looked in the parents' rights handbook given to her many times after each special education meeting on Lisa and found the telephone number of the local legal advocate's office. After discussing her concerns with Mr. Layton, Mrs. Layton made an appointment with Mrs. Black, an attorney.

On the day of the meeting with Mrs. Black, Mr. and Mrs. Layton arrived early with a box of school records, which they had saved since Lisa was in kindergarten. They explained to Mrs. Black their concerns with Lisa's possible graduation. Mrs. Black was very encouraging and said she would review Lisa's records and contact them in a week.

Two weeks later, Mrs. Layton received a telephone call from Mrs. Black. She said, "Mrs. Layton, I think there is reason to believe that Lisa has never received an appropriate education from this school district."

Mrs. Layton was shocked as she said, "What do you mean?"

Mrs. Black continued, "When Lisa was in second grade, a report suggested that Lisa receive a speech and language evaluation. She was apparently not evaluated, because there is no report in the file. Every year after that—in third, fourth, and fifth grade—it is written on the IEP that Lisa should receive speech and language services. However, she was never evaluated for those services, nor do I see any speech and language services indicated on any IEPs. In fact the only speech and language evaluation was the one you pursued after Lisa's brain surgery. Even that evaluation suggests services in speech and language, and no services were ever included in her IEP. In addition, Lisa should have been reevaluated in fourth grade, and she wasn't. After her initial evaluation in second grade, she wasn't reevaluated until sixth grade. The law states that Lisa is entitled to a reevaluation every three years."

Mrs. Layton said, "I remember being told that Lisa's speech and language needs were addressed in the LD classroom."

"That is not the same. An evaluation should have been conducted, and services should have been a part of Lisa's IEP. This constitutes an inappropriate education for Lisa. Based on my review of the records, I suggest the following actions. First, you need to locate an appropriate program for Lisa. I know of an excellent residential school only an hour from your home for students with serious learning disabilities. There are qualified LD specialists and speech and language therapists on staff. Because Lisa would live at the school, she would be provided with the necessary skills to live independently. I suggest that you initiate placement at the school immediately. I can help you make the contacts. Second, I suggest that you file for an impartial due process hearing to request that the school district pay Lisa's tuition and residential costs at the private school. At the hearing, it will be important to demonstrate that the school district made significant procedural errors affecting the appropriateness of Lisa's education. In other words, because the school district did not diagnose and provide services for Lisa's speech and language disorder, how could they say her education was appropriate? They can't, and we'll demonstrate this in the hearing. Also, we'll emphasize the fact that the school district did not properly evaluate Lisa by not reevaluating her in a timely manner. Last, we will need an independent evaluation of Lisa. I work with a team of professionals from the local university, and I can put you in contact with them. We will also ask at the due process hearing for reimbursement for any costs associated with the evaluation. Now, I know you may be concerned about my fees. Don't worry about the fees. We'll request reimbursement of my fees at the due process hearing or in court. My experience with cases like this is that we will likely prevail. Lisa will then receive the excellent education she deserves."

Mrs. Layton talked with her husband at length about her conversation with Mrs. Black. Both were somewhat reluctant to pursue what they considered radical means. However, they decided that Lisa's welfare should come first. The residential school sounded great for Lisa, and it would help her adjust to adult life and properly meet Lisa's speech and language needs.

Mr. and Mrs. Layton followed Mrs. Black's suggestions. Lisa was enrolled in the Caps Preparatory School the next month. The due process hearing was held two weeks later. The due process hearing was lengthy and emotionally draining for Mr. and Mrs. Layton. Two weeks after the hearing, Mrs. Black called the parents with the bad news. The hearing officer, in the order, acknowledged that the school district had made some significant procedural errors. However, those errors did not affect the quality or appropriateness of Lisa's educational program. Therefore, the hearing officer denied requiring the school district to pay tuition to the private school and denied requiring the school district to pay for an independent evaluation.

Mr. and Mrs. Layton were very upset with the outcome of the hearing. However, they decided not to appeal the decision. Because the tuition to the private school was so costly, they decided to reenroll Lisa in her original high school program. Lisa graduated at the end of the next school year.

QUESTIONS

Legal Issues to Consider

1. What were the legal reasons for requesting a due process hearing?

2. What was the reasoning used for denying reimbursement for private school tuition?

3. What procedural errors did the school district make?

Other Issues

1. Do you think Mrs. Black gave good legal advice? Why or why not?

2. Should procedural errors that occurred 10 years ago and were not part of the current dispute be considered in a due process hearing? Why or why not?

3. Based on the facts stated, do you think Lisa's education was compromised? Why or why not?

4. Because the parents agreed with Lisa's program, are they partly responsible for ensuring an appropriate education for Lisa? Why or why not?

5. Do you agree with the hearing officer's decision? Why or why not?

CASE 11.3

MICHAEL/SEXUAL MISCONDUCT

Michael was a 15-year-old African American boy who had been adopted by Mr. and Mrs. Mitchell at the age of 3. He was currently attending tenth grade at Pearson High School, which was located in a rural area in the Midwest about 60 miles from a large city. Michael attended Pearson County schools for his entire school career. Michael was an only child, and the Mitchells were always very involved in and supportive of Michael's education. At Pearson High School, Michael's teachers viewed him as a bright, college-bound student who was boisterous, loud, and playful. On occasion, teachers talked to Michael about his "playful" touching of girls. In fact, his English teacher once approached him about harassing a girl in English class. Michael laughed and said that he was teasing and didn't mean to harass anyone. However, he didn't tease the girl again. Even though Michael was seen as somewhat difficult and bothered girls, he had never been involved in a disciplinary situation and certainly was not viewed as a potential student in special education.

At the end of September during Michael's tenth-grade year, an incident occurred that changed Michael's life. Michael became angry at his math teacher one day because he failed a math test. The teacher said that he should have studied more and publicly made the statement in front of the class. After school, Michael smashed in the side window of the teacher's car and ran home. Apparently, someone saw him, and an hour later the police arrested him. Michael plead guilty in court and received probation. Michael was suspended from school for 10 days and then expelled from the school for the remainder of the semester.

Michael's mother, Mrs. Mitchell, happened to be a legal advocate for an attorney in a neighboring town. She was very unhappy that Michael was not allowed to attend school, and, after consulting with an attorney, she requested that an evaluation be conducted on Michael to determine if he were eligible for behavior disorders services. She felt that if he were eligible for special education services, he could not be expelled.

During his expulsion, his mother and father went to work daily, and Michael was left alone at home. One day, Michael was aware that a 10-year-old cousin was at home with the flu. Michael went to the cousin's home and went in uninvited and unnoticed. The cousin's mother heard her daughter crying and walked into her bedroom to observe Michael attempting to rape the girl. The cousin's mother screamed and ordered Michael out of the house. Michael's mother was immediately contacted and came home from work. The cousin's mother and Michael's mother had a long discussion with Michael about what had happened. Michael's mother convinced the cousin's mother not to call the police and not to tell anyone else in the family. Michael agreed to stay away from his cousin.

Two weeks later, the local sheriff arrested Michael for breaking into his home through his 15-year-old daughter's bedroom window and attempting to molest the girl. Michael said he was invited into the house by the girl. The girl said that Michael came into the room while she was asleep and tried to molest her. Michael was placed on house arrest for the remainder of the year.

The school district completed an evaluation on Michael by December. An evaluation conference was held, and Michael was labeled behavior disordered. The team based its decision on Michael's recent misbehavior at school (i.e., breaking the teacher's car window and sexually harassing girls) and misbehavior at home (i.e., home invasion and attempting to molest a girl). The team decided to provide an alternative program for Michael at home, with a teacher visiting him for one hour per day. Mrs. Mitchell was somewhat unhappy with the program but agreed to it so that Michael could continue to work toward earning graduation credits.

Michael returned to Pearson High School at the end of January, the beginning of the second semester. The IEP team revised Michael's IEP to include regular college-bound course work, monitoring of progress by the BD teacher, and psychotherapy through the local mental health center paid by the school district. For the first three weeks, Michael adjusted well. However, he then began teasing girls and touching in an inappropriate manner. He also began to talk back to teachers, leave assigned areas without permission, disrupt class, throw objects in class, curse at teachers, and make noises in class. At the end of the third quarter, Michael had failed all classes.

Mrs. Mitchell was very upset with Michael and the school staff. In March, she wrote a letter (Figure 11.3.1) to Dr. Keene, the school superintendent. Two weeks after the first letter was sent, Mrs. Mitchell sent another letter (Figure 11.3.2) to Dr. Keene.

FIGURE 11.3.1   A Letter to the School Superintendent

Dear Dr. Keene:

    I am writing this letter to request a due process hearing for my son, Michael Mitchell, who is a behavior disorder student at Pearson High School. I feel that he was treated unfairly by his teachers when they failed him in their classes. I believe that they deliberately set him up to fail his classes.

                    Sincerely,

                    Margaret Mitchell

FIGURE 11.3.2   Addendum to the First Letter

Dear Dr. Keene:

    This letter is an addendum to my request for a due
process hearing for my son, Michael Mitchell. Michael was out
of school from October through February. At the time Michael
was expelled, I was told by the school that it was because he
broke a window. However, on or about December 13, I was told
by both you and the special education administrator, Dr.
Haus, that he was being kept out of school because of his
potential to sexually act out. There were no incidents in
which he was caught sexually acting out in school. The school
psychologist also said that he had a potential to do this.
Therefore, he was not permitted to go back to school.

    Although Michael is back in school now, I feel that his
human rights were violated by keeping him out of school
several months for crimes he might commit on the school
grounds in the future. Also, as a result of being on the home
program, Michael's grades suffered.

    I feel that Michael is being deprived of a fair and equal
education. The teachers at Pearson High School are not
trained or equipped to deal with children like Michael.
Therefore, I am requesting that Michael be placed in a
residential school with teachers who are equipped to deal
with him so that he can reach his highest potential. Prior to
the residential placement, I am requesting that Michael
receive compensatory education for eight weeks during the
summer to make up for the time he was expelled from school.

    I want these matters included in the due process hearing.

                      Sincerely,

                      Margaret Mitchell

    Dr. Keene contacted an attorney specializing in special education law. The attorney
reviewed Michael's records and interviewed the teachers and administrators. After consulting with the school administrators, the attorney forwarded a settlement offer to Mrs.
Mitchell's attorney. The settlement offer included a provision for compensatory education
during the summer at school-district expense and an agreement to place Michael in a residential school.

    Mrs. Mitchell and her attorney reviewed the settlement offer and agreed to the terms.
The agreement was signed by both parties. Mrs. Mitchell then withdrew her request for a

due process hearing. Michael attended summer school and was placed in a residential school during the fall semester.

QUESTIONS

Legal Issues to Consider

1. Was it appropriate to continue Michael's expulsion after he was found eligible for behavior disorders? Why or why not?

2. Why did the school district agree to provide compensatory education in the settlement offer?

3. What is a settlement offer, and why was it used in this case?

Other Issues

1. Why do you think the school district agreed to a residential placement for Michael?

CASE 11.4

KRISTEN/ESSENTIAL THERAPY

It was May 5, and Mr. and Mrs. Boyer were feeling hopeful as they walked into Kristen's school. Kristen was finishing second grade, and they were so pleased with her progress. When Kristen was born without hands, the doctors felt that she probably would need special education assistance for her entire school career. However, for the past three years in school, Kristen had been placed successfully in a regular classroom. Although her teachers were initially apprehensive about having Kristen in class, they quickly saw that she was bright and able to compensate for her disability. She learned to write using both arms to hold the pencil. In PE, she was easily able to throw a ball with both arms. In fact, she was able to do most tasks independently, except open a milk carton and ride a bike. This year in second grade had been especially successful because Kristen had become a proficient reader and was receiving occupational therapy for her fine motor skills from Mrs. Williams, the occupational therapist. Kristen didn't directly receive services from the teacher of the physically handicapped, but the teacher consulted with her teacher regularly.

As Mr. and Mrs. Boyer walked into the annual review, they were very happy. Just as they anticipated, Kristen's teacher, Mrs. Stevens, was very pleased with Kristen's progress.

Mrs. Stevens began by saying, "Kristen has learned a great deal this year. She is reading on grade level, and she is compensating for her lack of hands beautifully. She has friends and is an enthusiastic learner. The occupational therapy has really helped her with writing and developing independence."

Mrs. Blackwell, the teacher of the physically handicapped, stated, "I agree. Kristen has advanced this year. Mrs. Stevens has made minor adaptations in her classroom, and this has made a great difference for Kristen. As indicated on the IEP, Mrs. Stevens and I talk once every two weeks for about 30 minutes. I suggest that Kristen receive the same services next year."

Mr. Springer, the special education administrator, said, "It seems that Kristen has had a great year in the regular classroom. Mrs. Williams, can you review her progress in occupational therapy?"

"Yes. As just stated, Kristen has adjusted well to the regular classroom environment. I see Kristen twice a week for 20 minutes each session. We work on two skills: writing and becoming functionally independent. Kristen has met her goals and objectives. Mrs. Boyer, you mentioned earlier this year that Kristen might be receiving myoelectric hands this summer. Is that still a possibility?"

Mrs. Boyer answered, "Yes, the hands have been ordered. For those of you who don't know what they are, let me explain. Myoelectric hands are a type of prosthesis that are strapped to Kristen's arms. They have two hooks that can be activated electronically by Kristen. After she learns to use them, she should be able to perform more complex motor skills, like opening a milk carton and holding a pencil with one hand. She should have the myoelectric hands this summer and will receive some rehabilitation from the hospital to learn how to use them. However, it will be very important to reinforce her learning during the school year. I understand that, at first, the hands are awkward and uncomfortable, so Kristen will probably need encouragement at home and at school to use them."

Mrs. Williams said, "I have worked with another patient in the past with myoelectric hands, so I'm familiar with them. You're right when you say that they are initially uncomfortable. It will be very important to reward and encourage Kristen to wear and use the hands. In time, she won't want to do anything without them. Next year, in third grade, she may need more assistance from me, so I suggest increasing her time with me to three times per week for 25-minute sessions. I will also work closely with Kristen's teacher and Mrs. Blackwell."

Mrs. Boyer said, "That would be great, Mrs. Williams. Kristen is not very enthusiastic about wearing the hands at this time, but we know in the long term it will be best for her. We will have to work together to encourage her and train her to use the hands."

The team discussed goals and objectives for Kristen in third grade. Then they discussed special services. Kristen would remain in the regular classroom for all subjects. She would receive occupational therapy (OT) three times per week for 25 minutes each session. Mrs. Blackwell would consult with the regular classroom teacher and the occupational therapist for 20 minutes per week. After the services were determined, the team discussed the extent to which Kristen would be involved in the state and local-district achievement tests. The team decided that Kristen would participate in the assessments with only extended time as a modification. The IEP was completed, and Mr. and Mrs. Boyer were given a copy.

During the summer, Kristen received the myoelectric hands. They were, as expected, uncomfortable and awkward. Gradually, Kristen began using the prostheses. When school began in September, Kristen came to school wearing the myoelectric hands. Although the prostheses were a curiosity for other students, Kristen adjusted well. Mrs. Williams worked with her three times a week for the first month of school.

At the beginning of October, Mrs. Williams walked into Mr. Springer's office. She began the conversation by stating, "You know, Mr. Springer, I have been very happy working in this school district. However, I have to tell you that I have been offered an excellent position with a pediatric hospital for a considerable salary increase. I have given much thought to the offer, and I feel that I must accept it. Therefore, I am resigning my position as occupational therapist effective October 15."

Mr. Springer looked shocked as he responded, "I am so sorry to hear this, Mrs. Williams. You've done an excellent job working with the children in this district. I know the students and their parents will be unhappy to hear you are leaving."

Mrs. Williams said, "Thank you. I had a hard time making this decision, but I feel it is best for me and my career at this time."

Mr. Springer asked, "Do you know anyone who might be interested in taking your place?"

Mrs. Williams said, "Unfortunately, no, I don't. There aren't many OT graduates, and those who do complete a degree in OT usually work for hospitals because the salaries are much greater. However, if I hear of anyone, I'll let you know."

With regret, the board of education accepted Mrs. Williams's resignation. Mr. Springer began a search to find a replacement. After four weeks, no replacement had been found.

Meanwhile, Mr. and Mrs. Boyer were told by Mrs. Williams that she was leaving. They were very sad because they had worked well with her during the past few years and Kristen had responded to her. One reason that Kristen was adjusting so well to the myoelectric hands was due to the extra encouragement from Mrs. Williams. After Mrs. Williams left, Mrs. Boyer asked Kristen weekly if anyone had taken Mrs. Williams's place. Kristen responded that no one had.

Out of concern, Mrs. Boyer contacted Mr. Springer. Mr. Springer stated that he was conducting a national search to locate a replacement. At this time, there were no applicants.

After six weeks without services, Mrs. Boyer contacted the local hospital and inquired about OT services. The hospital had a therapist, and Mrs. Boyer made arrangements to take Kristen to the hospital three times a week after school for the service. Although it wasn't as effective as providing the services at school, at least Kristen was receiving the services.

Periodically, Mrs. Boyer contacted Mr. Springer to inquire about a replacement. She was told that the search was continuing but that there were no candidates.

In February, Mr. and Mrs. Boyer were reaching the financial limit to what they could afford to pay for private OT services. They couldn't continue paying for the services. After consulting an attorney, they wrote a letter (Figure 11.4.1) to Mr. Springer.

Mr. Springer consulted with the school superintendent and responded to Mr. and Mrs. Boyer. He said that they were, in good faith, searching for a replacement therapist and would not agree to paying the cost of services at the hospital. He also said that the school district would not agree to provide compensatory services.

Mr. and Mrs. Boyer felt that they had no other choice but to request a due process hearing. The hearing was held before the school year ended. It lasted two hours, with each side presenting its case. Two weeks later, the Boyers received the due process hearing order. It stated that the Boyers were to be reimbursed fully for any cost incurred to this point in providing OT services. The order also stated that the school district would assume any future cost in providing the services at the hospital until a new therapist could be located. In addition, the order stated that Kristen was to receive six weeks of compensatory OT service during the summer, at no cost to the parents.

FIGURE 11.4.1   A Letter to the Special Education Administrator

---

February 22

Mr. Springer, Special Education Administrator
Franklin School District

Dear Mr. Springer:

    Our daughter, Kristen Boyer, has an IEP and is to receive
occupational therapy three times per week for a total of 75
minutes. As you know, Kristen was born without hands, and she
recently received myoelectric hands. It is essential that
Kristen receive these services, and the services are clearly
outlined in her IEP.
    In October, Mrs. Williams, the occupational therapist,
resigned to accept another position. You indicated to us on
several occasions that a search was in process to locate a
replacement. To date, we have been told that there are no
applicants for the position.
    Because it is essential that Kristen receive occupational
therapy services, we have taken her to the local hospital for
the services. She has been receiving services since November
20. Because we have incurred considerable cost in providing
these services, we are requesting that the school district
reimburse us for the cost of the services. In addition,
because Kristen missed six weeks of services, we are
requesting compensatory services during the summer to make up
for the missed occupational therapy services.
    We understand that finding an occupational therapist is
difficult, but we cannot compromise the needs of our
daughter, and the services were agreed on in her IEP. Thank
you for your attention to this matter.

Sincerely,

Mr. and Mrs. Boyer

QUESTIONS

Legal Issues to Consider

1. Why did the hearing officer order the school district to reimburse the parents for providing OT services at the local hospital?

2. Why did the hearing officer order the school district to provide compensatory services?

Other Issues

1. Is it fair for the school district to pay for services such as in this case when it is beyond the district's control to locate replacement personnel? Why or why not?

2. Can you think of another way the district could have proceeded to provide services?

━━━━━━ **CASE 11.5** ━━━━━━

JANET/IDENTIFICATION OF PROBLEMS

The due process hearing was held on May 9 at 9:00 A.M. in the school district's board meeting room. In the room, furniture was arranged in a semicircle. At the middle of the semicircle was a long table with one folding chair where the hearing officer, Mr. Goodman, was arranging papers. On either side were long tables with three chairs. On one side, the parents' attorney, Ms. Hudson, was organizing papers while she talked with her clients, Mr. and Mrs. House. On the opposite side, the school district's attorney, Mr. Gregory, talked with Ms. Sullivan, the special education administrator. In the middle of the semicircle was a high-school student desk, which was empty. Off to one side were a small table and desk where the court reporter was organizing her equipment. In the back of the room, other witnesses quietly sat and waited for the hearing to begin. Mr. Goodman asked the court reporter if she was ready to begin recording the proceedings and she nodded.

Mr. Goodman began the hearing by stating, "This hearing will come to order in the due process hearing to consider the case of Janet House. The primary issues in this case are:

1. Whether the school district shall pay for the student's placement in St. Mary's Academy, including tuition, fees, and books, for the past two school years for a total of $10,000.
2. Whether the school district shall pay for tutorial services of $1,000.
3. Whether the school district shall pay for an independent, private evaluation of $2,500.
4. Whether the school district shall pay for attorney fees of $15,000.

"This hearing will be conducted in a fair and impartial manner. The parties shall have the right to question witnesses. The parties have been advised of their rights.

"The first thing I'd like to do is to ask both sides if there are any questions regarding the records that have been transmitted."

Both attorneys indicated that there were no questions regarding the records.

Mr. Goodman continued, "Okay, we are ready for opening statements from the school district and then from the parents."

Mr. Gregory, the school district's attorney, began by saying, "Thank you. My name is Brian Gregory. I'm an attorney representing the school district in this case. The parents have asked for a due process hearing in this matter on several issues, and I'll just briefly outline our position on them."

Mr. Gregory glanced at some notes, then continued, "Janet attended first grade in the public school. However, because of poor performance and lack of progress, the first grade was repeated at the request of the parents. Janet did somewhat better as a result of being retained and was promoted to the second grade. Although making some progress, the parents still were not satisfied with the student's achievement and began exploring alternatives to the public school placement. Testimony will show that, at the initiative of the parents, the child was placed in St. Mary's Academy, a parochial school. This placement occurred at the beginning of the fall semester, two years ago, for second grade. Janet is now 11 years old and is currently completing third grade in the private school. Soon after placement in the private school two years ago, the staff of the private school suggested to the parents that additional testing of the child might be in order to determine more about Janet's learning difficulties. This recommendation was made based on observation, behavior, and characteristics of the child. As you will hear in testimony, this recommendation was never forwarded to the public school. It was given to the parents, who unilaterally contracted with a private testing firm for psychological testing of Janet. This testing revealed that Janet had a full-scale IQ score in the low-average range and could become a significant suicide risk. The parents, being unhappy and upset with the results of the private testing, requested that the public school conduct additional testing. At this time, the parents made a referral to the public school. The district conducted an evaluation of Janet in January of her second-grade year at the private school. Testimony will show that the public school evaluation indicated that Janet had an average IQ with no tendency to be suicidal and that she had a learning dis-ability. It was recommended that Janet receive LD resource services in February of her second-grade year at the private school. This service continued through the fall of Janet's third-grade year at the private school, when services were terminated with parent consent. The parents began home tutoring at the same time Janet began to receive LD services. The private home tutoring continues to the present.

"The parents, on their own accord, removed Janet from the public school and placed her in the private school, contracted for private testing, and employed a tutor. The school district has no responsibility to pay any of these costs."

The hearing officer said, "Thank you Mr. Gregory. Ms. Hudson?"

Ms. Hudson said, "Thank you. My name is Katherine Hudson, and I am an attorney representing Janet and her parents, Mr. and Mrs. House. It is Janet House's position and that of her parents that the public school is responsible for paying all costs associated with the private placement because the public school failed to properly identify the student's special education problems when she was in the public school. Janet was having difficulty in first grade, and it was the parents, not the school district, who suggested retention. At the begin-ning of second grade, the parents had no choice but to seek an appropriate education in a private setting. It was the parents, not the school district, who initially located an evaluation for Janet. It is Janet's position and that of her parents that the public school failed to provide the student with an appropriate educational program. Again, the parents had no choice but to seek a private tutor because the LD services provided were not appropriate. Our testi-mony will support this position."

Mr. Goodman stated, "Thank you. Mr. Gregory, call your first witness. When the wit-nesses are called, would you please state your name clearly and the position that you hold within the school district or what you do so that the court reporter can get that on the record?"

Mr. Gregory said, "I'd like to call Ms. Sullivan as my first witness."

Ms. Sullivan walked to the desk in the middle of the room and sat down.

Mr. Gregory continued, "Ms. Sullivan, would you please state your name and posi-tion with the school district?"

Ms. Sullivan answered, "My name is Susan Sullivan. I am the special education ad-ministrator in this school district."

Mr. Gregory began the questioning, "Ms. Sullivan, are you knowledgeable of Janet House's case?"

Ms. Sullivan answered, "Yes, I am. I have been directly involved with Janet and her parents since a referral was made to the school district from St. Mary's Academy. I am also aware of Janet's progress prior to that time, when she attended first grade in the district."

Mr. Gregory asked, "When did the school district first become aware of Janet's difficulties in learning?"

Ms. Sullivan answered, "When Janet was in first grade, she experienced difficulty. In January of her first-grade year, the first-grade teacher consulted the teacher assistance team in the building. She attempted some strategies, some of which were successful. At the end of the first-grade year, Mr. and Mrs. House stated that they were very unhappy with Janet's progress. They insisted that Janet be retained in first grade. Janet's teacher agreed, and Janet was placed with another first-grade teacher the next year. During the year Janet was retained, she progressed nicely. She learned to read and complete simple addition and subtraction problems. The teacher assistance team continued to periodically work with Janet's teacher during the year. At the end of Janet's second year in first grade, Mr. and Mrs. House decided to place Janet in St. Mary's Academy. In October after Janet began attending the private school, it was suggested by the private school teacher to Mr. and Mrs. House that Janet needed testing to determine exactly what her problems were. Mr. and Mrs. House contracted with a private firm to conduct the testing. At this time, I was not aware of the assessment. After the assessment was complete, it is my understanding that the parents were unhappy with the results. The private school then made a written referral to the public school to complete an evaluation on Janet. The sequence of events leading up to the referral is documented on the written referral from the private school."

Mr. Gregory said to the hearing officer, "The referral information is on Document Number 45."

Mr. Gregory continued the questioning by asking, "Ms. Sullivan, was there any reason to believe that Janet should have been referred for an evaluation at the end of her first year in first grade?"

Ms. Sullivan answered, "No, I don't think so. Janet's teacher was working with the teacher assistance team with some success. Then Janet was retained, again with some success. At that time, there was no reason to believe that a referral needed to be made."

The questioning by Mr. Gregory continued for the next hour. The hearing officer then called for cross-examination of Ms. Sullivan by Ms. Hudson.

Ms. Hudson began by asking, "Ms. Sullivan, are other children in first grade referred for evaluations?"

Ms. Sullivan answered, "Yes, on occasion."

Ms. Hudson continued, "And what is the most common academic reason for a child to be referred for an evaluation in first grade?"

Ms. Sullivan answered, "It's difficult to generalize, because all referrals are unique, but probably the most common reason for a referral in first grade is not learning to read."

Ms. Hudson asked, "Did Janet have difficulty learning to read in first grade?"

Ms. Sullivan answered, "Yes, but her teacher worked with the teacher…"

Ms. Hudson cut her off and said, "I asked you if she had difficulty learning to read and you said yes. Now, if the most common reason a child would be referred for an evaluation in first grade is lack of progress in learning to read, and Janet was having difficulty reading, would you agree that she should have been referred for an evaluation at that time?"

Ms. Sullivan looked frustrated as she answered, "No. I said her teacher was working with the teacher assistance team and…"

Ms. Hudson again cut her off and said, "I asked for a yes or no answer. It seems to me that any child experiencing great difficulty reading in first grade would be referred for an evaluation and Janet was not. Therefore, her parents had to seek a private school and a private evaluation."

The cross-examination continued for another hour and a half. The hearing officer then recessed for lunch. The afternoon included questioning of witnesses for the school district, including the school psychologist and LD teacher. The parents' witnesses were also questioned, and they included the parents, a private psychologist, and private school teachers. At 10:00 P.M. that evening, the due process hearing concluded. Both attorneys made closing statements, and the hearing officer made a final statement.

Mr. Goodman stated, "My closing statement will be brief. The hearing officer's decision will address oral testimony and written evidence. The decision will contain orders related to all issues. The school district is responsible for the official, written, verbatim record of this hearing. After completing the decision, all materials will be returned, and I will have no further contact with the parties about this matter. The written findings of fact and decision will be mailed by certified mail within 10 days of the close of the hearing. The requesting party and the respondent will receive copies of the decision, as well as the state board of education. The decision will be binding upon the parties unless the decision is appealed. The decision will completely detail the procedures for appeal. This hearing is concluded."

Two weeks after the hearing ended, both parties received a decision from the hearing officer. The order stated, in part, the following:

1. The school district shall not pay for the student's tuition, fees, books, and related costs at the parochial school.
2. The school district shall not pay for tutorial services provided at home by the parents.
3. Attorney fees are a matter left to the courts.
4. The school district shall continue to provide special education services to the child based on the specifications outlined in the IEP.

QUESTIONS

Legal Issues to Consider

1. Why wasn't the school district ordered to pay tuition to the private school?

2. Why wasn't the school district ordered to pay for the private, independent evaluation?

3. If the parents requested attorney fees within the court system, would a judge have ordered reimbursement to the parents? Why or why not?

Other Issues

1. What if the hearing officer had ordered the school district to pay tuition to the private school and the school district refused? How can the hearing officer demand compliance with an order?

2. Should hearing officers be allowed to award attorney fees? Why or why not?

▰▰▰▰▰▰▰   **CASE 11.6**   ▰▰▰▰▰▰▰

GABRIEL/VOCATIONAL TRAINING

The impartial due process hearing was convened on behalf of Gabriel Richards in the administration center of the local school district on Thursday, December 10. The hearing was closed to the public at the request of the parent. The school district was represented by its legal counsel, who served as the primary spokesperson for the school district. The parent was represented by a legal advocacy service provided by a local law-school legal clinic. Two law students served as the primary spokespersons for the parent. Both parties presented witnesses, and the student, Gabriel, did not attend the hearing.

The parent, Ms. Mary Richards, requested the hearing. The following issues were presented before the hearing officer:

1. Whether the school district provided Gabriel with FAPE when it failed to provide the vocational hours required by the IEP developed for Gabriel for the past school year.
2. Whether the school district violated Gabriel's rights when it failed to promptly develop alternative job sites when a job in a retail store deteriorated during the past school year.
3. Whether the school district denied Gabriel his procedural rights by subjecting him to suspensions from school.
4. Whether the school district was financially liable for two years of postsecondary compensatory education requested by the parent as a remedy for the alleged violations.

The school district's position was that Gabriel's rights had not been violated, that he had been provided with FAPE, that his vocational planning and IEP were appropriate, and that the school district was not responsible for providing postsecondary compensatory education.

Throughout the hearing, nine witnesses were called to testify—six for the parent and three for the school district. Through the testimony, the following background and sequence of events emerged.

Gabriel was a 21-year-old male with the disability of autism. He received special education and related services throughout his school years. Gabriel exhibited the characteristics of a behaviorally disordered and language-impaired student. He communicated utilizing gestures, a few words in sign language, and communication (picture) books. Inappropriate behaviors included flapping his arms, head-slapping, yelling, pinching himself, biting his arms, smearing feces with hands on walls, head-banging, and crying.

Gabriel was educated by the local high school until he became 21 years old. When at high school, Gabriel was involved in extensive vocational training. The training included job sites on school grounds and in the community and coursework focusing on daily living skills and recreational skills. While working on a job, Gabriel was assigned a job coach who monitored behaviors and job performance. The job coach also encouraged appropriate job-related behaviors such as following directions and meeting employer expectations.

In the workplace and at school, Gabriel often exhibited inappropriate behaviors. On three occasions, the inappropriate behaviors resulted in suspensions from the work site, but not suspension from school. When Gabriel displayed inappropriate behaviors, attempts first were made by the job coach to assist Gabriel in gaining control over his behaviors. When these attempts failed, he was removed from the job site and allowed to complete his day at school.

During Gabriel's school years, the parent and school district developed a positive working relationship. Ms. Richards attended all IEP and multidisciplinary meetings and was actively involved in Gabriel's education. On one occasion, Ms. Richards obtained an independent evaluation, which was considered by the IEP conference, and its recommendations were implemented. The independent evaluator praised Gabriel's program and teacher as being progressive and appropriate.

In July, prior to Gabriel's last year in high school, Ms. Richards met with Gabriel's teacher and job coach to develop a behavioral intervention plan. A work evaluation revealed several inappropriate behaviors. In one instance, Gabriel punched in for work but would not move to his work area for 45 minutes. Another observation documented that Gabriel required almost continuous verbal prompting because he was very loud and engaged in excessive self-stimulating behaviors. On another day, Gabriel worked for the entire time, and his production was equal to or better than most of his coworkers. It was difficult to determine clear antecedents for Gabriel's behaviors, but possible antecedents could have included lack of sleep, mouth pain, illness, lack of motivation, new school staff, or being asked to perform a task that he did not want to perform. The team included a detailed behavioral intervention plan in Gabriel's IEP for the past school year.

During testimony, it was apparent that Ms. Richards did not want a change in placement, but rather a commitment from the school district to pay for two additional years of compensatory education so Gabriel could remain in his current placement. Gabriel continued to be served by the state department of rehabilitation services after he left school, and services at his job site were continued. Ms. Richards stated that Gabriel no longer had an entitlement for services from the school district because he was 21 years old, and there were no assurances that the state department of rehabilitation would continue to pay for services for any specific period of time. If the school district were ordered to pay for Gabriel's continuing vocational program, the placement would be ensured.

The hearing concluded, and two weeks later each party received an order from the hearing officer. The order, in part, included the following:

1. The school district provided Gabriel with FAPE through the age of 21 years. There is no evidence to substantiate the allegation that the school district failed to implement Gabriel's IEP. When Gabriel's behavior prevented him from working at the community work site, he returned to his local high school and received vocational programming at school. The school district acted in good faith to implement Gabriel's IEP to the maximum extent possible.

2. When Gabriel's behavior began to deteriorate during the past school year, the school district appropriately attempted behavioral interventions to encourage him to adapt to his work environment. The school district did not move Gabriel quickly from one work site to another, but attempted numerous behavioral interventions over a period of several months before moving him to a new job site.

3. There is no evidence to support the allegation that the school district violated Gabriel's rights. Gabriel was not suspended from school, but was removed only from the job site when necessary due to inappropriate behaviors. He continued to receive an appropriate vocational education at his home school.

4. Gabriel is not entitled to compensatory education at the expense of the school district. Because the parent is satisfied with the student's current vocational placement and has requested compensatory funding to ensure the continuation of this placement, and because this placement was initially developed and planned by the school district (but now is funded by another agency), the parent's argument that the school district did not appropriately plan for Gabriel's vocational needs is clearly not founded in fact.

QUESTIONS

Legal Issues to Consider

1. Under what circumstances would compensatory education be ordered by a hearing officer?

2. Why wasn't Gabriel's removal from the job site not considered a suspension?

3. According to IDEA, what responsibilities does a school district have when a student is displaying inappropriate behaviors?

Other Issues

1. Should the law be changed to require school districts to provide appropriate services to adults with disabilities past the age of 21? Why or why not?

2. Should students with Gabriel's characteristics (i.e., severe communication disorder and inappropriate behaviors) be allowed to work in the community, or should they receive services in a shelter-care environment? Why or why not?

ANSWERS TO LEGAL ISSUES TO CONSIDER

JODI/SPECIAL EDUCATION SERVICES

1. According to the basic principles of IDEA, did the team make a good decision not to provide special education services to Jodi? You may want to consider FAPE and equal access. Why or why not?

> The team did not make a good decision regarding special education services for Jodi. Jodi had a profound disability, and it was incorrect not to offer special education services based on her ability to benefit from the services. Under equal access, Jodi had a right to be offered the opportunity to develop to her own capability. FAPE means special education services that are provided at public expense, under public supervision, and without charge; that meet the standards of the state education agency, including standards under IDEA; that include ages 3 to 21 in the state involved; and that are provided in congruence with the child's IEP. Under the equal access doctrine and FAPE, Jodi would be offered special education services. It can be assumed that she had a disability that adversely affected her learning.

2. Describe any prominent court cases that address the issue of zero reject and educability.

> Three prominent cases address the issue of educability: *Mills v. D.C. Board of Education* (1972); *Pennsylvania Association for Retarded Citizens (PARC) v. Commonwealth of Pennsylvania* (1971, 1972); and *Timothy W. v. Rochester School District* (1988). The first two cases focused on the right of children with disabilities to an education, and the last specifically focused on educability.

3. Would Jodi be considered handicapped under Section 504 of the Rehabilitation Act of 1973? Why or why not?

> Under Section 504, people are handicapped if they meet the following definition: have or have had a physical or mental impairment that substantially limits a major life activity or are regarded as handicapped by others. Major life activities

include walking, seeing, hearing, speaking, breathing, learning, working, caring for oneself, and performing manual tasks. The handicapping condition only has to substantially limit one major life activity in order for students to be eligible. Jodi would be handicapped under this definition.

4. If Jodi were considered handicapped under Section 504, what kinds of services could be provided?

Under Section 504, Jodi would be entitled to an appropriate education. Appropriate means an education comparable to the education provided to nonhandicapped students, requiring reasonable accommodations. Related services (e.g., physical therapy) or specialized education services may be the reasonable accommodation.

■■■■■■■■■■ **CASE 3.2** ■■■■■■■■■■

LINDA/HOMESCHOOL

1. What responsibilities did the school district have under the federal mandate for child find? Did the school district fulfill its responsibilities?

It is questionable that the school district fulfilled its responsibilities for child find. IDEA mandates that each state education agency and local education agency conduct annual activities to identify, locate, and evaluate all children with disabilities residing within their boundaries, regardless of the nature or severity of their disabilities. The elementary school staff had direct knowledge that Linda was living within the boundaries of the school district and that she wasn't attending school. The staff also had knowledge that Linda might be a student with a disability, based on her performance in kindergarten. It might have made sense to pursue the reasons that Linda was out of school and to offer to conduct appropriate evaluations. Perhaps Linda's mother would have reconsidered her decision to homeschool Linda.

2. What responsibilities did the school district have under the federal mandate for transition? Did the school district fulfill its responsibilities?

The case suggests that the school district fulfilled its responsibilities for transition. Transition is defined in IDEA as "a coordinated set of activities" for the student that must be designed "within an outcome-oriented process" to "promote movement from school to postschool activities, including postsecondary education, vocational training, integrated employment, continuing and adult education, adult services, independent living, or community participation." Linda participated in the high school work–study program and was transitioned to an adult agency upon completion of high school.

3. How does transition in IDEA relate to the zero reject principle?

Transition forces schools to focus on the future of all students with disabilities within their programs. Students will not be discontinued from services at graduation if services are needed. School districts have to take responsibility for providing this transition to the community and adult world. No longer can they assume that students will be successful simply because they finished high school.

━━━━━ **CASE 3.3** ━━━━━

DANNY/EXPULSION

1. How does IDEA address the issue of expulsion?

IDEA's 1997 reauthorization addresses the issue of expulsion directly. If it is determined through a manifestation-determination review that the behavior is not a manifestation of the disability, disciplinary procedures applicable to children without disabilities may be used with the child in the same way they are applied to children without disabilities. However, the school district must continue to provide FAPE. FAPE includes the provision of services necessary to enable the child to progress in the general curriculum and advance toward the achievement of IEP goals. The child's IEP team must determine these services.

2. Was it legal for the district to expel Danny? Why or why not?

Yes, it was legal, because the district determined through a manifestation-determination review that Danny's behavior was not a manifestation of his disability.

3. Was it legal for the district to expel Danny from school during his ongoing suspension from school? What evidence supports your answer?

It was not legal to discontinue special education services for Danny during his expulsion, according to IDEA. Danny must continue to receive the services necessary to enable him to progress in the general curriculum and advance toward his IEP goals.

━━━━━ **CASE 3.4** ━━━━━

PETER/HEALTH IMPAIRED STUDENTS

1. Was Peter eligible for services under IDEA? Why or why not?

IDEA provides special education and related services to any student who has a disability and whose disability adversely affects education or whose disability causes the student to need special education services. It is possible that Peter could be considered to have the disability "health impaired." However, it is questionable whether Peter's disability adversely affected his education and made it necessary for him to receive special education or related services.

2. Was Peter eligible for services under Section 504? Why or why not?

Peter was clearly protected by Section 504. He met the Section 504 definition of handicapped. He had a physical impairment and was regarded as having a handicap that substantially limits a major life activity (i.e., learning). The reaction of people to Peter's handicap significantly limited him from benefiting from school. A Supreme Court decision—*Board of Education v. Arline* (1987)—also clarified the protection of students with communicable diseases. Peter had a communicable disease, and it was clearly the intent of Section 504 to prohibit discrimination for students with these diseases.

3. Should the school district have excluded Peter from the general population? Why or why not?

Case law regarding Section 504 has supported the position that students with AIDS should be educated in the regular classroom, but individual determination for each case must be made by a panel of medical experts. If, for an individual case, it were likely that the child could transmit the disease (e.g., bite others), it would be possible for the child to be provided an education in a more restrictive setting. This was not the case with Peter. Therefore, under Section 504, it would be discriminatory to exclude Peter from his peer group.

------ **CASE 3.5** ------

KATE/PHYSICAL DISABILITIES

1. Based on the evidence given, was Kate eligible for services under IDEA? Why or why not?

IDEA states that a child has a specific learning disability if the child does not achieve commensurate with the child's age and ability level in one or more of the areas listed, and the team finds that a child has a severe discrepancy between achievement and intellectual ability in one or more of these areas: oral expression; listening comprehension; written expression; basic reading skill; reading comprehension; mathematics calculation; and mathematics reasoning. A child cannot be labeled as having a specific learning disability if the severe discrepancy between ability and achievement is primarily the result of a visual, hearing, or motor disability; mental retardation; emotional disturbance; or environmental, cultural, or economic disadvantage. In addition, the disability must have an adverse affect on the child's education. Given this definition and the data presented, Kate would not be eligible for the category-specific learning disability. Kate might have been eligible for physically handicapped if it could be demonstrated that her lack of hands interfered with her education.

2. What other federal law might provide legal protection to Kate? Would she have been entitled to special services?

Section 504 would offer protection from discrimination for Kate. Under Section 504, a person is identified as handicapped if that person has or has had a physical or mental impairment that substantially limits a major life activity (i.e., learning) or is regarded as handicapped by others. Kate would have to be provided an education comparable to education provided to nonhandicapped students, requiring that reasonable accommodations be made. Reasonable accommodations would be provided by making an accommodation plan that might include related services or special education services.

3. Was cost the legal basis for denying occupational therapy?

It was not legal to refuse special education services on the basis of cost. IDEA has no provisions to limit the FAPE required simply because the district may not have the funds.

■■■■■■ CASE 3.6 ■■■■■■

ANDRE/AGE AND SPECIAL EDUCATION SERVICES

1. Is it legal for the school to reject Andre at age 18? Why or why not?

Legally, a student cannot be excluded between the ages of 18 and 21 if that student has not graduated from high school. IDEA mandates services for students until the age of 21, and the courts—for example, *Tuttle v. Evans* (1993)—have clarified the federal law. In this case, other issues also surface. Because Andre failed even special education classes, and no meetings were held to address this failure, the district did not provide FAPE.

2. What obligation does the school have for Andre's transition into the community?

IDEA mandates transition services for Andre. Students age 16 and above must have a statement of needed transition services in their IEPs. Transition is defined as a "coordinated set of activities for the student designed within an outcome-oriented process to promote movement from school to postschool activities, including postsecondary education, vocational training, integrated employment (including supported employment), continuing and adult education, adult services, independent living or community participation." In this case, the evidence suggests that transition services were not properly considered.

▬▬▬▬▬ **CASE 4.1** ▬▬▬▬▬

CARLOS/DISCRIMINATORY EVALUATIONS

1. What mistakes does Mr. Simpson make when evaluating Carlos?

Mr. Simpson made several errors in evaluating Carlos.

(a) The assessment was discriminatory. The WISC III was not standard-ized on Spanish-speaking children, and the student was not assessed in his native language.

(b) The assessment did not appear to focus on the student's educational needs. Carlos was simply labeled as a result of the assessment.

(c) The assessment was not comprehensive and multidisciplinary. The intelligence test appeared to be the only test used, and the school psychologist appeared to be the only professional involved in the assessment.

(d) The rights of the student and his parent were not protected. The eval-uation was not comprehensive and multidisciplinary, the school psy-chologist refused to consider an outside evaluation, and it appeared that an evaluation conference was not held.

2. What is the school's responsibility regarding the independent evaluation?

The school district is obligated to consider an independent evaluation submit-ted by the parent. This consideration must occur in an IEP meeting. The dis-trict is not obligated to follow recommendations in the independent evaluation, only to consider the evaluation.

3. From the information provided, does Carlos have a disability? If yes, what is the dis-ability? If no, what information would lead you to believe that he does not have a disabil-ity? What other information might be needed to answer this question?

It is uncertain whether Carlos has a disability, considering that he did not re-ceive a comprehensive evaluation. Assessments were not specific to Carlos' area of educational need, and related areas such as hearing were never tested. If the independent evaluation was determined to be appropriate, it appears that he would not be considered eligible to receive special education services under the categories of specific learning disability or mental impairment.

▬▬▬▬▬ **CASE 4.2** ▬▬▬▬▬

TONY/INADEQUATE EVALUATIONS

1. Describe the issues of parent participation that were ignored during this evaluation.

There were many parental rights that were ignored during this evaluation, according to IDEA. They include:

(a) written notice to the parent that the district proposed to evaluate the child, including why the district proposed the evaluation and on what basis

(b) informed parental consent prior to the evaluation

(c) notice of parental rights

(d) the parent did not participate and provide input into the evaluation

(e) notice to the parent that the district was convening a meeting to discuss the evaluation (and possibly plan a program)

(f) after the meeting, notice to the parent of the outcome of the meeting

(g) parental permission for special education placement before the placement

Because of these major errors, the child and parent were not afforded their rights under IDEA.

2. Describe the issues of appropriate evaluation that were ignored during this scenario.

There were numerous errors, including the following:

(a) Tests used might have been discriminatory based on the norming process described in one test.

(b) A variety of assessment tools and strategies were not used to gather relevant functional and developmental information about the child.

(c) The parent did not participate or have input into the evaluation.

(d) The tests used did not appear to be validated for the specific purpose for which they were used.

(e) The person administering the tests did not appear to be trained and knowledgeable about the tests.

(f) The testing did not appear to be administered in a standardized format or using standard conditions (i.e., the back of the classroom).

(g) Tests were not tailored to assess specific areas of educational need.

(h) The child was not assessed in all areas related to the suspected disability.

(i) Eligibility and placement were determined based upon one person's judgement.

CASE 4.3

SCOTT/PROCEDURAL ERRORS

1. What was wrong with Scott's evaluation, according to IDEA?

Many procedural errors occurred during this evaluation. They included:

(a) The parent did not receive information on parental rights.

(b) The school counselor assessed Scott without prior written notice to the parent and informed consent from the parent.

(c) It appeared that the school counselor was not trained to administer the tests used.

(d) Scott was not assessed in all areas related to his suspected disability, and a variety of assessment tools and strategies were not used. Progress in the general curriculum, for example, did not appear to be part of the evaluation.

(e) The evaluation was not multidisciplinary. It appeared to be conducted by two people.

(f) The parent was not notified in writing of the meeting to discuss the results of the evaluation.

2. From the information provided, does Scott have a disability of emotional disturbance? Why or why not?

According to IDEA, emotional disturbance means that a child exhibits one or more of the following characteristics over a long period of time and to a marked degree that adversely affects a child's educational performance:

- an inability to learn that cannot be explained by intellectual, sensory, or health factors
- an inability to build or maintain satisfactory interpersonal relationships with peers and teachers
- inappropriate types of behavior or feelings under normal circumstances
- a general pervasive mood of unhappiness or depression
- a tendency to develop physical symptoms or fears associated with personal or school problems

Emotional disturbance includes schizophrenia and does not apply to children who are socially maladjusted, unless they are also emotionally disturbed.

Given this definition and the procedural errors that occurred during the evaluation, it is difficult to determine if Scott met the definition. From the information reported, one might conclude that he met some of the characteristics, but the faulty evaluation does not substantiate the presence or absence of disability.

3. Based on the meeting to discuss Scott's evaluation, what could Fred do next?

Fred has several options. They include:

- requesting an independent evaluation at school district expense
- requesting mediation
- requesting due process hearing

The options might result in another evaluation, which would clarify the presence or absence of a disability.

━━━━━━━━━━ **CASE 4.4** ━━━━━━━━━━

TINA/CLASSIFICATION ISSUES

1. Based on the test results and the definition of a learning disability, did the school make the correct decision concerning Tina's classification during the first evaluation? How do you know?

> One might assume that the school district followed correct procedures (e.g., consent and notification) during the evaluation. If this were the case, the focus would be on the definition of learning disability in IDEA. The operational definition of learning disability in IDEA regulations indicates that a written report must document that the child has a severe discrepancy between achievement and ability that is not correctable without special education and related services. Assuming all other pieces of the definition were met, the evaluation did not show this discrepancy.

2. After Tina's accident, was it appropriate for Justine to request additional testing? Why or why not?

> Justine had the right to request another evaluation from the school district. After the request (i.e., referral), the school district would have reviewed existing evaluation data and identified what additional data, if any, were needed to determine if Tina had a disability. The school district would have notified Justine of its decision to conduct or not to conduct an additional evaluation. If Justine disagreed with the decision, she could have requested a due process hearing or mediation.

3. Should the school consider the test results from Nancy Bertel? Why or why not?

> According to IDEA regulations, the school district was obligated to consider the evaluation results presented by the parent. The results should have been considered in an IEP meeting, but the school district was under no obligation to agree with the evaluator's recommendations. If Justine did not agree with the outcome of the meeting, she could have requested due process or mediation.

━━━━━━━━━━ **CASE 4.5** ━━━━━━━━━━

JOAN/REFUSAL TO EVALUATE

1. Should Joan have been required to take a state group achievement test such as the IAT? Why or why not? If Joan had been identified as a student with a disability, would your answer be different? How?

> Individual states have different rules about who should and should not take state tests of achievement. Generally, most states require that all students take

the test. If Joan were identified as a student with a disability, the answer would be different. IDEA requires that children with disabilities be included in general state and districtwide assessments, with appropriate accommodations and modifications, if needed. The IEP team must determine and document the IEP modifications in the administration of state or district assessments of achievement. If the IEP team determines that the child will not participate in an assessment, the IEP must include a statement of why the assessment is not appropriate and how the child will be assessed.

2. After the parents requested that Joan be tested for LD, was the school under any obligation to evaluate her? How should school district personnel have proceeded?

The request by Joan's parents for evaluation would become a referral. School-district personnel were obligated to consider if the referral was appropriate. The school district could then reject or accept the referral. The parents should have been notified in writing of the district's decision to evaluate or refuse to evaluate Joan. This notice should have included information on parents' rights. If Joan's parents disagreed with the decision, they could have requested a due process hearing or mediation.

3. Was the school district under any obligation to consider the results from the independent tests obtained by the parents? Why or why not?

IDEA requires that a school district consider independent evaluations only if the child has been identified as having a disability. The real issue in this case is the school district's refusal to conduct an evaluation and the parent's disagreement. The parents could request a due process hearing or mediation to request an evaluation. The parents could also request that the school district pay for the independent evaluation. If, through a due process hearing, the district is ordered to evaluate the child and the child is found eligible for special education, the district could be ordered to reimburse the parents for the independent evaluation.

◼◼◼◼◼◼◼ **CASE 4.6** ◼◼◼◼◼◼◼

LATIFA/BIASED TESTING PROCEDURES

1. Describe how the school district handled the issue of parental consent for evaluation and its impact on the evaluation process.

The school district did not obtain written informed consent for the evaluation before the evaluation. Therefore, the parent's and child's rights were not observed during the evaluation. The district should not have proceeded with the evaluation. If questioned in a due process hearing, the district would not be able to defend itself on this issue. The foundation of IDEA is that parents are informed and consent to any activities that might result in the child being labeled as having a disability.

2. Should the school have tested Latifa in her native French? Why or why not?

The school should have tested Latifa in her native language. IDEA states that tests should be administered in the child's native language or other mode of communication, unless it is clearly not feasible to do so. There was no reason to believe that it was not feasible to assess Latifa in her native French.

3. How have the courts interpreted issues of cultural or racial bias of standardized tests?

According to *Larry P. v. Riles* (1979), the court banned the use of standardized intelligence tests to evaluate African American children for placement in classes for children who were mentally impaired. This was affirmed by the Ninth Circuit Court of Appeals in 1986 and was expanded to ban the use of these tests for African American children in any special education placement. Another case, *PASE v. Hannon* (1980), held that certain IQ tests may contain items that might be considered racially biased. The court also held that the school district had not used an IQ test as the sole determination for placement in special education.

▄▄▄▄▄▄▄▄   **CASE 5.1**   ▄▄▄▄▄▄▄▄

WALTER/TRANSITION SERVICES

1. Was Mr. Watson justified in keeping Walter in his current classroom?

Provided Walter is achieving his IEP goals and objectives, Mr. Watson is justified in keeping Walter in his current placement. According to the Rowley case, the purpose of appropriate education does not mean that schools should provide services to maximize the student's education.

2. Were the Thompsons justified in requesting that Walter be placed in the vocational setting?

The Thompsons would have to show that Walter's current education is inappropriate by showing that he is not achieving his IEP goals and objectives (i.e., inappropriate education), and they would have to show that the vocational placement is more appropriate for Walter.

3. If Walter is achieving the goals and objectives set forth in his IEP, should he be moved?

No, Walter should not be moved if he is achieving his IEP goals and objectives.

━━━━━ **CASE 5.2** ━━━━━

VERNON/IMPROPER PLACEMENT

1. Is Vernon achieving the goals and objectives set forth in his IEP?

It is questionable whether Vernon is achieving the goals and objective set forth in his IEP. The Reweys should request documentation that Vernon is achieving his goals and objectives.

2. Did the MDT make the proper decision in the placement of Vernon?

Dealing with IDEA's LRE principle in court cases has been tenuous at best. Thus far, "the results of these cases has been mixed, with some decisions favoring inclusive placements and others restrictive placements" (Yell, 1998, p. 251).

3. Is the full continuum of placement available at this district?

It does not appear that the full continuum of services is available in this district. A less-restrictive option would be to place Vernon in a resource room with appropriate mainstreaming.

━━━━━ **CASE 5.3** ━━━━━

YANCY/GENERAL EDUCATION PARTICIPATION

1. Did Mr. Mendel make the proper decision by allowing Yancy to remain in the classroom for a 10-week trial period?

Allowing Yancy to remain in the class for longer than the agreed on period shows a *good faith* effort, provided the classroom teacher is also making and documenting a "good faith" effort.

2. Does Hanna have any grounds for requesting that the aide, Mr. Hudson, receive more training?

To date, there does not appear to be much support about the role that the quality of an aide's training has on appropriate education.

3. Should Hanna request a placement closer to Yancy's home? Is the school obligated to create such a placement?

Hanna can request a closer placement, but the district is under no obligation to provide it, as long as they have in place a proper continuum of alternative placements.

━━━━━━ **CASE 5.4** ━━━━━━

NICHOLAS/PARENT PARTICIPATION

1. What members should be present at an MDT meeting?

The MDT should be composed of a group of persons, including at least one teacher or other specialist with knowledge of the suspected area of disability.

2. What members should be present at the IEP meeting?

Members of the IEP team should include the parents of the child; at least one general education teacher of the child (if the child is or may be participating in general education); at least one special education teacher; a representative of the school district who is qualified to provide or supervise special education, is knowledgeable about the general education curriculum, and is knowledgeable about the availability of resources within the school district; a person who can interpret the instructional implications of evaluation results; other persons who have knowledge of the child at the discretion of the parent or school district; and the child, if appropriate.

3. What procedures or processes did the team fail to follow concerning the evaluation, parent participation, and IEP development? What role does parental consent play in the school's responsibility in the IEP process?

Among the errors, the MDT members failed to

(a) arrange for an alternative date for the MDT meeting so that Nicholas Drumage's parent(s) could attend

(b) obtain parent input and consent for Nicholas' IEP (in addition, the use of the NITPIC is questionable)

(c) failed to obtain and reach agreement from the parents concerning the IEP

━━━━━━ **CASE 5.5** ━━━━━━

KELLY/RELATED SERVICES

1. From the information provided, was Kelly receiving an appropriate education?

Provided the school was following the goals and objectives from Kelly's IEP, then Kelly's education was appropriate.

2. What is meant by *appropriate education*? How have recent court cases or IDEA defined it? Was a good faith effort made to provide appropriate education?

The IEP should serve as the major tool for acquiring an appropriate education. Furthermore, according to standards from the *Board of Education v. Rowley*

(1982) case, the intent of IDEA is to provide students with "a reasonable opportunity to learn," not to provide students with "opportunities to reach their maximum potential" (Turnbull, 1993).

3. By law, what would prevent the district from purchasing a machine and training an assister for Kelly?

Provided the school is providing an appropriate education, without the machine and assister, it is under no obligation to provide them.

■■■■■■■■   **CASE 5.6**   ■■■■■■■■

HAROLD/ADEQUATE SERVICES

1. From the information provided, was Harold receiving an appropriate education without the tutoring program?

Provided the school was following the goals and objectives from Harold's IEP, then Harold's education is appropriate.

2. Is the school obligated to provide a tutor or aide for Harold? What role should cost play in deciding an appropriate education?

Provided the school is providing an appropriate education without the tutor, it is under no obligation to provide Harold with one.

3. What can Harold's parents do to get better services for him in the general education classroom?

The parent could argue that Harold needs more time from the special education teacher and request that this should occur in the general education classroom. Or, she can take her case through due process, if she feels that an appropriate education could be provided through better services.

■■■■■■■■   **CASE 6.1**   ■■■■■■■■

JOHN/DISRUPTIVE BEHAVIOR

1. What is the legal basis for the proposed placement of John in a private day treatment facility for students with behavior disorders?

IDEA requires that school districts establish procedures to assure that "to the maximum extent appropriate, children with disabilities ... are educated with children who are not disabled, and that special education, separate schooling, or other removal of children with disabilities from the regular educational environment occurs only when the nature or severity of the disability is such that education in regular classes with the use of supplementary aids and services cannot be achieved satisfactorily." In this case, John was being removed from the regular school due to the nature and severity of his behavior disorder. The school district had documented numerous attempts to assist John by providing supplementary aids and services.

In addition, IDEA requires that school districts provide a continuum of alternative placements to meet the needs of children with disabilities. The continuum must include regular classes, special classes, special schools, home instruction, and instruction in hospital and institutions, and it must make provisions for supplementary services (i.e., resource room or itinerant instruction) to be provided in conjunction with regular-class placement. In this case, the district considered options along the continuum.

2. Did the parents have a legal basis to demand that John stay in Martin Luther King Middle School (e.g., John would pick up severe behaviors from other BD students)?

The parents stated their opinion, which may, in fact, have been correct. However, there was not a legal basis to support their concern. As long as the placement was individually determined to meet John's special needs and was based on an appropriate IEP, the placement could legally be made in a private day treatment program for students with behavior disorders.

3. If the district had not attempted to assist John by selecting particular teachers, changing his schedule, providing a behavior management program, and so forth, would that have changed the outcome of this case? Why or why not?

If the district had not made numerous attempts to meet John's needs within the public school placement, the outcome might have been different. In fact, the district might have been required to provide supplemental services within the public school setting before proposing a more restrictive program. If a district made no attempt to provide supplemental aids and services and it made a placement outside of the district, it would be apparent that the district was not following the IDEA in its implementation of LRE. In addition, the district, by not providing supplemental aids and services, would not be providing an appropriate education for John based on the needs stated on his IEP.

━━━━━━ **CASE 6.2** ━━━━━━

BEN/INCLUSION

1. According to IDEA, was the principal correct when he made the statement, "We don't have inclusion here. Ben will have to go to the special education class in the building"? Why or why not?

The principal did not make a wise or legal statement. IDEA states that decisions for children should be made on an individual basis and should be made based on the child's IEP. The principal did not consider the child's needs, nor did he base his statement upon the child's IEP. His statement appeared to be based on current resources available and current structure of the special education program.

2. Describe some of the case law that has helped set standards for determining FAPE and LRE. Did the school district in this case meet the standards?

Judicial interpretation of FAPE and LRE include the following cases:

Board of Education of the Hendrick Hudson Central School District v. Rowley (1982). The court developed a two-pronged test for FAPE: Did the school district follow procedural compliance? Was the IEP reasonably calculated to confer educational benefit?

Daniel R. R. v. State Board of Education (1989). Can education in the regular classroom, with the use of supplemental aids and services, be achieved satisfactorily for a given child? If it cannot and the school intends to provide special education or to remove the child from regular education, we ask whether the school has mainstreamed the child to the maximum extent appropriate.

Sacramento Unified School District v. Holland (1994). The court used a four-factor balancing test to determine LRE: (1) educational benefits of placing the child in a full-time regular education program; (2) the nonacademic benefits of such a placement; (3) the effect the child would have on the teacher and the other students in the class; and (4) costs associated with this placement.

If these questions and factors were considered in light of Ben's case, it would be determined that the school district met all of the standards to appropriately make the decision to place Ben in special education classes 60 percent of the school day.

3. How does Section 504 address the issue of LRE? Did the district in this case meet the intent of Section 504?

Section 504 addresses LRE in academic settings and nonacademic settings. The regulations state that handicapped children should be educated with non-handicapped children unless it is not possible, even with the use of supplemental aids and services. In nonacademic settings, extracurricular services and activities, including meals and recess periods, are addressed. Handicapped children are to participate with nonhandicapped children to the maximum extent possible. The school district in this case appeared to meet the intent of Section 504.

4. Is the term *inclusion* a legal term? How does IDEA address inclusion?

The term *inclusion* is not a legal term, nor is it addressed directly in IDEA. IDEA addresses the legal terms of LRE, FAPE, continuum of alternative placements, and placements. If the child is placed appropriately in an individualized program designed to meet the child's needs and the regulations of IDEA are met, the concept of inclusion becomes a moot point, legally speaking.

━━━━━━━━   CASE 6.3   ━━━━━━━━

JAMES/TEACHER BIAS

1. Did the team meet the requirements for LRE as stated in IDEA? Why or why not?

The team did not meet the requirements of LRE as defined in IDEA. IDEA specifically states that, to the maximum extent appropriate, children with disabilities are educated with children who are not disabled. Removing students with disabilities from the general education environment should occur only when the nature and severity of the disability is such that education in regular classes with the use of supplementary aids and services cannot be achieved satisfactorily. There is no evidence in this case that James' disability was severe enough to warrant placement in a full-time special education placement. There is also no evidence in this case that supplementary aids and services were even discussed. The placement appears to have been made based on the convenience of the teachers involved and existing configurations of services available.

2. Did the team meet the requirements for continuum of services as stated in IDEA? Why or why not?

IDEA specifically requires that a continuum of services be available and include instruction in regular classes, special classes, and so forth. There must also be provisions for supplementary services such as resource room or itinerant instruction to be provided in conjunction with regular class placement. From the data provided in this case, it seemed as though a full continuum of services was not available for consideration. Resource placement was indirectly rejected and not truly considered as a placement option.

3. Was James' IEP individualized to meet his special needs? What evidence supports your statement?

It is questionable that James' IEP was truly individualized to meet his needs. His general education teacher stated that James was progressing well in all areas except reading. This statement was not considered when writing James' IEP. Instead, the special education teacher suggested that if a child had difficulty with reading, all other academic areas would be affected. She stated that James fit this profile and would likely benefit from full-time special instruction. The special education teacher assumed that James was similar to other children who had difficulty in reading and suggested his placement be based not on James' needs, but on the assumed needs of other, similar children. There is little evidence indicating why James did not stay in the general education classroom.

■■■■■■■■   **CASE 6.4**   ■■■■■■■■

DAVID/THREATENING BEHAVIOR

1. Was it legal for the special education teacher to tell the parents that David would not be considered for a residential placement before the evaluation and evaluation conference? Why or why not?

> The special education teacher made an error when she told the parents that one option along the continuum—residential—would be eliminated before the evaluation, conference, and IEP. Although IDEA states that students with disabilities should be educated with students without disabilities as much as possible, it is also states that school districts must maintain a continuum of alternative placements, including instruction in regular classes, special classes, special school, home instruction, and instruction in hospitals and institutions. The placement should also be based on the IEP and should be individualized.

2. According to IDEA, what issues of eligibility did the evaluation team consider in deciding if David were eligible for special education?

> The team had to consider if David had a disability as defined by IDEA that affected his learning. The definition for emotional disorders is very broad, and David's profile could fit the definition. There was also evidence that David's deficits interfered with his learning.

3. Should the evaluation team have placed David in a residential program initially? Why or why not?

> The team made a defensible decision not to place David in a residential placement initially, as long as they considered all options along the continuum of possible placements. LRE requires that children with disabilities are educated with children who are not disabled as much as possible. The removal of students with disabilities from general education occurs only when the nature or severity of the disability is such that education in general education with the use of supplementary aids and services cannot be achieved satisfactorily.

■■■■■■■■   **CASE 6.5**   ■■■■■■■■

JANE/REFUSAL TO CONSIDER

1. According to IDEA, describe how the school district failed to follow the LRE doctrine.

> IDEA states that children with disabilities should be educated with nondisabled children to the maximum extent possible, and the removal of children from the regular classroom should occur only when the nature or severity of

the disability is such that education in regular classes with the use of supplementary aids and services cannot be achieved satisfactorily. The school district failed to do the following:

(a) the school district did not truly consider placing Jane in first grade with supplementary aides and services. All school staff rejected the idea of including Jane in first grade without consideration of the possibility;

(b) the placement decision was not truly individualized and did not consider Jane's special needs; and

(c) the placement decision was based on the current configuration of special education services in the building and not a full continuum of services. It appears that the only service available to Jane was a self-contained special education classroom with speech and language therapy services.

2. According to case law on LRE, what factors should the district have considered in making the placement decision?

Daniel R. R. v. State Board of Education (1989) provided a two-pronged test for making LRE decisions: Can education in the regular classroom, with the use of supplemental aids and services, be achieved satisfactorily for a child? If it cannot, and the school intends to provide special education or to remove the child from regular education, ask whether the school has mainstreamed the child to the maximum extent appropriate.

Another case from the U.S. Court of Appeals for the Ninth Circuit, *Sacramento Unified School District v. Holland* (1994), provided school districts with a four-factor balancing test to use when making LRE decisions:

(a) consideration of educational benefits of placing the child in a full-time regular education program

(b) consideration of the nonacademic benefits of such a placement

(c) consideration of the effect the child would have on the teacher and the other students in the class

(d) consideration of costs associated with this placement

<hr>

CASE 6.6

JARED/LEGAL RIGHTS

1. According to IDEA, does a child with a disability have a right to be placed in general education? Why or why not?

A child with a disability does not have a legal right to be placed in regular education. IDEA states that "to the maximum extent appropriate" children who are disabled are to be placed with nondisabled children. Providing an individually appropriate program to meet the needs of the child takes precedence over placement in regular education.

2. According to IDEA, does a child with a disability have a right to be placed in the child's home school? Why or why not?

Although IDEA expresses preference for placement in the neighborhood school, there is no statutory right for that placement. Case law has also supported this position.

3. To what extent did the school district follow the LRE doctrine concerning continuum of services?

IDEA requires that the school district maintain a full continuum of services for students with disabilities. In this case, the IEP team made a decision to place Jared in a more restrictive environment (i.e., a private day treatment facility), instead of his current placement (i.e., self-contained special class) or a less restrictive environment (i.e., regular class placement with supplementary aids and services). It appears that a full continuum of services was available.

━━━━ CASE 7.1 ━━━━

AMY/PARENTS IN CLASS

1. What factors should be used in making a decision about Amy's placement?

First, consideration of Amy's placement should occur in an IEP meeting, and the decision made should be based on Amy's strengths and parental concerns, the results of her most recent evaluation, and, if appropriate, results of her performance on any state or districtwide assessments. Goals for Amy should be based on how her disability affects her involvement and progress in the general education curriculum.

Case law—*Sacramento Unified School District v. Holland* (1994)—suggests consideration of the educational benefits of placing the child in a fulltime general education program, the nonacademic benefits of such a placement, the effect the child would have on the teacher and the other students in the class, and the costs associated with this placement.

2. Was the district justified in returning Amy to Mrs. Keller's self-contained special classroom? Why or why not?

Assuming the district made a decision to return Amy to a special class in a procedurally correct IEP meeting, the decision was procedurally correct. However, if challenged, district personnel might have to provide evidence that real attempts were made to include Amy in the general education class. Given that the district provided only a part-time aide and no other supplementary aids and services were considered, the district might have difficulty defending its decision.

3. What is meant by *parent participation,* and did Amy's parents have the right to show up in the classroom or to serve as part-time aides?

IDEA gives parents rights in several areas, including:

- informed consent prior to evaluations and initial placement
- participation in meetings concerning the child
- involvement in placement decisions
- the right to question decisions made about the child in regard to evaluation and placement
- the right to an independent educational evaluation
- opportunity to examine records of the child

IDEA does not address the issue of the parents' right to show up in the classroom on a daily basis or to serve as part-time aides.

<hr>

■■■■■■■   **CASE 7.2**   ■■■■■■■

LANSKY/PARENTAL CONSENT

1. According to IDEA, how should a school district gain parental permission for an initial evaluation? Did the school district in this case meet this standard?

The district must inform the parent in writing that the district proposes to evaluate the child. The notice should include the following:

- an explanation of why the child should be evaluated
- a description of other options that the district considered and why those options were rejected
- a description of each evaluation or procedure used as a basis for determining that the evaluation is needed
- a description of parents' rights
- a listing of sources for the parents to contact in understanding the notice

The notice must be written in the native language of communication of the parent and be understandable to the general public. In addition, written consent in the parents' native language must be obtained before an evaluation.

In this case, the school district did not meet this standard. There was no evidence that the parents received written notice in their native language of what the district was proposing, nor did the parents give informed consent to the evaluation.

2. Was the school district justified in placing Lansky at Mountain Road Elementary? Why or why not?

> Probably not. The district should provide a full continuum of placement options for Lansky, particularly because there are other students with similar disabilities. The Reskis could request that Lansky be tested by an independent evaluation, or they could request a due process hearing to contend Lansky's placement.

3. Should an interpreter have been present for the evaluation meeting? Why or why not?

> The Reskis have quite a few parental rights, including being informed about testing, providing consent to be tested, and having information explained to them in their native language.

<hr>

CASE 7.3

TUNITA/SETTING GOALS

1. What are Kersha's rights concerning input into her child's ITP?

> Kersha could make changes in the ITP; however, the school could reject those changes. If this occurred, Kersha could take her case through due process.

2. What can Kersha do if she feels that Tunita's ITP needs to be changed but the school district refuses?

> She can seek due process.

3. Did the district provide appropriate education to Tunita?

> This decision would be based on her ITP goals and objectives, and in accordance with *Board of Education v. Rowley* (1982), the school district does not have to provide opportunities for the student to achieve to their maximum potential.

<hr>

CASE 7.4

KAMI/IMPROPER EVALUATION

1. Do the parents have a right to a second evaluation?

> If they disagree with the first evaluation, they can request an independent evaluation. In this case, they could tell the school that they are seeking an independent evaluation and that they expect the district to pay for it. Next, they should request a due process hearing should the district refuse to pay for evaluation.

2. Should the school provide a full-time aide to assist Kami in Mrs. Sootherby's classroom?

> This is an appropriate education issue. The intent of IDEA was not to provide opportunities for students to achieve their maximum potential, but only to provide an equal opportunity for an education.

▬▬▬▬▬▬   CASE 7.5   ▬▬▬▬▬▬

WASHINGTON/DIVORCED PARENTS

1. Does Washington's father have a legal right to be at Washington's IEP meeting?

> Traditionally, the general practice is to invite only the parent who has custody of the child in cases of divorce or separation.

2. If he has a legal right to be a full participant in the IEP process, based on what information would he have a right to request that Washington be moved into an LD classroom?

> He would have to request that Washington be evaluated for learning disabilities, and then, from that information, the MDT would have to determine the primary disability. If the district refused, he would have the right to an independent evaluation and procedural due process.

3. If the natural parents lose their rights to participate in the child's education, what must the state do to make certain that the child's rights are well protected?

> In cases where the natural parents lose their rights, they may ask foster parents to represent the child or assign a surrogate parent.

▬▬▬▬▬▬   CASE 7.6   ▬▬▬▬▬▬

ARMSTRONG/DENIAL OF BEHAVIOR

1. When a child with a disability is being suspended for longer than 10 days, or more than 10 cumulative days, what should the district personnel do?

> Long-term suspension and expulsion (more than 10 days) are not permitted for students whose behaviors are related to their disabilities. If a child's behavior is suspected of being related to a disability, the district should hold a *manifestation-determination* meeting to determine the relationship. If there is a relationship between the behavior and disability, the district could hold a meeting (with the parents of the child) and request that the child be placed in a more restrictive setting. If the parents disagree, they may seek due process. If there is no

relationship between the disability and the behavior, the school can suspend for longer than 10 days, but educational services still must be continued for the child.

2. Can the parents request that information from a child's records be expunged? What happens if the school refuses to expunge information from a child's records?

Parents can request that information in records be amended. If the district refuses, the parents have the right to seek due process.

3. Guns and drugs are two reasons for expulsion from school. How does IDEA address these issues concerning students with disabilities?

The 1997 IDEA amendments allow schools to unilaterally place students who bring guns or drugs to school in an interim alternative setting.

■■■■■■■■   **CASE 8.1**   ■■■■■■■■

JAMES/EXPULSION

1. Describe the rights of both parties during a due process hearing. Were those rights observed in this case?

Each party in a due process hearing has the right to be represented by counsel or any person with special knowledge or training with respect to students with disabilities. Each party can present evidence and confront, cross-examine, and compel the attendance of witnesses. Evidence that has not been disclosed to each party at least five days before the hearing is inadmissible. Either party has the right to obtain a verbatim record of the hearing, written findings of fact, and the decisions. In this case, it appears that the rights of both parties were observed.

2. Parents have two additional rights during a due process hearing. Describe these additional rights and how these rights were displayed in this case.

Parents also have the right to have the child who is the subject of the hearing present and to open the hearing to the general public. In this case, it did not appear that the child was present. It was difficult to determine if the hearing was open to the public.

3. According to IDEA, what does the term *impartial* mean when used to describe the hearing officer?

An impartial hearing officer is a person who is not an employee of a public agency that is involved in the education or care of the child or by anyone having a personal or professional interest that would conflict with the officer's objectivity.

4. Under what circumstances can a party request an impartial due process hearing?

A parent or public agency (e.g., school district) can initiate a due process hearing if (1) the district proposes to initiate or change the identification, evaluation, or educational placement of the child or the provision of FAPE to the child or (2) refuses to conduct the above. In addition, due process may be initiated if the district requests consent for placement or evaluation and the parent refuses consent.

5. Why was this hearing initiated?

This hearing was primarily initiated because the consequences of a disciplinary incident threatened to change the student's special education placement—that is, possible expulsion—without the agreement of the parent. The parent also challenged the appropriateness of the school district evaluation, the type of disability, and the outcome of the IEP conference held to determine the relationship between James' misbehavior and his disability.

━━━━━━━━ **CASE 8.2** ━━━━━━━━

BOBBY/DISCIPLINE

1. What was the primary issue that prompted the due process hearing? How did the school district respond to this incident in terms of a change in placement? From the evidence given, was this an appropriate response?

The primary issue prompting the due process hearing was the discipline incident involving Bobby hitting the teacher. The district apparently responded by holding an IEP conference to determine whether Bobby's behavior of hitting the teacher was related to his disability. The team found that the behavior was related to the disability and responded by changing Bobby's IEP and placement. The proposed action was to place Bobby in a day treatment facility for students with behavior disorders. Procedurally, the district acted appropriately. However, a decision to place Bobby outside of the district should be based on more than one incident, and it should include more than one intervention to maintain Bobby in the regular school. It is possible that the district built a case on other episodes of violence, with hitting the teacher as the latest example. It is also possible that many interventions were attempted to maintain Bobby in the regular school without success.

2. The parents' attorney stated that Bobby was placed in two regular classes simply because of the parents' request. Was this appropriate? Why or why not?

The right to FAPE, according to IDEA, belongs to the child, not to the parents. It was not appropriate for the school district to change Bobby's placement simply because the parents requested a change when it was clear that the change was not in the student's best interest (i.e., appropriate).

3. The parents' attorney alleged that the school district did not consider an outside report on Bobby. What is the school district's responsibility to consider the report?

When presented with an independent evaluation, the school district is obligated to consider the findings. The school district does not have to follow recommendations in an independent evaluation, but it must consider the evaluation. In this case, it was not clear from the evidence reported whether the district had actually received the outside report, as the parents' attorney alleged.

━━━━━━━ **CASE 8.3** ━━━━━━━

ANN/TUITION REIMBURSEMENT

1. Did Mrs. Spencer have to give permission for Ann to receive increased LD services in eighth grade? Why or why not?

Mrs. Spencer did not have to give permission for Ann to receive increased LD services. IDEA requires parental permission in three instances: (1) when the child is initially evaluated for special education services; (2) when the child is reevaluated; and (3) when the child initially receives special education or related services. If a change is made in placement, the parent must be afforded an opportunity to participate in a meeting to discuss the change and must be properly notified of the meeting. The parent must also be properly notified of the outcome of the meeting.

2. Describe the case law that requires that an IEP be reasonably calculated to confer educational benefit.

Board of Education of the Hendrick Hudson Central School District v. Rowley (1982) was a Supreme Court case that formed the cornerstone for all subsequent appropriate education cases. In this prominent case, the court established a two-pronged inquiry for determining compliance with IDEA: (1) Did the school district follow procedural compliance? (2) Is the child's IEP reasonably calculated to provide educational benefits? If these requirements have been met, the school district has complied with IDEA.

3. Why did the hearing officer deny tuition reimbursement for the private school to the parent?

IDEA requires that a student who is the subject of a due process hearing stay in the current educational placement unless the parent and school district mutually agree otherwise until the conflict is resolved. In this case, there was no evidence that the parent and school district agreed to the private school placement. There was also no evidence that the student's needs could not be met in the public school setting. IDEA does not prohibit the parent from unilaterally enrolling a child in a private program, but the parent does so at the parent's own financial risk. The hearing officer in this case ruled that the IEP proposed by the public school for Ann was appropriate to meet her needs. In addition, prior IEPs were determined to be appropriate. Therefore, there was no reason to think that Ann's needs could not be met by the public school. It was the parent's right to enroll Ann in a private school, but the district had no obligation to reimburse the parent for the tuition.

CASE 8.4

LUKE/STAY PUT

1. What is the primary issue of due process in this scenario?

Stay put is the primary issue of due process in this scenario. IDEA states that during the pendency of due process or judicial proceedings the child involved in the conflict must remain in the current educational placement unless the parent and school agree otherwise or unless (1) the child had a weapon or was involved in the sale, use, or possession of illegal drugs or (2) the child presented a danger to himself or others. In a case involving weapons or drugs, the district could have placed the child in an interim alternative educational setting for 45 days. On the forty-sixth day, the student would return to the original placement unless the parent and district agreed otherwise. If the child presented a danger to himself or others, as this case illustrated, the school district could request an injunction from the hearing officer to remove the child to an interim alternative educational setting. In this case, the hearing officer denied the request, and the student had to return to the original placement after the suspension.

2. On what basis could the school district have pursued an injunction to remove the child from school pending the outcome of the due process hearing?

Reauthorization of IDEA (1997) states that the school district may request that a hearing officer issue an injunction to temporarily remove a dangerous student. To issue such an order and to determine that a student was dangerous, the hearing officer would have to determine that there was a substantial likelihood of injury, and reasonable steps to minimize the likelihood of harm would have to be taken. In addition, the current IEP would have to be appropriate, and an interim educational setting that allowed the student to progress in the general curriculum and to continue to receive IEP services that would enable the student to meet IEP goals would have to be in place.

3. Why was the school district unable to expel the student?

According to IDEA, school districts cannot expel students with disabilities for more than 10 days on the basis of behavior that is caused by their disabilities.

4. The PE teacher stated that he had no idea the student was in special education. If this is true, will there be a legal concern? If so, what will the concern be?

The PE teacher should have been aware of the student's disabilities and the student's IEP. The student's IEP is supposed to be individualized to meet the student's needs. It would be impossible to demonstrate that the student's IEP was individualized and appropriate if general education teachers had no knowledge of the student's disability and IEP.

5. What were the issues of LRE in the settlement offer?

IDEA clearly states LRE provisions. In this case, the district proposed a change of placement for this student to an out-of-district day treatment facility for BD students. The parent then proposed, and the district agreed to, a settlement offer to place the student in a more restrictive placement, a residential facility. According to the LRE doctrine of IDEA, it might be difficult for the school district to defend its agreement to place the student in the more restrictive setting when it had proposed a less restrictive setting.

━━━━━━━━   **CASE 8.5**   ━━━━━━━━

SUSAN/PARENT INPUT

1. Describe the legal errors made by the school district and their basis in IDEA.

The school district made at least three legal errors. The first was failure to submit the parents' request for a due process hearing. IDEA has specific timelines for reaching a final decision in a due process hearing (45 days). In this case, the timelines were exceeded because the due process hearing was not submitted immediately. The second error was the failure to carry out services listed on the IEP—that is, occupational therapy. IDEA specifically states that services on a child's IEP must be carried out for the child to receive an appropriate education. The third error was the failure to provide parental input into the IEP. One of the main principles of IDEA is to provide the opportunity for parental input into the IEP process. In this case, the parents were told that they did not have input into the selection and evaluation of goals.

2. The hearing officer indicated that Susan was receiving educational benefit from her educational program. What was the basis in case law for affirming Susan's placement in the early childhood classroom?

A Supreme Court decision, *Board of Education of the Hendrick Hudson Central School District v. Rowley* (1982), outlined a standard for determining appropriate education. The standard was a test that included: (1) the school district's procedural compliance and (2) whether the IEP was reasonably calculated to confer educational benefit. This standard was used to determine that Susan's program was appropriate.

3. What was the legal basis for returning Susan to her original placement during the pendency of due process hearing proceedings?

During the pendency of due process proceedings, IDEA requires that the child who is the subject of the conflict remain in the current placement unless the parents and school district mutually agree to an alternate placement.

CASE 8.6

LORI/INDIVIDUALIZED IEP

1. Was Lori's IEP individualized? How do you know?

Lori's IEP did not appear to be individualized. The special education teacher, Ms. Bolen, indicated that all special education students took general education classes in social studies and science. She indicated this was the reason that Lori was placed in these classes.

2. Why might Lori's IEP be inappropriate?

There were several reasons that Lori's IEP might be inappropriate. The major reason was that the IEP did not appear to be individualized. Other evidence that would support the hypothesis that the IEP was inappropriate included the following:

(a) The parents were apparently not notified about the IEP held on May 15 to plan Lori's eleventh-grade IEP.
(b) Ms. Bolen maintained no communication with Lori's general education classroom teachers, even though Lori was failing all of her regular classes.
(c) There was no evidence that an individualized transition plan was developed for Lori. Discussing what Lori planned to do after high school was inadequate.
(d) Lori's schedule (and special education service) was changed without a formal IEP meeting, and the IEP was changed based only on parental request.
(e) The extent of time in special education listed on the IEP for eleventh grade did not match a schedule change made in September (see **d** above).
(f) The IEP team did not review Lori's progress on her previous IEP.

3. What legal rights concerning due process did Lori's parents exercise in this scenario?

Lori's parents exercised the following rights:

(a) The right to request an impartial due process hearing.

(b) The right to be represented by counsel.

(c) The right to examine/cross-examine witnesses.

<hr>

CASE 9.1

DARRELL/PERSONAL NOTES

1. Were the director of special education's personal notes considered part of the school record? Why or why not?

The issue central to answering this question is whether or not the director's notes are considered a record. The Family and Educational Rights and Privacy Act (FERPA) states that records of personnel that are kept in the sole possession of the maker of the record and that aren't shared with any other person except a temporary substitute are not considered an educational record. If the director has made notes about school personnel, they probably would not be considered as a record. One could construe this to include any record in the sole possession of the maker and not shared with anyone. However, if the notes relate directly to the subject of the conference, it is possible that the notes could be interpreted as an educational record, although this might be debatable.

2. Did the parent have the right to bring an advocate and another relative to the meeting? Why or why not?

The parent had every right to bring anyone she wanted to attend the conference, according to IDEA.

3. Was the advocate correct in stating that the child had a right to be placed in a regular classroom in his home school? Why or why not?

The advocate was not correct in making this statement. IDEA states that the child's placement should be determined individually and that the child should be placed to the maximum extent appropriate with other nondisabled children (LRE). School districts must also maintain a full continuum of services. Therefore, it may be individually appropriate for a child to be placed outside of the district in a day treatment facility. This type of placement may represent a child's LRE.

━━━━━━━━   **CASE 9.2**   ━━━━━━━━

JEFF/IMPROPER DISCLOSURE

1. Was the information that Mrs. Baker shared with the other teachers and the parent considered an educational record? How do you know?

> The information shared, even by oral means, was considered an educational record under the definition in FERPA. The records were disclosed orally, were directly related to a student, and were maintained by the school district. The disclosure also contained personally identifiable information about Jeff.

2. Was it appropriate for Mrs. Baker to talk about Jeff to other teachers in the teachers' lounge? Why or why not?

> According to FERPA, it probably was not appropriate for Mrs. Baker to talk specifically about Jeff in the teacher's lounge, if one makes the assumption that the other teachers did not have any legitimate educational interest in Jeff. However, if the teachers had a legitimate educational interest in Jeff, it would have been appropriate to share the information.

3. Was it appropriate for Mrs. Baker to talk about Jeff to another parent (Dr. King)? Why or why not?

> According to FERPA, it was not appropriate for Mrs. Baker to disclose personally identifiable information from Jeff's educational record without prior written consent from the parent.

4. If Mrs. Baker's analysis of why Jeff was placed in her class was correct—that is, by parent request—was this an appropriate action by the placement team?

> If Mrs. Baker's analysis was correct, it was not appropriate for Jeff to be placed in her regular classroom based only on parent request. According to IDEA, the right to an appropriate education belongs to the child, not to the parent. If the school district placed Jeff in the regular classroom based only on parent request and with knowledge that the placement was not totally appropriate, the district would put itself at risk and would not be providing an appropriate education for Jeff.

━━━━━━━━   **CASE 9.3**   ━━━━━━━━

KEVIN/DELAYED RECORDS

1. Why was it a problem for the school district to wait two months to send the bulk of Kevin's records to Mrs. Allen?

Both FERPA and IDEA require that school districts allow parents and their representatives to inspect personally identifiable information (records) concerning the child within a reasonable time, and in no case more than 45 days. In this case, Mrs. Allen had to wait about 60 days for the bulk of the records and longer for other pieces of the record.

2. Mrs. Gregory indicated that the behavioral graphs were her personal records, and she didn't have to give them to the parent. Was this true? Why or why not?

The BD teacher, Mrs. Gregory, was in error. Educational records, according to FERPA and IDEA, mean records that contain personally identifiable information about the child that are maintained by the school district. Mrs. Gregory indicated that the behavioral graphs were her personal records. However, it is indicated that the graphs were shared with Mrs. Allen when discussing Kevin's progress in school. Therefore, Mrs. Gregory's information is defined as a school record and is covered under FERPA and IDEA. The graphs should have been immediately released to the parent.

3. Was Kevin's "therapy" day at home considered a suspension from school?

Kevin's therapy day at home would likely be considered a suspension from school without being afforded the protective rights of IDEA and case law. See, for example, *Goss v. Lopez* (1975).

4. Was Dr. Whitford correct when he told Mrs. Allen she would be charged a fee for copying Kevin's records? Why or why not?

Both FERPA and IDEA state that the school district may charge a reasonable fee to the parents for copying the records, unless imposing a fee effectively prevents the parents from reviewing the records.

━━━━━━━━━ **CASE 9.4** ━━━━━━━━━

JOHN/WITHHOLDING INFORMATION

1. Did the receiving school have legal access to John's discipline records? Why or why not?

John's teachers at Lincoln High School, as the receiving school, had legitimate educational interests in the behavior of John and therefore should have had access to all records for John. FERPA also states that information concerning discipline action taken against a student for conduct that posed a significant risk to the safety or well-being of that student or other students could also have been disclosed to John's teachers and administrators at Lincoln High School. IDEA includes stipulations for the requirement that disciplinary records be transferred with students so that teachers are aware of students' previous behavior.

2. Assuming that John's violent behavior was not addressed in his IEP, was his IEP appropriate? Why or why not?

If the most-recent evaluation of John determined that his violent behavior was a special need for John, or if his behavior interfered with his or other students' learning, the violent behavior should have been addressed in the IEP, either as a goal or in a behavior management plan. Even if the threat to kill another student was an isolated incident, the behavior should have been addressed in the IEP. Assuming the above, the IEP might not be appropriate and might not have resulted in an appropriate placement because John's special needs were not adequately addressed.

CASE 9.5

DEAN/INVASION OF PRIVACY

1. Was it necessary for Pam to sign a consent for reevaluation? Why or why not?

It was proper for Pam to sign a consent for reevaluation. IDEA, as reauthorized in 1997, requires consent for reevaluation.

2. Was it legal for the school district to expel Dean, assuming his behavior was found to be related to his disability? How do you know?

Assuming Dean's behavior was found to be related to his disability, Dean should not have been expelled. His placement could have been changed (which it eventually was), but he could not be unilaterally removed from school for more than 10 school days. The support for this is found in case law and the 1997 amendments to the IDEA. See, for example, *S-1 v. Turlington* (1981) and *Doe v. Maher* (1986). The 1997 amendments to IDEA state that if the child's behavior is not related to the disability, the child can receive the same disciplinary actions as other students, provided there would be no complete cessation of services. This does not seem to be the case with Dean.

3. Under what conditions did Pam have the right to a records hearing?

FERPA states that a parent shall have the opportunity for a hearing to challenge the content of the student's educational records on the grounds that the information in the records is inaccurate, misleading, or in violation of the privacy rights of the student.

4. Was the records hearing conducted appropriately? Why or why not?

The records hearing was conducted in an appropriate manner. FERPA states that the hearing must be held within a reasonable time after it is requested and that the parent receive prior notice of the date, time, and place of the hearing.

It is also states that an official of the school district who doesn't have a direct interest in the outcome of the hearing may be the hearing officer and that the hearing should give the parent the opportunity to present relevant evidence and be represented by counsel. The hearing officer should make a decision in writing within a reasonable period of time after the hearing and it should be based solely on the evidence presented at the hearing. The decision must include a summary of the evidence and the reasons for the decision.

CASE 9.6

CARLOS/FALSIFYING DOCUMENTS

1. Was it legal for Mary to create an IEP document in the manner requested by Mr. Bing? Why or why not?

It was highly improper for Mary to create an IEP document unilaterally. Ethical issues aside, IDEA has many regulations surrounding the proper convening of a meeting for the purpose of writing an IEP. These regulations were completely ignored. The parent did not receive notice of the meeting, and Mary wrote the IEP by herself without proper participants. The IEP was only written to cover for the school district's error in not writing an IEP for Carlos. Two major principles of IDEA, writing an appropriate IEP and parent participation, were totally ignored.

2. Was it legal for Mr. Bing to forward a document to the parent's attorney two days before a due process hearing?

IDEA states that evidence for a due process hearing must be disclosed five days before a due process hearing to be admissible. In this case, those timelines were not met.

3. Was Carlos' placement appropriate? Why or why not?

Case law—*Board of Education of the Hendrick Hudson Central School District v. Rowley* (1982)—clearly states that procedural compliance is essential to demonstrate that a child is receiving FAPE. In this case, procedural compliance was nonexistent; therefore, the program was not appropriate.

CASE 10.1

DONNIE/BRINGING A GUN

1. On what legal basis was the IEP team able to place the child in an alternative placement?

Until June 1997, school districts relied on case law for guidance in disciplining students with disabilities. For example, see *Honig v. Doe* (1988). In June 1997,

IDEA was reauthorized and included specific guidance on the discipline of students with disabilities. IDEA now states that a student can be placed in an interim alternative educational setting for a maximum of 45 calendar days if the student brings a dangerous weapon to school or sells, has possession of, or uses drugs in school. The principal can make the decision to place the student in the alternative setting. However, the IEP team determines the nature of the placement.

2. What would have occurred if the parent had not agreed with the alternative placement?

If the parent had initially not agreed to the placement of her son in the alternative school (interim alternative educational setting), she could have requested an impartial due process hearing. During the pendency of the hearing, the student would remain in the interim alternative educational setting. The student would have returned to his original placement (i.e., regular high school) on the forty-sixth day unless the school went before the hearing officer to prove that the student was dangerous—that is, beyond a preponderance of the evidence— and requested an injunction to keep him in the alternative placement until the dispute was resolved.

3. Could this student have been expelled from school (i.e., removed from school for a lengthy period of time)?

This student could not have been expelled because the IEP team determined in its manifestation determination that the student's behavior was related to his disability. Because an expulsion is considered a change in placement, the child's placement, beyond the 45-day alternative placement, could not have been changed outside of an IEP meeting.

CASE 10.2

ANDY/IMPULSIVE BEHAVIOR

1. According to IDEA and the information given, did the IEP team make an appropriate manifestation-determination decision? Why or why not?

It appears that the IEP team made an appropriate manifestation determination given the information described. The most recent evaluation was reviewed (including the functional behavioral evaluation), observations were considered, and the IEP was reviewed in terms of Andy's behavior. To determine that there was no manifestation, the team would have had to find that the IEP and placement were appropriate, supplementary aids and services were provided, behavioral interventions were provided, and the child understood his behavior and could control the behavior. Because the IEP was revised in light of the incident, one may presume that the IEP was not appropriate. It cannot be determined whether supplementary aids or services were provided, but one could assume that behavioral interventions were not provided. In addition, it was clearly determined that Andy did not understand his behavior and was unable to control the behavior. Because of this, the team could not make a determination of no manifestation.

2. Could the school district have expelled the student? Why or why not?

The school district could not have expelled the student because the IEP team determined that Andy's behavior was a manifestation of his disability.

3. Why couldn't the school district place the child in an interim alternative educational setting for 45 days?

According to IDEA, a student can be placed in an interim alternative educational setting for 45 calendar days if the student brings a dangerous weapon to school or has possession of, sells, or uses illegal drugs at school. Hitting a teacher, or in this case, running into a teacher, does not qualify as one of those behaviors.

CASE 10.3

KATIE/MARIJUANA CIGARETTE

1. What other action could the school district have taken regarding the student's placement after the suspension?

According to IDEA, Katie could have been placed in an alternative setting for 45 calendar days because she had drugs at school. The IEP team would have determined the setting.

2. How closely did the school district follow IDEA procedures in regard to the manifestation determination at the IEP meeting held after the incident?

In order to find no manifestation between the behavior and disability, the IEP team must determine the following:

(a) The IEP and placement were appropriate.
(b) Supplementary aids and services were provided.
(c) Behavioral interventions were provided.
(d) The child understood the behavior and could control it.

The IEP team did not directly address the first three items, but it did address the last issue. Therefore, the conclusion of the team members that the behavior was unrelated to the disability could have been questioned.

3. Was it proper to expel the student with no education? Why or why not?

It was highly improper to expel the student with no further education. IDEA clearly states that FAPE is available to all children with disabilities residing in the state between the ages of 3 and 21, including children with disabilities who have been suspended or expelled from school. The school district remained responsible for providing an education to this student.

━━━ **CASE 10.4** ━━━

MIKE/VIOLENT THREATS

1. Did the school district follow correct procedures in conducting the IEP meeting? How do you know?

According to IDEA, it appeared that the school district followed correct procedures in conducting the IEP meeting. The IEP team considered the most recent evaluation (including a functional behavioral evaluation), observations of the student, and the IEP of the student. Based on this information, the team determined that the IEP needed to be revised, the student understood his behavior, and he could not control the behavior. It appeared that the team discussed and determined that supplementary aids and services and behavioral interventions were provided for the student.

2. What is *stay put* and why was it used?

According to IDEA, stay put means that during the pendency of due process proceedings, the child must remain in the then-current educational placement unless the school district and parent agree otherwise. A school district may request an injunction from a hearing officer to keep the student out of school (in an interim alternative educational setting) during the pendency of the hearing if the student is dangerous. The only exception to the stay put rule would be if the child were placed in an alternative setting for having drugs or weapons at school. In this case, the child would remain in the alternative setting until the dispute was settled.

3. What are the required elements for determining that a student with a disability is dangerous?

IDEA outlines four elements that a hearing officer must consider in determining if a student is dangerous and should be kept out of the current placement during the pendency of the due process hearing.

  (a) The school district must demonstrate by substantial evidence that maintaining the child in the current placement is substantially likely to result in injury to the child or to others.
  (b) The school district has taken reasonable steps to minimize the risk of harm should the child remain in the current placement.
  (c) The current IEP is appropriate.
  (d) The school district has an plan for an interim educational setting that will allow the child to make progress in the general curriculum and continue to receive IEP services.

■■■■■■■ **CASE 10.5** ■■■■■■■

TIM/TEACHER AND PARENT REBELLION

1. Was it proper for Mrs. Bush to talk to a parent other than Mrs. Singleton about Tim? Why or why not?

It was improper, illegal, and unethical for Mrs. Bush to share information about Tim to another parent. Even though the information was shared orally, it would be considered an educational record under FERPA. The information was directly related to Tim and maintained by the school district, and it disclosed personally identifiable information about Tim.

2. Was it proper for Mrs. Lefton to unilaterally remove Tim from Mrs. Bush's classroom for two weeks to work in another room with the aide? Why or why not?

It was improper for the principal to remove Tim from the first-grade classroom for two weeks. By removing Tim from his regular daily activities in first grade, it could be interpreted that he was functionally excluded from school, even though he received instruction from the aide in a separate room. If one makes this interpretation, then Tim was excluded (i.e., suspended) without basic rights available to all children. See *Goss v. Lopez* (1975). These rights include (1) oral or written notice of the charges and (2) the chance to present his side of the story.

IDEA indicates that a student can be removed from school without a placement change for 10 school days or more if a pattern of exclusion does not exist. Although Tim was denied appropriate services on his IEP, the most important issue was that Tim's parent apparently was not notified of the change.

3. Legally, can parents of general education students insist that a child with a disability be removed from a particular classroom?

The right to appropriate services based on the IEP belong to the child with a disability, not to other children in the classroom and their parents. A petition to remove a child with a disability from a particular regular classroom might put pressure on the IEP team to change the child's placement, but this should not be considered a valid factor in making placement changes. Placement changes should be based on the individual child's needs and services required, not on other parents' opinions.

■■■■■■■ **CASE 10.6** ■■■■■■■

MARIO/EXPULSION PROCEEDING

1. What errors were made in the IEP meeting when the behavioral incident was discussed?

IDEA requires that the IEP team conduct a functional behavioral assessment, implement a behavior intervention plan, and conduct a manifestation determination within 10 days of a serious behavioral incident like this one. In this case, there is no evidence that a functional behavioral assessment or behavior intervention plan were even discussed.

IDEA also requires the following three considerations to be discussed during the IEP meeting to make the manifestation determination: evaluation results, observations, and the IEP and placement. It appears that these areas were discussed by the IEP team. To determine that there is no manifestation, the team must determine that the IEP and placement were appropriate, that supplementary aids and services were provided, that behavioral interventions were provided, and that the child understood his behavior and could control the behavior.

In Mario's case, the team determined that Mario understood his behavior and that his IEP and placement were appropriate, although this might be open to question. The team did not address behavioral interventions and supplementary aids and services, nor did they discuss whether Mario could control his behavior. Some information (i.e., the evaluation) indicated that Mario had difficulty with impulsivity and was a follower, although this information was not fully discussed. In addition, one might question why behavioral interventions or supplementary services were not necessary, given that several school staff knew that Mario was hanging around known drug users in the school.

2. What other discipline action could the school district have immediately taken, along with suspension from school?

IDEA allows, in the case of a dangerous weapon or drugs, the school district to place the child in an interim alternative educational setting for a maximum of 45 calendar days. The IEP team would determine the setting, and the child would return to school on the forty-sixth day. This would have been an option in Mario's case.

3. The special education administrator told the parents at the IEP meeting not to send Mario back to school until a decision was made on his possible expulsion. Was this appropriate? Why or why not?

This clearly was not appropriate. In essence, the principal unilaterally extended Mario's suspension without the rudimentary rights required in *Goss v. Lopez* (1975). In addition, Mario was effectively suspended 14 school days, and IDEA states that 10 consecutive school days is the maximum allowed without procedural protections of a placement change (i.e., IEP meeting). The principal could have suspended Mario more than 10 days if there were not a pattern of exclusion to effectively change his placement. However, an IEP meeting would have to be convened to conduct a manifestation determination. A functional behavioral assessment would have to be conducted and discussed in the IEP meeting. Therefore, the principal also changed Mario's educational placement without following correct procedures (e.g., notice and IEP meeting).

4. Was the school district able to legally expel Mario without providing services? Why or why not?

> The school district was able to legally expel Mario from school given the outcome of its manifestation determination. However, according to IDEA, Mario would have to be afforded the right to FAPE in another setting.

━━━━━ **CASE 11.1** ━━━━━

JANIS/INADEQUATE BUILDING

1. What was the hearing officer's rationale for not ordering compensatory education?

> Under IDEA, a school district must provide FAPE. In this case, the evidence suggests that the school district met this requirement. For any compliance technique to be applied (i.e., compensatory education), the school district must be found to have not provided FAPE to the child. Therefore, there were no grounds for requiring the district to provide compensatory education. In addition, the parent unilaterally placed Janis in the private school, even though an appropriate education would have been available in the public school.

2. Under what circumstances would the parent have been eligible to receive tuition reimbursement for the private school placement?

> For a compliance technique to be applied (i.e., tuition reimbursement, compensatory education), the hearing officer would have to make the judgement that the school district did not provide FAPE. If this had been the case, tuition reimbursement (or compensatory education) might have been ordered. The position would have been that Mrs. Vaughn *had* to seek private school placement for Janis to receive FAPE.

3. If the school district had not provided an appropriate education for Janis in junior high, would this have changed the outcome of this case? Why or why not?

> Yes, the outcome would have been different. See answers to questions 1 and 2.

━━━━━ **CASE 11.2** ━━━━━

LISA/GRADUATION FEARS

1. What were the legal reasons for requesting a due process hearing?

> It was alleged that the school district had not provided Lisa with FAPE and that the parents were entitled to reimbursement for expenses in locating and placing Lisa in an appropriate program.

2. What was the reasoning used for denying reimbursement for private school tuition?

The hearing officer reasoned that the school district made some procedural errors in evaluation and carrying out Lisa's program. However, although serious, the errors did not render the school district's program for Lisa inappropriate. Lisa did receive FAPE despite the procedural errors.

3. What procedural errors did the school district make?

First, the school district failed to provide a speech and language evaluation in the second grade even though one had been suggested. Second, the independent speech and language evaluation submitted by the parents in fourth grade suggested speech and language services. Subsequent IEPs continued to indicate that Lisa needed speech and language services, but no services were ever detailed in the IEP. Apparently, the speech and language services were provided by the LD teacher in the special education classroom.

============   **CASE 11.3**   ============

MICHAEL/SEXUAL MISCONDUCT

1. Was it appropriate to continue Michael's expulsion after he was found eligible for behavior disorders? Why or why not?

No, it was not appropriate to continue expulsion after Michael was found eligible for behavior disorders. IDEA states that a child cannot be expelled for behavior that was a manifestation of the disability. Although Michael was not identified as a special education student at the time of the expulsion, his mother requested an evaluation for possible special education services, thereby notifying the school district of that possibility. If a school district has knowledge that a child may have a disability (i.e., parent requesting an evaluation), the child is entitled to all protections of IDEA. If the child is eligible for special education services, a manifestation determination and a functional behavioral assessment must be held. In this case, the evidence suggests that neither was conducted. However, one might conclude that Michael's disability might have been related to the behavior. In fact, the behavior causing the expulsion was stated as one piece of evidence that Michael did indeed have a behavior disorder. Although the school district did provide home services for Michael in special education during the expulsion, the evidence suggests that the expulsion was carried out, and this was an error.

2. Why did the school district agree to provide compensatory education in the settlement offer?

One might assume that the school district was advised by the school district's attorney that Michael was wrongly expelled from school (see above) and that a hearing officer in all likelihood would order the school district to provide the compensatory services. This was possibly a strategy to avoid a costly due process hearing.

3. What is a settlement offer, and why was it used in this case?

A settlement offer is a written offer made by one party (either parent or school district) to resolve the case before a due process hearing or court hearing. The settlement offer was possibly used in this case as a strategy to avoid a costly due process hearing and to avoid being ordered to pay attorney fees. The school district's attorney apparently thought that the school district might have difficulty prevailing in a hearing. The Handicapped Children's Protection Act allows attorney fees to be awarded after the time the school district makes a written offer of settlement to the parents if the offer is timely (i.e., within 10 days before a due process hearing begins), the offer is not accepted within 10 days after it is made, and the hearing officer finds that the relief finally obtained is not more favorable to the parents than the settlement offer. In this case, the school district probably had a losing case and offered what the parent was requesting. If the case had gone before a hearing officer or a judge, it is likely that the district wouldn't have been ordered to provide anything more than the settlement offer. Therefore, attorney fees wouldn't have been ordered.

━━━━━ **CASE 11.4** ━━━━━

KRISTEN/ESSENTIAL THERAPY

1. Why did the hearing officer order the school district to reimburse the parents for providing OT services at the local hospital?

A school district, according to IDEA, must provide at no cost to the parents an appropriate education to any child identified as having a disability. The vehicle for providing an appropriate education is the IEP. In this case, Kristen was a child identified as having a physical disability. An IEP was planned and written as the vehicle for providing an appropriate education for Kristen. Part of the services included the related service of OT. Through no fault of its own, the district's occupational therapist left for other employment, and the district was unable to provide services in Kristen's IEP. Because the district was unable to provide all services listed on the IEP, the district was unable to provide an appropriate education. Because the parents had to spend funds to obtain the related service of OT that the school district agreed to provide on Kristen's IEP, the parents were entitled to recover costs of services they incurred when the district refused to pay for them.

2. Why did the hearing officer order the school district to provide compensatory services?

As stated above, the school district is obligated to provide an appropriate education to any student identified as having a disability. In this case, the school district was unable to meet this obligation because special education personnel were unavailable. Consequently, Kristen did not receive all services on her IEP (i.e., OT) for a period of six weeks. Essentially, Kristen did not receive an appropriate education for a period of six weeks. When a student has not received an appropriate education in the past, one means of addressing the problem can be by providing compensatory education. In this case, the school district was ordered to provide six weeks of compensatory OT services during the summer.

CASE 11.5

JANET/IDENTIFICATION OF PROBLEMS

1. Why wasn't the school district ordered to pay tuition to the private school?

Hearing officers will not award tuition if the parent unilaterally places a child in a private program. The question here was, "Did the child have a disability that went undetected by the school district prior to private school placement?" The evidence suggests that the school district was acting in a reasonable manner with this child because the first-grade teacher was working with the building's teacher assistance team with some success, and the child was retained with some success. Therefore, at the time the parents placed Janet in a private school, a referral was not appropriate. Because Janet did not have an IEP at the time of her parochial school placement, it is clear that the parents unilaterally placed the child. In addition, when a referral was made to the school district for an evaluation, the district responded promptly by completing the evaluation and providing appropriate special education services.

2. Why wasn't the school district ordered to pay for the private, independent evaluation?

The evidence suggests that the parents unilaterally sought the private evaluation and, when dissatisfied with the results, made a referral to the public school. Therefore, it would not have been appropriate to order the district to pay for the private evaluation. If the parents sought the initial evaluation from the public school and were dissatisfied with the results, the parents could have requested an independent evaluation at public expense. The parents would then have had to prove that the school district's evaluation was inappropriate.

3. If the parents requested attorney fees within the court system, would a judge have ordered reimbursement to the parents? Why or why not?

A judge would likely not order reimbursement of attorney fees. A judge will order attorney fees to the prevailing party if the prevailing party is the parent. Of the four issues brought before the hearing officer, the school district prevailed on all four. Therefore, it is unlikely that attorney fees would be awarded.

━━ **CASE 11.6** ━━

GABRIEL/VOCATIONAL TRAINING

1. Under what circumstances would compensatory education be ordered by a hearing officer?

Compensatory education may be awarded if it is determined that a school district did not provide FAPE. Compensatory education is intended to provide for "lost time" due to an inappropriate education. Often, compensatory education is awarded by requiring the school district to provide services above and beyond the services normally afforded a student. This could include extended school-day services, summer services, or education beyond the age of 21.

2. Why wasn't Gabriel's removal from the job site not considered a suspension?

To be considered a suspension, Gabriel would have to have been denied appropriate services based on his IEP. The hearing officer concluded that Gabriel continued appropriate educational services despite removal from the work site.

3. According to IDEA, what responsibilities does a school district have when a student is displaying inappropriate behaviors?

IDEA states that if a child's behavior impedes the child's learning or that of others, the IEP team must consider strategies, including positive behavioral interventions, strategies, and supports, to address that behavior.

REFERENCES

Americans with Disabilities Act of 1990, 42 U.S.C.A. § 12101 *et seq.* (West 1993).

Board of Education v. Arline, 480 U.S. 273, 107 S. Ct. 1123, 94 L. Ed. 2d 307 (1987).

Board of Education of the Hendrick Hudson Central School District v. Rowley, 458 U.S. 176 (1982).

Daniel R. R. v. State Board of Education, 874 F. 2d 1036 (5th Cir. 1989).

Doe v. Maher, 793 R. 2d 1470 (9th Cir. 1986).

Family Educational Rights and Privacy Act, 20 U.S.C. § 1232 *et seq.*

Goss v. Lopez, 419 U.S. 565, 95 S. Ct. 729 (1975).

Honig v. Doe, 484 U.S. 305 (1988).

Individuals with Disabilities Education Act Amendments of 1997, Pub. L. No. 105-17, 105th Cong., 1st sess.

Individuals with Disabilities Education Act Regulations, 34 C.F.R. § 300.121 *et seq.*

Larry P. v. Riles, 343 F. Supp. 1306 (N.D. Cal. 1972), 502 F.2d 963 (9th Cir. 1984), 793 F.2d 969 (9th Cir. 1984).

LRP Publications (1999) *Making sense of the new IDEA regulations:* Vol. 1. Alexandria, VA: Author.

Mills v. D. C. Board of Education, 348 F. Supp. 866 (D.D.C. 1972).

PASE v. Hannon, 506 F. Supp. 831 (N.D. Ill. 1980).

Pennsylvania Association for Retarded Citizens (PARC) v. Commonwealth of Pennsylvania, 334 F. Supp. 1257, 343 F. Supp. 279 (E.D. Pa. 1971, 1972).

Rehabilitation Act of 1973, Section 504, 29 U.S.C. § 706 (7)(B).

Rehabilitation Act of 1973, Section 504 Regulations, 34 C.F.R. § 104.3(j)(2)(i).

S-1 v. Turlington, 635 F. 2d 342 (5th Cir. 1981).

Sacramento Unified School District v. Holland, 14 F. 3d 1398 (9th Cir. 1994).

Timothy W. v. Rochester School District, EHLR 559:480 (D.N.H. 1988).

Turnbull, H. R., & Turnbull, A. P. (2000). *Free appropriate public education: the law and children with disabilities* (6th ed.). Denver, CO: Love.

Tuttle v. Evans, 613 N.E. 2d 854 (1993).

Weishaar, M. K., & Borsa, J. C. (2001). *Inclusive educational administration: a case study approach.* Boston: McGraw-Hill.

Yell, M. L. (1998). *The law and special education.* Upper Saddle River, N.J.: Prentice Hall.

INDEX

Americans with Disabilities Act of 1990,
20–23
Title I: employment discrimination, 20
Title II: public services and state and local
governments, 21
Title III: privately owned public
accommodations and services, 21–23
Title IV: telecommunications, 23
Amy/Parents in Class, 100–103, 210–211
Andre/Age and Special Education Services,
48–51, 195
Andy/Impulsive Behavior, 154–157, 225–226
Ann/Tuition Reimbursement, 120–122,
216–217
Armstrong/Denial of Behavior, 110–112,
213–214

Benchmarks, in IEP, 11
Ben/Inclusion, 83–86, 205–207
*Board of Education of the Hendrick Hudson
Central School District v. Rowley*, 26–27
Bobby/Discipline, 116–120, 215–216

Carlos/Discriminatory Evaluations, 52–54, 196
Carlos/Falsifying Documents, 146–150, 224
*Cedar Rapids Community School District,
Petitioner v. Garret F., a Minor, by His
Mother and Next Friend, Charlene*,
27–28
Child find, 4. *See also* Zero reject/child find
Compliance techniques, 170–190
Gabriel/Vocational Training, 188–190, 234
Janet/Identification of Problems, 184–187,
233
Janis/Inadequate Building, 170–173, 230
Kristen/Essential Therapy, 180–184,
232–233
Lisa/Graduation Fears, 173–177, 230–231

Michael/Sexual Misconduct, 177–180,
231–232
Confidentiality and privacy, 132–150
Carlos/Falsifying Documents, 146–150, 224
Darrell/Personal Notes, 132–135, 220
Dean/Invasion of Privacy, 144–146,
223–224
Jeff/Improper Disclosure, 135–138, 221
John/Withholding Information, 141–144,
222–223
Kevin/Delayed Records, 138–141, 221–224

Daniel R. R. v. State Board of Education, 28–29
Danny/Expulsion, 40–42, 193
Darrell/Personal Notes, 132–135, 220
David/Threatening Behavior, 89–92, 208
Dean/Invasion of Privacy, 144–146, 223–224
Discipline
definitions, 5
under IDEA, 6, 7, 8, 9
in principle of zero reject/child find, 4
Donnie/Bringing a Gun, 151–154, 224–225
Due process, 113–131
Ann/Tuition Reimbursement, 120–122,
216–217
Bobby/Discipline, 116–120, 215–216
James/Expulsion, 113–116, 214–215
Lori/Individualized IEP, 129–131, 219–220
Luke/Stay Put, 123–125, 217–218
Susan/Parent Input, 125–128, 218–219

Education for All Handicapped Children Act of
1975, 20. *See* Individuals with
Disabilities Act (IDEA)
Employment discrimination, under ADA, 20–21
Evaluation and classification, 52–66
Carlos/Discriminatory Evaluations, 52–54,
196

Evaluation and classification *(continued)*
  Joan/Refusal to Evaluate, 61–63, 199–200
  Larry P. v. Wilson Riles, 25
  Latifa/Biased Testing Procedure, 64–66,
    200–201
  *Parents in Action on Special Education
    (PASE) v. Joseph P. Hannon*, 26
  principle of nondiscriminatory, 4–8
  Scott/Procedural Errors, 57–59, 197–198
  Tina/Classification Issues, 59–61, 199
  Tony/Inadequate Evaluations, 54–56,
    196–197

Free and appropriate public education (FAPE),
  1, 8

Gabriel/Vocational Training, 188–190, 234

Harold/Adequate Services, 77–79, 204
*Honig, California Superintendent of Public
  Instruction v. Doe*, 30–31

Individual education plan (IEP), 67–79
  *Board of Education of the Hendrick Hudson
    Central School District v. Rowley*, 26–27
  *Cedar Rapids Community School District,
    Petitioner v. Garret F., a Minor, by His
    Mother and Next Friend, Charlene*,
    27–28
  components of, 10–12
  Harold/Adequate Services, 77–79, 204
  Kelly/Related Services, 75–77, 203–204
  Nicholas/Parent Participation, 73–75, 203
  principle of, 8–13
  Vernon/Improper Placement, 69–71, 202
  Walter/Transition Services, 67–69, 201
  Yancy/General Education Participation,
    71–73, 202
Individuals with Disabilities Act (IDEA), 1–15
  changes made in revisions, 2–3
  disability categories, 2
  need for, 1–2
  principle of individual action plan, 8–13
  principle of least restrictive environment,
    13–14

  principle of nondiscriminatory assessment,
    4–8
  principle of parent participation, 15
  principle of procedural due process, 14–15,
    16
  principle of zero reject/child find, 3–4

James/Expulsion, 113–116, 214–215
James/Teacher Bias, 86–89, 207
Jane/Refusal to Consider, 92–95, 208–209
Janet/Identification of Problems, 184–187, 233
Janis/Inadequate Building, 170–173, 230
Jared/Legal Rights, 96–99, 209–210
Jeff/Improper Disclosure, 135–138, 221
Joan/Refusal to Evaluate, 61–63, 199–200
Jodi/Special Education Services, 35–37,
  191–192
John/Disruptive Behavior, 80–83, 204–205
*John Sessions v. Livingston Parish School
  Board*, 30
John/Withholding Information, 141–144,
  222–223

Kami/Improper Evaluation, 107–108, 212–213
Kate/Physical Disabilities, 45–48, 194–195
Katie/Marijuana Cigarette, 157–160, 226–227
Kelly/Related Services, 75–77, 203–204
Kevin/Delayed Records, 138–141, 221–222
Kristen/Essential Therapy, 180–184, 232–233

Lansky/Parental Consent, 103–105, 211–212
Larry P. v. Wilson Riles, 25
Latifa/Biased Testing Procedure, 64–66,
  200–201
Least restrictive environment (LRE), 80–99
  Ben/Inclusion, 83–86, 205–207
  Daniel R. R. v. State Board of Education,
    28–29
  David/Threatening Behavior, 89–92, 208
  James/Teacher Bias, 86–89, 207
  Jane/Refusal to Consider, 92–95, 208–209
  Jared/Legal Rights, 96–99, 209–210
  John/Disruptive Behavior, 80–83,
    204–205
  principle of, 13–14

Sacramento City Unified School District v. Rachel H., 29
Linda/Homeschool, 37–39, 192–193
Lisa/Graduation Fears, 173–177, 230–231
Lori/Individualized IEP, 129–131, 219–220
Luke/Stay Put, 123–125, 217–218

Mario/Expulsion Proceeding, 166–169, 228–230
Mediation, under IDEA, 14–15
Michael/Sexual Misconduct, 177–180, 231–232
Mike/Violent Threats, 160–163, 227

Needs, educational, 6
Nicholas/Parent Participation, 73–75, 203

Objectives, in IEP, 11
Office of Civil Rights, U.S., 18

Parent participation, 100–112
    Amy/Parents in Class, 100–103, 210–211
    Armstrong/Denial of Behavior, 110–112, 213–214
    Kami/Improper Evaluation, 107–108, 212–213
    Lansky/Parental Consent, 103–105, 211–212
    principle of, 15
    Tunita/Setting Goals, 105–107, 212
    Washington/Divorced Parents, 108–110, 213
Parents in Action on Special Education (PASE) v. Joseph P. Hannon, 26
The Pennsylvania Association for Retarded Children v. the Commonwealth of Pennsylvania, 24–25
Peter/Health Impaired Students, 42–45, 193–194
Peter Mills et al., Plaintiffs v. Board of Education of the District of Columbia, 25
Placements
    annual determination, 13–14
    continuum of, 13

Privately owned public accommodations, under ADA, 21–23
Procedural due process
    John Sessions v. Livingston Parish School Board, 30
    principle of, 14–15, 16
Public services, under ADA, 20–21

Reliability, of assessment, 7

Sacramento City Unified School District v. Rachel H., 29
Scott/Procedural Errors, 57–59, 197–198
Section 504, Rehabilitation Act of 1973, 15–19
    IDEA compared with, 17–18
    persons protected under, 16
Student misconduct and compensatory education, 151–169
    Andy/Impulsive Behavior, 154–157, 225–226
    Donnie/Bringing a Gun, 151–154, 224–225
    Honig, California Superintendent of Public Instruction v. Doe, 30–31
    Katie/Marijuana Cigarette, 157–160, 226–227
    Mario/Expulsion Proceeding, 166–169, 228–230
    Mike/Violent Threats, 160–163, 227
    Tim/Teacher and Parent Rebellion, 163–166, 228
Susan/Parent Input, 125–128, 218–219

Telecommunications, under ADA, 23
Timothy W. v. Rochester School District, 24
Tim/Teacher and Parent Rebellion, 163–166, 228
Tina/Classification Issues, 59–61, 199
Tony/Inadequate Evaluations, 54–56, 196–197
Transition services, 12
Tunita/Setting Goals, 105–107, 212

Validity, of assessment, 7
Vernon/Improper Placement, 69–71, 202

Walter/Transition Services, 67–69, 201
Washington/Divorced Parents, 108–110, 213

Yancy/General Education Participation, 71–73,
    202

Zero reject/child find, 35–51
    Andre/Age and Special Education Services,
        48–51, 195
    Danny/Expulsion, 40–42, 193
    Jodi/Special Education Services, 35–37,
        191–192

Kate/Physical Disabilities, 45–48, 194–195
Linda/Homeschool, 37–39, 192–193
*The Pennsylvania Association for Retarded
    Children v. the Commonwealth of
    Pennsylvania*, 24–25
Peter/Health Impaired Students, 42–45,
    193–194
*Peter Mills et al., Plaintiffs v. Board of
    Education of the District of Columbia*, 25
principle of, 3–4
Timothy W. v. Rochester School District, 24